In This Place Called Prison

In This Place Called Prison

WOMEN'S RELIGIOUS LIFE IN THE SHADOW OF PUNISHMENT

Rachel Ellis

UNIVERSITY OF CALIFORNIA PRESS

University of California Press
Oakland, California

© 2023 by Rachel Ellis

Library of Congress Cataloging-in-Publication Data

Names: Ellis, Rachel, 1988– author.
Title: In this place called prison : women's religious life in the shadow of
    punishment / Rachel Ellis.
Description: Oakland, California : University of California Press, [2023] |
    Includes bibliographical references and index.
Identifiers: LCCN 2022037224 (print) | LCCN 2022037225 (ebook) |
    ISBN 9780520384538 (cloth) | ISBN 9780520384545 (paperback) |
    ISBN 9780520384552 (ebook)
Subjects: LCSH: Mapleside Prison (not real name) Religion and/in
    prisons United States 21st century Women prisoners "shine a light on
    the tension between freedom and constraint experienced through reli-
    gion in prison"(p4) | Women prisoners—Religious life—United
    States—21st century.
Classification: LCC HV8738 .E44 2023 (print) | LCC HV8738 (ebook) |
    DDC 365/.43—dc23/eng/20221123
LC record available at https://lccn.loc.gov/2022037224
LC ebook record available at https://lccn.loc.gov/2022037225

Manufactured in the United States of America

32 31 30 29 28 27 26 25 24 23
10 9 8 7 6 5 4 3 2 1

Religious instruction should be provided by law for those under detention. . . . Are the souls of those entombed in the City Prison less valuable? Are these men and women less reclaimable? . . . Is society less concerned in their moral renovation? Amazing is the apathy with which too many look on this subject. The idea would seem to have taken possession of the public mind that prisoners have no souls and no sensibilities.

R. N. Havens, 1846, Prison Association of New York

I look and see a woman who God loves. I don't see a "criminal."

Chaplain Harper, 2014, Mapleside Prison

Contents

Introduction

Asabi was 18 years old when she and a few friends plotted a robbery.[1] They would enter a bar, flash a gun, and leave with cash. But that night, things did not go according to plan. A bartender was killed. Asabi was not the person holding the gun. Nor was she the person who pulled the trigger. Asabi was sentenced to 30 years in prison as an accomplice to this crime.

Nearly two decades later, I met Asabi at Mapleside Prison, a state women's correctional facility on the East Coast of the United States. "I grew up in here," she motioned, her upright posture making her look taller than her 5'2" frame. Prior to the robbery-gone-wrong, Asabi's life was not easy. Her childhood was marked by sexual abuse and family strain. The racially segregated city of her youth was hollowed out by economic divestment and policymakers' neglect, offering little in the way of resources to low-income Black neighborhoods like hers. Now in her mid-30s, Asabi has spent nearly half her life in prison.

Asabi explained that for years, she reckoned with the night of the murder. Was she "as guilty as the person who actually *did* the killing?" she wondered aloud. Asabi said she eventually came to terms with the events that changed her life—the events that fated her to incarceration until nearly 50 years old. "Now I realize I am just as responsible," she continued, in carefully measured words. Her face drawn with regret, Asabi declared, "I don't want you to think that we are consumed by this [imprisonment]. We are free." Asabi's voice resounded against the cavernous room cast in concrete. "We are grateful for the freedom that God has allowed in this place called prison."

Religion has powerfully transformed Asabi's life behind bars. Throughout her sentence, Asabi experimented until she found a religion that felt right. She came to be a devout Baptist, firmly believing that forgiveness and salvation come from accepting Jesus Christ as Lord. "It's been a process," she conceded, "but now I can say I am finally free. I know the *only* thing I can't do is walk out that gate." Asabi gestured toward the towering gates wrapped in razor wire that kept her locked in. Nurturing her identity as a "child of God," Asabi went on to explain that her religious beliefs shape how she views her purpose in life. "I talk to God, and I know He loves me. I trust Him. I am God's child—I wouldn't change my life for anything."

Her words struck a chord. *For anything?* I wondered how many of us could so reverently say the same. In a cold, sterile room inside a crowded prison, not one moment unguarded, Asabi spoke words I would hear repeatedly throughout my year of ethnographic research spent observing and interviewing women at Mapleside Prison: she cared deeply about "making something out of her incarceration." What is more, her words matched her actions. Other women condemned to years, decades, or even a lifetime at Mapleside respected Asabi's sincere faith and described her devotion to God's transformative love. One friend said that Asabi "is nothing but truly spiritual," while another nicknamed her "the little pastor," seeing her as a role model for other Christians in the facility. Nearly 20 years into her sentence, religion offered Asabi a feeling of freedom in an environment designed to regulate her every move. With a serene smile, she remarked, "When God looks at us, He sees who we truly are."

. . . . .

Maria's experience with religion tells another story. If she serves every day of her 25-year sentence, Maria will leave prison at age 70. Like Asabi, Maria is a Black woman and a devout Baptist. In fact, Maria is so active in Protestant activities at Mapleside that the chaplain entrusted her to lead some of the programs herself. But religion functioned differently for Maria compared to Asabi.

"I don't care if they carry me out or if I walk out of here," Maria vowed. "All I want is that eternal life." When we met seven years into her incarceration, she said she has come to peace with the question "Why am I here?" Maria shared another refrain I would hear over and over again: "I'll get out in God's time." Rather than a freeing way to rise from incarceration, however, Maria's active participation in Protestant programs offered a framework that helped her embrace the logic of rehabilitation.

It was an unseasonably warm October afternoon when I observed Maria's class on Christian discipleship. With permission from the chaplain, Maria teaches a weekly course to recently born-again women—or "babes in Christ" as she calls them—on how to become good Christian disciples. The day before brought with it apocalyptic weather: the sun went dark, the winds howled, and the skies opened. Hearing news of a tornado warning, the women confined to Mapleside could do little else but pray the same towering walls holding them in would be strong enough to withstand the cruel storm.

Maria described peering through the narrow sliver of a window in her cell, wondering who would "make it."

Yvonne, a student in the class, chimed in. She recounted that during the storm, she got down on her knees and prayed: "Lord, I thank you. I repent now for all my sins."

Maria immediately admonished Yvonne. "Does that *work?* Can we just ask Him to forgive us when it look like the end is near?" For Maria, being a true disciple of Christ was more than having faith in the end times—day-to-day behavior must also be godly. "Unbelievers are looking at us 24 / 7. Everybody who come in here preaches that. We *got* to follow the rules," she chided. As I would soon learn, outside volunteers coming from local churches to preach the gospel routinely insisted that being a good Christian woman meant behaving like a role model, whether in prison or not. Maria pointed toward the sky as she asked, "If I can't be obedient to the rules of the prison, how can I be obedient to *Him?*"

As other students murmured in agreement, Yvonne jumped in again, this time to corroborate Maria's point: "The Bible says, Be obedient to your masters." She was referring to the New Testament verse Ephesians 6:5, which reads, "Slaves, obey your early masters with respect and fear, and with sincerity of heart, just as you would obey Christ."[2] Hearing this, my mind began to inventory the legal scholarship describing incarceration as "American slavery, reinvented."[3] At the same time, I remembered the vital role of Black Church activism in the abolition of slavery.[4] The tension was apparent. Next to Asabi's sense of freedom, religious teachings seemed to guide Maria, Yvonne, and others to a monastic sort of rule-adherence and constraint. Effectively, their religious expression was about self-enforcement of the prison's rules—a personal and pedagogical practice that dovetailed with the contours of carceral control. Maria's words bear repeating: "If I can't be obedient to the rules of the prison, how can I be obedient to *Him?*"

This book is an effort to shine a light on the tension between freedom and constraint experienced through religion in prison. To understand these nested institutions, I spent a year researching religious life inside Mapleside Prison. Several days per week, I conducted ethnographic observations, cataloguing the intricacies of hundreds of women's daily lives and religious activities. Roughly two-thirds of the women at Mapleside are Protestant Christians, and while I will occasionally discuss the beliefs and practices of other faiths, this book focuses on the dualities revealed in Protestant religious adherence. Recall Asabi's poignant remark regarding "the freedom that God has allowed in this place called prison" and hold it beside Maria's proposition, "If I can't be obedient to the rules of the prison, how can I be obedient to *Him?*" As Asabi and Maria's words so clearly illustrate, their religion and the freedom it offers are inescapably bound by the coercive environment of carceral control.

I chose to begin with Asabi and Maria's stories because they demonstrate religion's capacity to offer both *freedom from* carceral control and *constraint within* carceral control. On the one hand, religion offers a competing set of norms, practices, and values with the potential to displace the norms, practices, and values of prison and undermine its coercive aims. The chapters that follow will demonstrate how Protestant religion—the most active and dominant faith tradition at Mapleside—is a resource for dignity, humanity, and social support. In this respect, religion jockeys with the carceral system for institutional primacy by redefining key aspects of the meaning and social experience of incarceration. On the other hand, religion cannot fully free women from the environment of coercive control in which they live because religious practice itself does not escape its placement within an ultimately penal setting. In these conditions, religion ends up reinforcing some of the aspects of carceral control it seeks to undermine—this is a process I call *secondhand carcerality*. Secondhand carcerality is a reiteration of carceral control by a noncarceral actor that occurs via contact with the criminal legal system. Secondhand implies an indirect manifestation, an unavoidable and even unintentional reissuing of a primary force by a subordinate but ostensibly separate force. Through this process, we will see how even well-intentioned institutional actors take on punitive logics when they interact with the surveillance, regulation, and coercion of the intractable prison system.

RELIGION AND PUNISHMENT IN AMERICA

Historians tell us that religion has long been entwined with punishment in the United States. Despite what we might imagine given the country's constitutional emphasis on the separation of church and state, religious practice is not peripheral to the carceral experience but rather embedded in the very foundation of North American prisons as we know them today.

In the colonial era, European settlers adapted Western penal models of corporal punishment, stocks and pillories, fines, banishment, and gallows. Jails functioned as mere holding facilities prior to punishment being meted out. Later, incarceration became the punishment itself. Contrary to what we might think today, prison was designed as a more humane alternative to hew closer to Christian ideals of penitence and benevolence. One of the world's first penitentiaries, Eastern State, was built in Philadelphia, Pennsylvania, in 1829.[5] Linked with Quaker principles of moral contrition and self-reflection, its prisoners spent 24 hours a day alone in their cells. They were given nothing but food to eat and a Bible to read. A singular skylight built into every cell, meant to symbolize the watchful "eye of God," evoked the panopticon model of control—keeping cell occupants under constant, yet unverifiable, surveillance.[6] In 1831, Alexis de Tocqueville and French magistrate Gustave de Beaumont toured the nation's prisons, describing: "In America, the progress of the reform of prisons has been of a character essentially religious. . . . So also is religion to this day in all the new prisons, one of the fundamental elements of discipline and reformation."[7] Religion was central to the logic and structure of the penitentiary, just as it was central to its new purpose: the process of moral transformation to be achieved through religious reflection.[8]

Throughout the late eighteenth and nineteenth centuries, all of this was explicit and overt.[9] "It is not accidental," scholar and activist Angela Davis writes, "that most of the reformers of that era were deeply religious and therefore saw the architecture and regimes of the penitentiary as emulating the architecture and regimes of monastic life."[10] Decade after decade, U. S. religious leaders actively sought prison reform of various kinds. Historian Jennifer Graber describes how, preceding the Civil War, Protestant beliefs around moral redemption through physical suffering were used to justify harsh prison conditions, including physical discomfort and corporal punishment in the name of rehabilitation,[11] while others document how, decades later, prison reformers working to instate a "kinder, gentler" form of punishment, particularly for women, drew on Christian beliefs about femininity and motherhood.[12] The politics of punishment in the twentieth century were profoundly shaped by evangelical Christian leaders and missionary groups, who took an active role in promoting "tough on crime" policies and colorblind criminal legal reforms.[13] Whether religious activists hoped to make prisons more austere and punitive or more instructive and rehabilitative, it seems they called on the Bible to offer up a justification for change.

Today's prisons are ostensibly less focused on spiritual transformation, with a perception of greater separation between religion and punishment. Yet, plenty of public and political discourses around the purposes of incarceration are still inflected with religious undertones. Sentiments like "if you do the crime, you do the time" or "lock 'em up and throw away the key" describe men and women in prisons as dangerous, immoral, or irresponsible.[14] These are not a far cry from centuries-old discourses around sin, contrition, and the need for redemption.

Institutional logic aside, the right to religious practice is among the few constitutional guarantees afforded to incarcerated persons in the United States. That freedom is owed to Black Muslims. In the mid-twentieth century, the Nation of Islam (NOI) proliferated inside American prisons, spreading with intense fervor. It was an affirming force for incarcerated Black men and their lived experiences of white supremacy and oppression. Government and prison administrators, however, viewed it as quite the opposite, fearing NOI as a radicalizing force that could foment racial upheaval inside correctional facilities. An alarm-sounding report by the Federal Bureau of Investigation in 1960 characterized NOI in prisons as a guise to challenge prison authority rather than a sincerely practiced religious tradition.[15] Prison officials sought to undermine NOI practice by splitting up adherents, placing them in solitary confinement, and denying them access to basic necessities like drinking water and adequate health care. In the years that followed, incarcerated devotees filed myriad grievances, and NOI leadership brought a case to the U.S. Supreme Court, *Cooper v. Pate*, arguing that incarcerated persons could sue state prisons for religious discrimination under the 1871 Civil Rights Act. The Supreme Court ruled in their favor, thereby supporting greater religious protection inside correctional facilities.[16]

By the 1990s, federal legislation would take up prison religion amid the rapid rise of Christianity inside prison walls, particularly conservative and evangelical Christianity. In 1993, Congress passed the Religious Freedom Restoration Act (RFRA), drafted with help from groups like Charles Colson's politically powerful Prison Fellowship.[17] RFRA mandated that restrictions to religious practice behind bars must be based only on a "compelling government interest," primarily concerning the safety and security of the prison.[18] Four years later, the Supreme Court heard the case *City of Boerne v. Flores* and ruled that RFRA was unconstitutional as applied to states. Reasoning that local ordinances should not be subject to federal regulation, the decision held that state prisons were no longer required to abide by RFRA.

A few years later, legislators once again pushed to protect religious freedom in state prisons. The Religious Land Use and Institutionalized Persons Act (RLUIPA) mirrored RFRA's language almost identically, mandating that states accepting federal funds for prison operations should create no burden to restrict the exercise of religion among prisoners unless "in furtherance of a compelling governmental interest" and through the use of the "least restrictive means of furthering that compelling governmental interest."[19]

RLUIPA passed unanimously in the House of Representatives and the Senate, and was signed into law by President Bill Clinton in 2000.[20] Because most states do accept federal funds for the operation of their prisons, RLUIPA applies nearly nationwide.

Religious programs in prison garnered even more support during the George W. Bush administration, with federal funds supporting faith-based initiatives doing the work of social welfare.[21] As such, just as the federal government slashed state funding for correctional programming, RLUIPA facilitated an unprecedented influx of religious worship services and scriptural studies of all stripes in every jail and prison in the country. The constitutional protection of religious practice, for all incarcerated persons except for those in solitary confinement, combined with budgets strained by the rising forces of mass incarceration and reductions to government spending, created a symbiotic relationship between the state and religion within American prisons. Apart from hiring a full-time chaplain and using staff time to patrol religious programs, prisons incur no additional financial costs for these voluntary programs. Meanwhile, congregations donate holy books and ritual objects, and there is no shortage of volunteers who organize and lead religious gatherings inside prison walls.[22] It is clear the state has a number of compelling incentives to embrace these religious programs: they are cost-effective and they provide activities for incarcerated men and women. Thus, while religion's relationship to imprisonment may be less overt compared to centuries ago, it is still very much woven into the fabric of correctional facilities through legislative protection and ubiquitous programming.

What does religious practice look like in contemporary prisons? Again, we see the entanglement of religion and personal transformation—this time, operationally separate from rehabilitative efforts by prison officials. Researchers report on the morally transformative impacts of religious activities like Bible studies and worship services. Studies (primarily on men in prison and primarily on Protestant Christianity in prison) show that religion provides a deeply meaningful sense of hope and moral self-worth,[23] and that religious participation can have prosocial outcomes for the incarcerated, leading to increased civic engagement, lower measures of aggression, fewer disciplinary infractions, and even a reduced likelihood of recidivism.[24] Religion may even help with adjustment to prison by lessening symptoms of depression.[25] Certainly, because it is decentralized and reliant on volunteerism, the array of religious programming is wide-ranging and unstandardized. Evidence suggests making religious accommodations across the variety of faith traditions is a persistent challenge,[26] and my own research confirms religious minorities must sometimes affiliate with and worship with larger, more active religious groups if their own is underrepresented. That said, a recent study of prevalent prison programs across numerous states found a persistent and shared purpose: personal transformation.[27] These findings echo the themes of religious redemption from centuries ago.

Religion also has practical implications for the prison experience. For instance, religion scholar Joshua Dubler draws attention to the prison chapel as a site providing daily routine and structured social interaction to lifers from a variety of faith traditions at Graterford Prison. Furthermore, religion can serve a protective purpose among incarcerated men. Sociologist Andrew Johnson, studying prisons in Rio de Janeiro, shows how adherence to the religiously sanctioned activities of Pentecostalism encouraged incarcerated men to abstain from alcohol, tobacco, and gang involvement.[28] Although the research is limited with regard to women's facilities, a handful of studies have demonstrated that religious identities can help women behind bars avoid "the mix" of breaking the rules and getting into trouble with prison officials.[29]

In some ways, it may come as no surprise that many men and women in prison identify as religious. Outside prison walls, most Americans draw on religion to make sense of their lives. According to a 2014 survey of over 35,000 residents of all 50 states, nine out of 10 Americans say they believe in God. Over 70 percent of Americans identify as Christian, with a quarter of Americans identifying as evangelical Protestants and 6.5 percent identifying as Protestants from historically Black traditions.[30] Women are more devout than men, on average—women of color even more so,[31] resulting in many women seeking out religion in prison as a source of identity and familiarity.[32]

It is important to note, however, that religion in prison is not exactly a free market. The kinds of programs offered in any given facility depend on which religious groups or parachurch organizations have the money, time, and interest to volunteer. In practice, the majority of these programs come from socially conservative, evangelical Protestant groups for whom proselytizing and prison ministry are central to their belief system.[33] Earlier studies have highlighted legal and ethical concerns around the proliferation of evangelical faith-based programs, Christian-only housing units, and Bible colleges inside prisons.[34] Where adherence to a Protestant set of beliefs is required for access to particular resources, they argue, the separation of church and state is in jeopardy. Put differently, in contrast to the overt reliance on Christian ideas in earlier iterations of the penal state, religion in today's prisons is meant to be accommodated but not endorsed by the state. That said, evidence suggests religious accommodation is rarely so tidily neutral.

Taken together, we know religion—especially Protestant Christianity—is a major defining feature of the prison experience for many people living behind bars in America right now. This stems both from the historical entwinement of religion and state punishment and more recent legislation that paved the way for the constitutional protection of religious freedom behind bars. There are meaningful and prosocial outcomes associated with religious practice in contemporary prisons, although scholars also caution against privileging Christianity above other faith traditions, lest the separation of church and state be entirely eroded. I begin my inquiry with the premise that prison is a well-established site of formal religion. In this book, I argue one major variable has been missing from prior analyses: the overarching context of carceral control, in which actors working within the prison system seek to surveil, regulate, and discipline their wards.

To be sure, prior studies have taken their setting seriously: never are we unaware that scholars' findings emerged within prisons. Throughout this study, I go further. Rather than consider carceral control a fixed-category backdrop, I make it an object of study. After all, as other scholars have noted, "religious provision . . . [is] never beyond the reach of institutional power."[35] At the facility level, carceral control may be supported by religion, functioning as a complementary institution, or it may be challenged by religion, functioning as a competing institution—or something betwixt and between. Thus, my study examines how the institutions of Protestant religion and the state collide and collude at the interactional level, embracing recent calls for research on whether religious activities in correctional facilities "align with or quietly subvert the agendas and imperatives of the prison administration."[36] I also contend with the gendered aspects of both religious practice and regimes of punishment by siting this research within a women's prison.

THE SOCIOLOGY OF CARCERAL CONTROL

To understand religion's interactions with carceral control, we must first explore how state control operates in the carceral context—specifically, in prisons. Prisons are designed to punish. From a correctional standpoint, imprisonment has four main goals. The first is incapacitation, or stopping an individual from continuing to commit crime by removing them from their everyday settings. The second is deterrence, discouraging future crime through the threat of punishment. Then comes rehabilitation via therapeutic and social resources meant to remedy the psychological or sociological factors that lead to offending. The final goal is retribution: doling out state-sanctioned punishment deemed morally deserved for breaking the social contract by committing a crime. The relevance of each of these goals ebbs and flows, depending on the political moment.[37] At present, criminologists agree the "decline of the rehabilitative ideal" in favor of a "culture of control" has blunted the first three goals.[38] What remains steadfast and unwavering is the fourth goal of retribution, or punishment for punishment's sake.

Control can be understood as any effort, explicit or implicit, by actors vested with regulatory authority. My definition here is purposely broad because "control" evokes a variety of meanings, from unspoken constraint and situational manipulation to explicit coercion and domination. Classical meanings of "social control" suggest any group regulates its members and encourages conformity through socialization or repression.[39] When it comes to the carceral system (any institutional apparatus related to jails or prisons), control happens through direct coercion as well as subtler mechanisms that direct individuals' attitudes and behaviors.[40] In prisons, state actors are conferred authority to control the behavior of their wards through near-constant surveillance and the imposition of sanctions. Carceral control cuts across every aspect of life in prison: what to eat, what to drink, when to sleep, what to wear, whom to speak to, how to spend time, where one's body is allowed to be—the list goes on. For this reason, prisons have been characterized as "total institutions," or isolated, highly structured spaces of work and residence that transform individuals into the roles they inhabit, promoting conformity to the norms and rules of the institution.[41] In the name of security, carceral control seeks to regulate incarcerated individuals' every move.

More and more, carceral control has gone beyond the obvious bastion of the prison. Scholars refer to a "net-widening" of control extending beyond the purview of official state actors working within the criminal justice system. In what has been called a "pipeline" or "an enduring collusion" of "wraparound incarceration,"[42] numerous justice-adjacent organizations comply with and even strengthen carceral control by funneling individuals into the correctional system. The net widens to civil and administrative actors who have been granted authority to sanction justice-involved individuals.[43] The net widens to primary and secondary schools, through school resource officers and their links to surveilling institutions.[44] The net widens to medical institutions, when EMTs and hospital staff work as first responders alongside police officers.[45] The net even widens to social service organizations, welfare offices, and drug treatment programs "where the state's capacities to rehabilitate ... [are] offloaded onto community-based actors and organizations."[46] The organizations operating inside, around, and adjacent to official punitive institutions can perpetuate surveillance, regulation, and penalties in support of carceral control.[47] A wider net catches more fish.

As scholars concur that the net of carceral control has widened to incorporate nonpenal actors and nonpenal settings, they are less conclusive when it comes to the ways nonpenal actors operate within penal settings. There is mounting evidence, for example, that when educational programs and drug treatment programs operate within detention facilitates, they necessarily take on surveilling functions.[48] Medical professionals caught between care and disciplinarity[49] may find that risk assessment tools meant to assess whether individuals are safe for society simultaneously replicate notions of dangerousness and criminalization.[50] Closer to the case at hand, there is even a study of prison chaplains that finds the work of serving incarcerated communities' religious needs is marked by the pervasive sense of risk management: according to that study, "chaplains believe their primary role is to serve inmates, yet they also seek to control inmates in ways supportive of institutional needs."[51] Preliminary evidence suggests an irreconcilable tension between carceral and noncarceral institutions working side by side within the prison setting.

The purpose of this book is to interrogate how one institution— religion—interacts with the contours of carceral control when it is nested within another, more totalizing institution—the prison. Past debates have pitted religion as a potential form of resistance to state authority against prison as an institution of social control. This *either/or* framework misses the messier dynamism of the institutions' entanglements. If carceral control is not just a backdrop but an active variable, we can take a sociological approach to the interplay of religion and carceral control as seen through informal interactions and organizational-level mechanisms. Chronicling how religion offers both freedom from and constraint within carceral control, the chapters that follow will reveal how religion proves a formidable opponent. Religion vies for institutional primacy while reinforcing some aspects of carceral control through the process of secondhand carcerality discussed earlier. As I will discuss at greater length in the conclusion, there are reasons to believe that secondhand carcerality, a reiteration of carceral control by a noncarceral actor in moments of contact with the criminal legal system, is promulgated by a wide array of noncarceral institutions.[52] Here, religion is the focal institution, yet we must remember throughout: American punishment is a powerful and encompassing institution, and its coercive functions galvanize ancillary institutions—from schools to welfare offices, from religious organizations to medical settings—into enacting carcerality by proxy.

THE STUDY

The above argument is drawn from an intensive, up-close study of religious life in one U. S. state women's prison. I conducted ethnographic fieldwork inside the guarded gates of Mapleside Prison over a 12-month period. Each week, I spent several days observing religious life. Prison authorities' whims dictated whether it was a two-visit week or a four-visit week, whether it was a two-hour observation or a nine-hour observation. On average, I was permitted to conduct my research three days a week for three and a half hours at a time (for a total north of 500 hours of ethnographic observation). By observing religious life and talking to many of the people who live, work, and worship inside prison walls, I pieced together an understanding of the toxicity of carceral control and analyzed how secondhand carcerality defined the tension between freedom and constraint derived from religious practice inside prisons.

Gaining access to prisons for research is exceedingly difficult.[53] In the methodological appendix of this book, I detail how I went about obtaining the necessary permissions for this study, eventually securing approval for this yearlong work within a women's prison. In the appendix, I also detail my analytical procedure, contend with my positionality as a Jewish woman who was raised in an interfaith household, describe the privileges and pitfalls of my role as an "interested outsider," and grapple with the ethics of conducting this study as a nonincarcerated, middle-class white researcher.

Mapleside is a publicly funded state women's prison on the East Coast of the United States. Its population is about 1,000, with roughly equal numbers of Black and white women and a smaller share of Latina women. The majority are between the ages of 21 and 50, although women as young as 17 are incarcerated there having been tried as adults, as are octogenarians in need of intensive eldercare. It is common to meet women who have not graduated high school and are working toward GEDs, as well as women with high school diplomas but no college experience. Some women at Mapleside have attended college and earned an associate's or bachelor's degree, while a small handful have continued onto graduate education. The average sentence at Mapleside is three and a half years, and the most common convictions are drug offenses (around 17 percent) and homicide (around 20 percent), followed by larceny and assault (both around 15 percent). Some of the women are first-timers; others are repeat offenders.

With permission to observe activities in Mapleside's "Main Hall," the building that houses the cafeteria, gym, computer lab, classrooms, religious library, and chaplain's office, I had unparalleled access to the day-to-day rhythms of the women's lives. I observed a honeybee preservation program and yoga classes. I sat in on formal activities like victim's awareness and volunteer appreciation events. I spent hours on end talking with hundreds of women at Mapleside about their experiences. I got to know dozens of women exceedingly well, learning about their families, their crimes, their cliques inside prison, and their opinions on everything from pop culture to politics. I watched as they made friends, teased each other, argued, and fought. We ate hot lunches from the cafeteria off Styrofoam trays in cold, drafty classrooms, and we sat together as they typed up essays for their college-credit courses in the computer lab. I heard about their participation in secular activities like gardening club, Toastmasters classes, Zumba classes, college education courses, GED courses, the service-dog training program, and the cat companionship program. I witnessed physical altercations with corrections officers where voices were raised, handcuffs came out, and disciplinary tickets sent women to solitary confinement.

Religious life is vibrant within Mapleside's thick concrete walls. From minimum to maximum security, all of the women at Mapleside who are not in solitary confinement are permitted to attend religious programs. After all, it is their constitutional right. I observed religious programs nearly every day of the week. I spent time at Catholic, Sunni Muslim, Jewish, and Protestant worship services. I participated in Sunday church services that drew, on an average week, up to a quarter of the prison's total population, as well as Baptist, African Methodist Episcopal (AME), and nondenominational youth Bible study groups for women under 25; evangelism courses; ministry classes; Christianity-based self-help classes; Discipleship classes; and Christian movie screenings. I attended special events: "Gospelfest," where Christian women showcased their ministerial talents; a weekend-long nondenominational Christian "retreat" in the prison library; a Christmas caroling event held in the gym; and two weekend-long Christian revival meetings. I conducted observations on major holidays, including Good Friday, Easter, Pentecost, Mother's Day, Father's Day, Thanksgiving, and Christmas.

Nearly two-thirds (63 percent) of the women at Mapleside identified as Protestant (see table 1). Noting that "Protestant" was used as an umbrella affiliation for Baptist, AME, Pentecostal, Apostolic, and

Table 1   Religious Affiliation of Incarcerated Women at Mapleside

Religious Group	Percent Affiliated[1]
Protestant	63
Catholic	7
Sunni Muslim	5
Lutheran	4.5
Wiccan	3.5
Seventh Day Adventist	3
Jehovah's Witness	2
Nation of Islam	2
No Affiliation	2
Jewish	1.5
Moorish Scientist	0.6
Native American	0.5
No Response	5.4

1. Official records of the entire Mapleside population circa January 2015, coded by author. Parameters are presented in percentage form to disguise distinguishable characteristics of the prison (i.e., exact size of population).

nondenominational Christians, the sheer number of Protestant programs offered every day of the week encouraged my focus on this group's practices. The second largest group was Catholic, with 7 percent of women affiliated. As the third largest group, Sunni Muslim affiliation accounted for 5 percent of the women at Mapleside. Only 2 percent of women selected "None" on their Religious Preference Form, and just over 5 percent did not complete the form.

From informal conversations to field interviews, I sought as many perspectives as possible on the inner workings of prison life. I was not allowed to bring a tape recorder inside the facility, and the lack of privacy made it hard to schedule time and space for a candid exchange. Nevertheless, along with informal conversations with hundreds of incarcerated women, correctional officers, administrators, and outside volunteers, I conducted 18 formal, sit-down interviews. These interviews were with 9 Protestants, 3 Catholics, 2 Jews, 1 Jehovah's Witness, and 3 women who identified as agnostic or atheist.

WHAT IS RELIGION?

The term "religion" means different things to different people. In this book, "religion" will refer to a formal social institution organized around beliefs with reference to the sacred. I am guided by sociologist Émile Durkheim, who defines religion as "a unified system of beliefs and practices relative to sacred things, that is to say, things set apart and surrounded by prohibitions—beliefs and practices that unite its adherents in a single moral community."[54] The sacred is set apart from the profane, with congregants brought together through practices oriented around that which is holy. Today, sociologists of religion also attend to religion as a formal institutional affiliation: "Most often understood as voluntary participation in a denomination organized around theological and administrative structures, religion brings together powerful forces of socialization, pedagogy, and ritual."[55] This is closer to the meaning of religion as it is used by prison administrators, with firmer boundaries around religious membership.

Of course, many people have sacred beliefs and practices separate from formal religious institutions. This is typically called spirituality, signifying "an internal, personal, subjective, and private experience" with a higher power, deity, or realm "that transcend[s] specific religious traditions."[56] Sociologists of religion also describe a related concept called "lived religion," in which people cobble together bits and pieces of religious objects, rituals, and ideas as they embody faith in their own ways.[57] For some people, this precludes participation in any organized religion.

What does or does not "count" as religion, in a legal sense, has real consequences for those wishing to practice a particular faith tradition in prison. Although the Supreme Court of the United States has never formally defined "religion," lower courts and state governments have done so. The U.S. Court of Appeals for the Third Circuit used an "inherently vague definitional approach" to religion as a belief system "comprehensive in nature" that addresses "fundamental and ultimate questions," which are "often . . . recognized by the presence of certain formal and external signs."[58] The context of carceral control varies with regard to defining religion. The Montana Department of Corrections, for instance, defines "authentic religion" as a "definable, sincerely held moral system that includes belief, behavior, participation, proficiency, and exclusivity." Religions like Islam, Buddhism, Judaism, Christianity, Indigenous faiths, and Wicca are generally accommodated. Other religious traditions may require a formal request to the administration to accommodate practice. For example, New York's Department of Corrections and Community Supervision vets requests about religions deemed "unfamiliar" by seeking "advice on matters of religious doctrine, practice, and tradition from recognized religious authorities in the outside community."[59] In Virginia, however, no religion—familiar or otherwise—can be recognized as a religious group within prison facilities without a minimum of five incarcerated persons attesting to their desire to practice that religion.[60]

Inside prisons, what ultimately counts as religion is defined and regulated by state and federal governments and implemented by prison officials. Faith and spirituality, while absolutely central to the experience of religion, are peripheral concerns for carceral actors. For these reasons, when I refer to religion, I will use Mapleside's classifications. Later on, I will interrogate the practical meaning of such classificatory labels when exploring how women live out these top-down categories.

RLUIPA requires correctional facilities to accommodate religious practice and state-run Departments of Corrections issue official guidelines dictating the specifics of the accommodations. Prison administrators handle five main categories of accommodations: personal property, communal activities, grooming exceptions, work exemptions, and special diets.[61] Mapleside's religious accommoda-

MSP Inmate Religious Preference Statement

To: RAC Coordinator

From:_____   _____   _____
                    Inmate Name   ID/AO number   Housing Unit

Check one: ☐ Initial declaration of religious preference   ☐ Change of religious preference*

My religious preference is (check _one_):

☐Buddhist..(specify denomination or sect:_____)

☐Christian...(specify denomination or sect:_____)

☐Church of Jesus Christ of Latter Day Saints

☐Islam..(specify denomination or sect:_____)

☐Jehovah's Witnesses

☐Native American...(specify denomination or sect_____)

☐Odinist

☐Wicca

☐None

☐Other:_____

Figure 1. Montana State Prison Inmate Religious Preference Statement.

tions include weekly congregate worship services and a study forum (such as a Bible study or a Quranic study), kosher meals (which, according to officials, double for the halal diet), a limited number of ceremonial meals including Ramadan and Passover, religious clothing and jewelry, and holiday programming. Those in solitary confinement are not permitted to attend communal religious programs with Mapleside's general population, although they are entitled to holy texts and weekly visits from the chaplain.[62]

During a woman's first week at Mapleside, her "intake" procedure includes selecting a religious affiliation on a Religious Preference Form. This allows her to attend only that group's religious programs (as well as any nondenominational religious programs).[63] Notably, the administrative categories presented on these forms vary by state. A sample Religious Preference Form (see fig. 1) from the state of Montana demonstrates some of the options (while helping to keep

---

KANSAS DEPARTMENT OF CORRECTIONS
RELIGIOUS AFFILIATION INFORMATION

DATE_____

OFFENDER NAME_____NUMBER_____

PRESENT RELIGIOUS AFFILIATION:

___Asatru/Odinist	___Assembly of Yahweh	___Buddhist	___Catholic
___Christian Science	___Hinduism	___House of Yahweh	___Islam
___Jehovah Witness	___Judaism	___Krishna	___Mormon
___MSTA	___Native American	___Christian/Protestant	___Rastafarian
___7-Day Adventist	___Sikh	___Thelema	___Unity
___Wiccan	____Other (_____)		

NAME OF YOUR OUTSIDE RELIGIOUS GROUP:
_____

NAME OF RELIGIOUS LEADER (Priest, Pastor, Imam, Sheik, Medicine Man, etc.):
_____

ADDRESS OF RELIGIOUS LEADER:_____
                              Number   Street
                          _____
                              City   State   Zip Code

If I decide to change my religious affiliation, I will make my request to the Pastoral Care Department.

Signed:_____   _____ _____
       Offender Name   Number   Chaplain's/Warden's/Superintendent's Designee   Date

---

Figure 2. Kansas Department of Corrections Religious Affiliation Information.

Mapleside's location masked). On this form, for instance, a woman could select "Wicca," yet were she a Protestant or a Catholic, she would have to select "Christian." Another sample from Kansas (see fig. 2) provides 22 options, including "Catholic" and "Christian / Protestant." Depending on the specific state and facility, a wide variety of religious denominations may worship together in prison.

NEW YORK STATE DEPARTMENT OF CORRECTIONS AND COMMUNITY SUPERVISION

CHANGE OF RELIGIOUS DESIGNATION FORM

_____ Correctional Facility

Inmate's Name: _____ DIN: _____ Location: _____

Date of Last Change (Check with IRC or Guidance): _____ ____ _____
                                                  Month Day   Year

I profess to be of the _____ faith and not of the _____ faith as previously listed. (Inmates can not self designate to be Native American. Established policy requires inmates to provide verification of ancestry to the facility Chaplain who will forward to the Director of Ministerial, Family and Volunteer Services for review/approval.) I understand that subsequent changes of religion will only be permitted at twelve (12)-month intervals.

_____   _____
SIGNATURE OF INMATE   DATE SIGNED

_____
SIGNATURE, CHAPLAIN OF FORMER RELIGION

Approves Based On:

    ☐ Self-Declaration

or ☐ Documentation of Existing Status by an appropriate religious body

or ☐ Conversion

_____   _____
SIGNATURE, CHAPLAIN OF NEW RELIGION   DATE SIGNED

Figure 3. New York State Change of Religious Designation Form.

To convert religions, an incarcerated person must submit a new Religious Preference Form. In Virginia, incarcerated persons are permitted to submit conversion paperwork as often as four times per year, while in Montana, conversion is permitted only once per calendar year. In some states, Religious Change Forms are automatically approved, while in other states, conversion may require a formal interview with the Religious Activities Coordinator "to verify the inmate's newly declared religious preference."[64] A Change of Religious Designation Form from the state of New York requires the incarcerated person to obtain the signatures of three chaplains (the former religion's, the new religion's, and the prison's coordinating chaplain) (see fig. 3). Every U. S. state forbids evangelism by staff, volunteers, and incarcerated persons.[65] One's religious preference is meant to be a firm, personal commitment to an administrative category, free of others' influence. Declaration of religious preference, like many aspects of prison life, is decidedly bureaucratic.

ON TERMINOLOGY

There are many different terms used to describe women in prison. In this book, I use the term "incarcerated women" as person-first language that prioritizes the humanity rather than the carceral status of those who chose to share their stories with me. I join with the scholars, activists, and incarcerated persons who eschew terms like "felons" or "convicts" or "offenders," focusing on the crime that led to their incarceration, or terms like "inmates" or "prisoners" that emphasize their role within correctional institutions.

The terms used to describe the individuals who work in prisons are also fraught. The colloquial label "guards" is largely rejected by staff, who prefer to highlight their role as officers of the law by calling themselves "corrections officers" or "correctional officers" (shortened to "COs" in casual conversation). Here, I will use the term "officers," as it is readily recognizable and aligns with the term used by most of the people who live and work at Mapleside, describing their role within the system of carceral control.

I privilege the term "criminal legal system" over "criminal justice system," referring to the system of policing, courts, and corrections that processes individuals from arrest to conviction to punishment.

Critics of the latter term cite the lack of "justice" doled out by the contemporary system of U. S. punishment.

With regard to religious groups, terminology is likewise complicated. Among Jews, Catholics, Muslims, and Wiccans, readymade labels seem to fit. Categorization is more difficult when it comes to Mapleside's Protestants. Ask any Protestant incarcerated woman or volunteer their religious affiliation, and they might respond "Christian" or "Protestant." Or they might say, "It's not about religion, it's about relationship [with Christ]." Yet these labels do not help to differentiate Mapleside's charismatic and evangelical laity from the historically Black Protestants, nor to separate out the Lutheran, Seventh Day Adventist, and Jehovah's Witness adherents. Nevertheless, in this book I use "Protestants" because that is the classification used by prison officials and by incarcerated women themselves. Furthermore, its breadth is an asset, since it is perhaps the only accurate label to encompass this group's wide range of beliefs and practices.

PLAN OF THE BOOK

The first chapter of this book chronicles a typical day at Mapleside Prison, from the sterile setting to the monotonous routine to women's interactions with the arbiters of carceral control. Woven throughout is the larger landscape of what prison punishment looks like in the United States today, particularly for women.

Contrasting the bleak isolation of most of prison life, chapter 2 explores the vibrant, energetic atmosphere of religious practices and programs at Mapleside. This chapter sets the scene for religion as a source of interpretive freedom behind bars. Next, chapter 3 takes a closer look at how religious messages are relevant to individuals' carceral narratives and logics. As in other aspects of prison life, religious programs involve in-depth discussions about what it means to be incarcerated. For the many women practicing Protestant

Christianity who too often feel disposable to society, messages of God's love are paramount. This is also where we begin to see religion as a site of secondhand carcerality, detailing how messages that frame prison as "part of God's plan" can dovetail with punitive state discourses.

Gender, motherhood, and ideologies of family are the focus of chapter 4. We see Protestant religious programming pushing back against the prison's scrutiny of women's femininity and their maternal roles by casting incarcerated women as "women of God." At the same time, the predominant gender traditionalism imports messages about self-regulation of femininity and sexuality consistent with the normative narratives promoted by prison officials. Likewise, in championing women's motherhood, religious programs adopt a tenor of paternalism that is eerily similar to prison discourses. Secondhand carcerality is amplified when gender becomes central to the conversation.

Chapter 5 zooms into the practical side of religious programming at Mapleside. The constitutional right to religion creates a space for women to organize their own community and sense of social status within it. Religious programs, especially Protestant programs, cultivate important emotional support, personal attention, and access to material resources otherwise unavailable inside prison. They also implement an organizational structure of "church officials," or incarcerated adherents designated by the chaplain to facilitate activities. Religion thereby offers a source of moral dignity and status like the system of lay leadership in the Black church outside of prison. Alongside the important meaning derived from this social system, this sorting becomes another site of secondhand carcerality, insofar as it fosters an environment where women are forced to compete over scarce resources of material objects and social status. As such, women can experience religion within prison as a landscape of material and social inequalities.

In the conclusion, I step back to consider the big picture. How does religion offer both freedom and constraint from carceral control? When it comes to the institutional relationship between religion and the state, how does this study speak to their competition for primacy in the prison sphere? In and around the correctional system, where else do we see the reach of secondhand carcerality, and how can we disrupt it? Reviewing the lessons learned through this study, this chapter identifies key takeaways for academics, policymakers, and practitioners concerned with the expansion of carceral control within prison walls and across institutions. In the epilogue, I follow up with two women as they leave Mapleside, experiencing religion in reentry.

1 *Thou Shalt Not*

A DAY IN PRISON

This place isn't fit for anyone. It isn't fit for animals.
And they tell you it gets easier, that you learn to deal
with your time, but I don't know. You watch your life
pass by, out a window, or on the TV screen. At the
end of the day, when it's lights off and they cut off
the TV, and they lock you in your room—that's the
hardest part.

Vanessa, 25 years old, sentenced to 30 years in prison

"There's a darkness in here, can't you feel it?" Rosario asks me one
Sunday night in the prison gym. Rosario is a 31-year-old woman
serving life without parole. The oppressive weight of the summer's
heat sinks down over us. Everything looks beige, from the paint on
the cement walls to the drab tile floors to the khaki prison-issue uniforms. The skylights, set high in the ceiling, are inky black under the
cloak of night. Fluorescent lights beam overhead, bright and sterile.
"When I got here, all I saw was darkness," Rosario says.

The darkness Rosario sees describes not only how the prison
looks but also how it feels. This chapter sets the scene of daily life at
Mapleside Prison once the gates clang shut. It details what criminologist Gresham Sykes calls the "pains of imprisonment," including
the absence of privacy, lack of autonomy, separation from loved ones,
psychological degradation, and sense of threatened personal safety

that define prison life.[1] Whether overt or insidious, every aspect of the experience behind bars feels inescapably oriented toward oppressive carceral control, from the architecture of an institution designed to degrade to the monotony of the everyday routine, from the tensions between the people confined inside and those paid to confine them. Later on, we will see how religion offers a stark contrast to these grim realities.

IMPRISONMENT BY THE NUMBERS

Well into the twenty-first century, women's incarceration is at an all-time high. In fact, according to the U.S. Bureau of Justice Statistics, men's incarceration rates have begun to decline for the first time since the prison boom of the 1970s and 1980s, while women's rates remain elevated.[2] Women account for 7.5 percent of all those in state and federal prisons, to the tune of 200,000 women held in American jails and prisons on any given day.[3] The overall downward trend suggests that perhaps mass incarceration has peaked. Yet more than two million Americans are held behind bars each and every year. A population of that size can be hard to fathom. Add up everyone living in Atlanta, Boston, and Baltimore: the prison population is higher.

Not only are the numbers vast, but the system is notoriously costly. Private prisons get a lot of attention, although they confine just 8 percent of all incarcerated people.[4] The more enduring ties binding prisons and capitalism exist in the form of state and federal contracts with private companies and suppliers.[5] It is the state-run penal system that costs taxpayers some $43 billion annually (the average cost to incarcerate one person was $34,000 annually as of 2015).[6]

Beyond the strict confines of incarceration, scholars have documented immense racial disparities throughout the criminal legal system. Between policing and arrests to fines and fees, prosecution and sentencing, and community supervision, there is ample evidence of discrimination and disadvantage experienced by Black,

Latinx, and other minoritized groups at each inflection point.[7] For example, studies of police departments across the country have found that, after controlling for a variety of factors related to crime, demographics, and precinct variables, police are more likely to stop, search, handcuff, use force, and arrest Blacks than whites.[8] Despite credible evidence that white Americans are equally likely as Black Americans to use illegal drugs, Blacks are 2.7 times more likely to be arrested and 6.5 times more likely to be incarcerated for drug-related offenses.[9] Prosecutors are 25 percent more likely to drop a white defendant's most serious charge or reduce their charges than they are a Black defendant's,[10] and Black defendants are almost 50 percent more likely than their white counterparts to be detained at the time of their arraignment, with Latinx defendants about 15 percent more likely[11]—a variable scholars correlate with harsher sentences.

Racial inequalities persist in criminal sentencing. Black and Latinx defendants tend to be more often sentenced to confinement rather than the community-based sanctions afforded to whites for comparable crimes.[12] Together, Black and Latinx individuals comprise about 30 percent of the overall U. S. population, but nearly 60 percent of the prison population. In 2019, the rates of Black and Latinx imprisonment outstripped whites by a factor of 5 and 2.5, respectively. The racial disparity was most stark among men in the 18–19 age category, where Black male teenagers were 12 times more likely to be imprisoned than their white male counterparts.[13] Meanwhile, Latinx defendants are twice as likely as whites to receive mandatory minimum charges,[14] and Black defendants are disproportionately represented (56 percent) among those sentenced to life without the possibility of parole.[15] Looking specifically to women, racial disparities abound.[16] One study found that Black women are two times more likely than white women to have their sentences "enhanced" as "habitual offenders."[17] Likewise, scholars find that Black women are more likely than white woman to become incarcerated and serve more time in prison for comparable offenses.[18]

Along with people of color, the correctional system disproportionately locks up socioeconomically marginalized people of all
races. Often, low-income individuals are punished for nonviolent
crimes and drug offenses precipitated by their ongoing lack of access
to good schools, good jobs, and safe neighborhoods. As scholar and
activist Angela Davis writes, they "are sent to prison, not so much
because of the crimes they may have indeed committed, but largely
because their communities have been criminalized."[19] Indeed,
according to the 2004 Survey of Prison Inmates by the Bureau of
Justice Statistics, 4 in 5 people in prison lived in urban zip codes
prior to their incarceration.[20] Studies of returning citizens find evidence that over half of those released from prison live in neighborhoods with high concentrations of poverty, and are nearly 10 times
more likely to be homeless compared to the average American.[21]

Mere contact with the criminal legal system is a profoundly dis-
ruptive experience, even when it leads to no conviction or jail time at
all. An arrest generates records, including mugshots, which have
proven durable and damaging.[22] Going to court means, at minimum, an interruption to one's workday and/or childcare, and the
threat of social stigma whether or not found guilty. It can also mean
months spent sitting in jail awaiting trial, losing work and even
housing while legally presumed innocent.[23] Indeed, modern-day
social control is predicated on police and courts' punitive systems of
red tape and financial penalties. Imagine the intensity of these
impacts for those who undergo lengthy trials or plea bargains with
hostile prosecutors, only to be sentenced to years, decades, or even
lifetimes in prison.[24]

Furthermore, justice involvement at any level means being mired
in moral judgments: *Is this defendant a responsible and self-
disciplined person?* Detectives, prosecutors, judges, and juries make
normative assessments of a person's perceived character. Often, state
actors vilify "criminals" in an effort to support victims. Yet this
rhetorical disparagement ignores the well-established relationship
between victimization and offending, such that most convicted

individuals have themselves been victims of other crimes. One study reported that a mere 5 percent of arrestees had never been victimized or witnessed violence prior to their arrests.[25] Criminologists explain that offenders and victims are often one and the same people, describing these "blurred boundaries" as the murky reality of crime.[26] Even among the most serious violent crimes, circumstances that lead to offending are often highly situational—the so-called "worst of the worst" are actually *less* likely to reoffend once paroled compared to those convicted of nonviolent crimes.[27] What court actors deem immoral or irresponsible is all too often a chain of safety net failures that lead people to criminalized activity.

In the end, when we weigh how mass incarceration affects society, we must also consider collateral consequences after a prison sentence ends. Prison guts people's lives and devastates families. Incarceration substantially harms mental health and feelings of self-worth.[28] Those eventually released from confinement find their criminal records make it much harder to get a job.[29] A felony conviction also means being barred from public housing, food stamps, welfare, and even a driver's license in many states. It can mean losing the right to serve on a jury, eligibility for student loans and financial aid, and, in some jurisdictions, the right to vote. A criminal record can even be considered legitimate grounds for divorce or the loss of parental rights.[30] Those leaving prison often face significant financial debt, owing thousands of dollars in felony fines, court fees, restitution, and other legal financial obligations.[31] All of these factors compound disadvantage, worsening life chances by virtue of having spent time in prison. Those who "did the time" frequently find there is no past tense—they will continue to be punished well beyond their sentences, possibly for the rest of their lives.[32] Sociologist Reuben Jonathan Miller calls this the "afterlife" of mass incarceration, in which formerly incarcerated people are ushered into a "supervised society" that limits chances at success by design.[33] The effects of incarceration also reverberate through families. Nearly half of all U.S. adults report having an immediate family member who has spent one night or more in jail or prison.[34] Incarceration for any period of time is tough on partners and children—emotionally, financially, and socially—as they navigate physical separation, stigma, and myriad other personal strains.[35] The impact of the correctional system extends beyond the multitudinous numbers of those serving time, and well beyond their time served. Prison's key role in creating and perpetuating existing inequalities urges a careful look not only at what our society hopes prisons will accomplish but also at what *really* goes on inside their walls.

THE ARCHITECTURE OF CARCERAL CONTROL

Mapleside Prison rests in a clearing, up the way from farmhouses that betray their age with yellowed siding and rusting Chevy pickups parked on adjacent dirt driveways. Miles away from friends and loved ones—hundreds of miles in some cases—the rural setting of the prison feels more isolating than bucolic. True to form as a modern American prison, the border of the compound is traced by impossibly high fences wrapped in barbed razor-wire, with armed officers in watchtowers dotting the perimeter at regular intervals.

Seasons change, but Mapleside stays the same. Month after month, year after year, the prison is frozen in time, seemingly immutable on its perch amidst the landscape of rolling hills and deciduous trees. Beyond the towering fences and the steel doors that lock women in, the summer's clear blue skies feel just out of reach. In the winter, snowfall clings to the gates, transforming the prison walls into a sparkling white fortress.

Inside the prison compound is a set of brick buildings surrounding a small inner courtyard. The inner courtyard is abuzz during "Movement," time periods in which khaki-clad incarcerated women "move" from building to building. They snatch a few precious moments outdoors as correctional officers zip past, their navy uniforms and steel-toed boots accessorized with walkie-talkies beeping from their shoulders. The compound includes not only the cellblocks but also work buildings, where women earn about a dollar an hour sewing state flags and officer uniforms, building furniture for government offices and universities, processing vehicular registrations, or performing data entry for a private company that has contracted their labor with the state.[36]

The healthcare building houses a dental facility, medical ward, and psychiatric wing for women on round-the-clock surveillance. The library building offers access to fiction and nonfiction, legal texts, and classrooms for GED and college education classes. A processing wing houses "new admits" through the first two weeks of their sentences (from there, they will be transferred to "gen pop," or the general population, or to "ad seg," Mapleside's euphemistic shorthand for "administrative segregation"—solitary confinement or "lock").

Then there is the Main Hall where, as a condition of my research access, I spent the majority of my time at Mapleside Prison. The Main Hall is a bustling hub of daily activity. Every woman in gen pop visits the Main Hall for lunch and dinner and to access the gym, computer lab, visiting room, chaplain's office, and spaces used for voluntary programs. There, they navigate the building's cement-block walls slathered in bright white paint, while their shoes squeak on the Lysol-polished tile floors. Around mealtimes, the clean, lemon pine scent is displaced by the odor of pungent dishes piping out of the cafeteria, like sauerkraut on hotdog day. Double doors open to the courtyard, swinging constantly as people stream in and out of the Main Hall. Its corridors are usually noisy, with throngs of women comingling in a din of footsteps and conversation. An officer sits behind a centrally located desk, answering ringing phones and issuing loud commands that add to the cacophony.

Inside the Main Hall, there are five multipurpose classrooms. Bible studies, worship services, 12-step meetings, anger management classes, and other programs share these classrooms, whether for voluntary participation or mandated by a case manager. Each room is scattered with desks, plastic chairs, and large chalkboards. Half the year, noisy A/C units blare a clattering hum. In the colder months, depending on the disposition of the petulant heating system, the classrooms can be freezing and drafty. Gusts of wind whip through cracks in the unsealed windows that look out onto the courtyard, and many women take to wearing gloves indoors to keep warm. Contrary to popular notions about prison architecture, there are no security cameras in the rooms of the Main Hall—only in the hallways. Instead, the door to each room is cut out with a large, reinforced window, allowing anyone to peer inside at any time. A light clanging of keys signals imminent surveillance, notifying everyone that an officer is approaching.

The last, arguably most important, buildings on Mapleside's compound are the housing units: four buildings of cellblock-style rooms in which women are kept under lock-and-key for at least eight hours a day. Dim and dank, a single tiny window (narrow to prevent escape) provides the only natural light. In these double-occupancy cells, the ceilings are low, the floors are concrete, and twin-size bunkbeds jockey for space with a stainless steel sink and toilet set (each to be used within plain view). Toilet seat lids are contraband. "It's horrible," an early 40s white woman named Anne told me of the toilet setup. With no privacy, the incarcerated women adhere to an informal social etiquette—a set of norms that dictate a delicate defecation dance. Anne described:

> If you have to *use* the bathroom, at the first gas or anything, you have to turn around and flush down every single thing. And it's difficult, if you're tryin' to take a shit, to turn around and reach the handle to flush it down. And you're supposed to spray this chemical [deodorizer], but it's not allowed [by the prison], so we have to hide it.

Whenever possible, Anne explained, she waits to use the bathrooms in the work buildings or in the Main Hall, where shower curtains separate the stalls to offer a modicum of privacy. Finally, in the middle of each housing unit sits a "control room" for the purveyors of carceral control, commonly referred to as "the bubble," making its ubiquity clear as officers surveil their charges.

All of this is part of the punishment. At one point, I asked Maria, introduced earlier, whether the cells were climate controlled. She guffawed, shook her head, and called out to her friend Geneva, "You hear that? She just asked if we have air conditioning in our rooms!" Geneva clutched her chest and feigned a cough, playfully teasing my naïveté. The radiators barely worked, so why would I consider the possibility of air conditioners in the cells? Instead, women purchased box fans from a prison-approved vendor, both to cool them down on sweltering nights and to offer some auditory reprieve from the constant noise of walkie-talkies and surveilling officers. The lack of A/C units is one among a long list of deprivations: No cell phones. No internet access. No alcohol. No cigarettes. No "click" pens. No contact lenses. No scarves. No perfume. Even permission to own books and a television is tenuous, each a revocable resource. In sentences that stretch years, decades, or lifetimes, resources like these are a lifeline, offering a sense of humanity inside an institution that dehumanizes by design. When they are plucked away, it is a stark reminder that the incarcerated are not in control.[37] Stripping away any shred of privacy, creature comfort, or expression of individuality sets the baseline for carceral control.

Carceral control is all-encompassing by design, built into the very walls and walkways of Mapleside. This is our setting.

A TYPICAL DAY AT MAPLESIDE

Around 8 o'clock on a bitterly cold Thursday night, Lexi and Karen sit at a small table, ready for their weekly Jewish study in the Main Hall. This week, like most weeks, there is no outside volunteer to lead them—too few Jewish clergy and lay leaders volunteer at Mapleside to staff this program. Instead, Lexi and Karen use this time to talk about their weekly schedules. Karen chortled with dismay as she relayed a phone call with her boyfriend. When she described her day, "Yesterday I had yoga, today I have Pilates, then I'm going to a computer class," she recalled, "He said, 'Sounds like you're in Club Med!'" Karen bristled at his response, saying that she replied to him, "Would you rather I just sit in here depressed?" At this, Lexi nodded in my direction, corroborating Karen's point by adding, "We're all so desperate and sad, we just keep going and going, or we'll go crazy."

Karen and Lexi's active schedules were representative of the weekly routines of many women at Mapleside. Imprisonment in the U. S. is purposefully doled out in a structured, highly bureaucratic manner. Its repetitive schedules are rigid by design. The activities that Karen and Lexi described punctuate an otherwise monotonous cycle. *Work. Eat three meals. Call home. Sleep. Repeat.* They needed to break up the boredom, embracing the opportunities for self-determination that presented themselves.

To learn more about daily schedules, a Latina woman in her late 30s named Estrella walked me through a day in her shoes (table 2). On a typical weekday morning, the wake-up call sounds at 4:00 am. An hour earlier, officers make the rounds to be sure there is a body in every bed. "Count," which happens four times a day, requires that the incarcerated women demonstrate their presence. Asabi explained that "one of the escapes involved someone using a dummy in her bed to make it look like someone was there, so you've got to move around to show it's you." Like clockwork, officers shine a bright flashlight into every cell, rousing women from their slumber in the wee hours of the morning.

After Count, officers unlock the cells one by one. Women leave for breakfast in the cafeteria or to take their morning medications in the Medical Building. Anne said she relishes those tranquil hours: "It's still quiet and most people aren't up yet. I look at the trees, I look up at the moon, and I use that time to pray."

Breakfast is optional, and, unlike the majority of incarcerated women, Estrella is not on a medication regimen. Otherwise she

---

Table 2   A Typical Weekday at Mapleside

Time	Activity
3:00 am	"Count"
4:00 am	Lights on, wake-up
	Shower
4:30 am	Get medication from Medical Building
	Breakfast in cafeteria
6:30 am	Work assignment[1]
7:00 am	"Count"
10:45 am	Lunch in cafeteria
11:30 am	Work assignment
1:00 pm	Inside or outside recreation
2:30 pm	Voluntary programs (including religious programs) in the Main Hall
	Visit with family or friends (maximum of two per week)[2]
	Or Locked in cell
3:00 pm	"Count"
5:00 pm	Dinner in cafeteria
7:00 pm	Voluntary programs (including religious programs) in the Main Hall
	Phone calls home
	Visit with family or friends (maximum of two per week)
	Recreation within housing unit
9:00 pm	Locked in cell
10:00 pm	Lights out
11:00 pm	"Count"

---

1. "Unassigned" women, or those without a work assignment or GED classes, have showers and recreation from 9:00 to 10:30 am.
2. Visiting times dictated by housing unit. Visits may occur in either the afternoon or the evening, but not both.

would retrieve her medication from the Medical Building at 4:30 am. Instead, her mornings begin as follows: "I take a shower, I get dressed, and then I get back into bed and pray or read or watch TV until they call us out for jobs and school." Although it can take up to six months of full-time work in a prison job to earn enough money to purchase a television set from the prison's private vendor, it is one of the few comforts allowed. The markup is roughly double the going rate outside the prison, yet the $150 or $200 it costs to get a tiny flat-screen television becomes well worth it in this context.

Private vendors also sell uniforms to incarcerated women. Each morning, Estrella dresses in her prison-issue clothes, usually a combination of monochrome khaki T-shirts, sweatshirts, cardigans, or button-downs, paired with basketball shorts, sweatpants, or slacks. These uniforms help turn the state's wards from people into prisoners. They are meant to stymie expressions of individual identity. To some extent, it works. As Lexi lamented one day, "I miss clothes. I'm so sick of beige." She laughed, "We call it '50 Shades of Beige.'" Even so, as long as they are purchased from an approved vendor (a private company with a DOC contract), women can sport all brands and styles of sneakers, flip-flops, slides, ballet flats, Ugg boots, and Timberlands—just nothing with a high heel. Some women decorate their shoes with colorful markers. Nail polish is permitted, so intricate patterns and brightly colored manicures help break up the monotony of the khaki uniform. Makeup is allowed, as is limited jewelry (a wedding band, stud earrings, and a single hairclip). Necklaces are permitted only if they represent a religious faith, like a cross or a star of David. Women must inform the administration of any changes to the length or texture of their hair, " 'Cause we're property of the state," one woman explained, "so they can identify us if we escaped."

At 6:30 or 7:00 am, women's routines diverge, depending on work or school assignments. Those without a high school degree are required to take GED classes, while everyone else is required to work. Estrella is among the 200 or so women who work in the "sew shop," cutting and assembling prisoner uniforms, correctional officer uniforms, and the state flags that wave over every office in the county. Job positions are supposed to be filled by request, but often a recommendation from another incarcerated worker to a staff supervisor is enough to get a friend hired. As Chaplain Harper noted, "It's like the real world; it's about who you know. If you got someone working for [a department] and their friend vouches for them, then they'll get a job, when there were 12 other ladies waiting in line for the job."

One in ten women at Mapleside works for the prison's state-run company, which includes the sew shop, a woodcutting workshop where materials will be transformed into furniture for public workplaces like universities and governmental office buildings, and vehicle registration processing for the Department of Motor Vehicles. These are some of the best paid jobs in prison, offering anywhere from $5 to $9 for a full day's labor. A woman named Adelaide surmised that wages are calculated daily rather than hourly because the hourly rate would be paltry, as little as pennies to a few dollars an hour. All of the hourly pay rates are well below federal and state minimum wage. Maria, who prints state-sponsored public service materials in the "distribution shop," earns $7.30 a day. "It's not much," she cautioned, "but it's a lot for prison." Prison staff and administrators frame prison labor as a constructive and even rehabilitative way for incarcerated women to spend their time. "It gives them something to do to be productive, to give back," Chaplain Harper said, although admitting in the next breath, "Companies like to hire them because it's cheap labor, and companies are always trying to get the cheapest labor."

Mapleside's lower-paid jobs involve maintaining the prison operation: working in the mail room, landscaping the courtyard, cooking and serving food in the cafeteria, and performing sanitation work like mopping the floors, squeegeeing windows, and scrubbing toilets. Some women in prison are hired for jobs like caring for the elderly dementia patients in their midst or observing women placed on suicide watch. The administration fills as many jobs as possible with incarcerated workers. "It's a win-win," Chaplain Harper commented, "because the ladies make money and the state can get these goods and services for a cheaper price." Again, she recognized the dollars-and-cents reality: "But then again, of course, they don't get paid much." These workers earn about a dollar a day.

It is conceivable to imagine that incarcerated people have no living expenses. Yet this is not their reality. Women's obligations outside the prison do not vanish when they are locked up. Some have mortgage and car payments, childcare costs that escalate when a mother is incarcerated, and grocery bills to feed families on the outside. Recall the massive piling up of legal financial obligations, including felony fines, attorney's fees, court fees, restitution, and even "pay-to-stay" bills that charge incarcerated individuals per diem for some or all of their confinement.[38] Commissary items like clothing, food, and toiletries all come at a hefty markup: it would come as no surprise to pay $3.00 for a snack-sized bag of chips and a can of soda from the commissary or spend a whole day's wages on an hour-long phone call home.

On top of all that, many mothers send money home to support their children and interim guardians; others owe substantial sums in child support.[39] Deirdre, a mother of two, shared that she never wanted her children to "feel like they [were] going without." On a visit, her 11-year-old daughter mentioned a pair of earrings she hoped to buy from Claire's, a costume jewelry store at the shopping mall. "I told her, 'Don't worry about it, I'll take care of you,'" Deirdre recalled. "I mean, it's not essential, but I want her to feel like she's taken care of. So I mailed her $50 so she can get some earrings, get her lip gloss. And I sent her little sister $25, 'cause what you do for one, you should do for the other." Providing $75 to her children was a drastic hit to Deirdre's "books," yet she was proud she could manage it: "I've been going with less, but it made me feel good, 'cause it was something they wanted."

In the afternoons, once the workday is done, women have a degree of choice in how to spend their time: on the phone calling home, in the visiting room with guests (up to two visits per week for an hour per visit), in free recreation, or in the Main Hall attending voluntary religious and secular programs. On a typical day, Estrella would return to her housing unit to change out of her tan work scrubs, emblazoned "Sew Shop" on the back: "We can't wear our work clothes other places. So I put on some sweats." Then she would head to the Main Hall for religious programs like scriptural study or ministry classes. On other days, she joined the women who opt out of voluntary activities, locked into their cells from 2:30 to 5:00 pm, Estrella said wryly, for "mandatory naps."[40] Nevaeh, who was in her early 20s, described making every effort to avoid spending the afternoon this way. She told me, "I just don't like being in my room," and that she seized the chance to control a small portion of her life by spending most afternoons participating in voluntary programs in the Main Hall. Forty-some years older, Jocelyn similarly solved her boredom however she could. For example, she said, she "asked . . . if there was anything I could do to help the chaplain. I'm sure she has stuff. Apparently they were backlogged on these crosses." Jocelyn held up a two-inch needlepoint cross she was working on. "Women can write in [to the chaplain] and request a cross," Jocelyn continued, "so I offered to do it. It's nice to get out of my room. I'll do anything. I don't like to be in my room."

Mid-afternoon brings the third Count of the day: 3:00 am, 7:00 am, 3:00 pm, 11:00 pm. Counts run like clockwork. No escapes, no hiding, no unauthorized gatherings—Count is intended as a security measure, but, in practice, it is one of the clearest moments in which incarcerated women are reduced from a name to a number.

During my research, I witnessed dozens of afternoon Counts in the Main Hall. Everyone in the building is corralled into the gym, where women queue up based on their assigned housing units. Two officers are present: one to count the number of incarcerated women, the other to record each woman's DOC identification number on a clipboard. There is nothing for the women to do but stand and wait. Eyes are downcast, shoulders sag, ennui prevails on the best days. Reprimand and denigration prevail on the worst. Women must remain quiet and positioned in line; officers are outnumbered and use these behavioral control measures to abate any chance of collective uprising. Typically, it takes 20 minutes or so for the two officers to compare their numbers and report the official count over a walkie-talkie. Movement resumes after all the numbers add up to the daily tally of the confined (the official roster is updated each morning as women are admitted and processed out of the prison).

Dinner lasts from 5:00 to 7:00 pm, served in shifts. The meals call to mind public school offerings, with women called by housing unit to stare down rectangular slices of pizza, dry turkey slopped with gravy, and salads of wilted lettuce smothered in creamy dressing. After dinner, weeknight programs include Bible studies and 12-step meetings. Otherwise, most women return to their cells. On rare occasions, they might go to the visiting room, where they can sit across a table from a family member or friend to talk. Women may embrace their loved one once at the beginning and once at the end of their visit. Since Estrella did not receive many visitors, she listed her typical evening's activities as follows: "I'll take a shower, use the phone, and by 7:30 or 8:00, I'm in my room. I read, study, or watch TV from 9:00 to 11:00. I go to sleep at 11:00."

Long days of drudgery turn into even longer nights, according to Lexi, hinting again at the literal and figurative "darkness" Rosario had pointed out: "The night is when I really feel like I'm locked in. You can't get up in the middle of the night, you can't go get a snack from the refrigerator. There's no moment that's unguarded. Even in the middle of the night, you hear the walkie-talkies go off."

THE ARBITERS OF CONTROL

Carceral control is not automatic by architecture and daily schedules alone. People acting as agents of the state must enforce the rules, serving as the frontline arbiters of control. Journalist Ted Conover wrote of his year spent working as an officer at Sing Sing, "Prison . . . is actually a world of two sides—two colors of uniforms—the 'us' and the 'them.'" Conover called officers "society's proxies," responsible for doling out the punishment handed down by judges and juries in line with the laws crafted by elected officials.[41] Correctional officers are employed to supervise while maintaining order and security.[42] Their jobs are dual-purpose, devoted to both care (of "wards of the state") and custody (of "dangerous criminals").

Many of the incarcerated women I met described their treatment by correctional officers as squarely in the realm of coercive custody. It took a profound toll on their mental health and well-being. Normally cheerful Maria, for example, looked crestfallen one spring morning. Unable to muster a smile, she scoffed, "I am in no mood for prison today. I just can't deal with it today. All that stuff, I know you hear about it. I know you see it. I'm just in no mood." Maria had witnessed an officer berating a woman for something Maria knew she had not done. "The way they talk to us," she said of the officers, "they treat us like animals. We're all people in here. We're all humans."

Earlier in the day, Maria continued, her own humanity was disrespected in the Main Hall. She needed to use the bathroom. There is a lone private bathroom that officers must lock and unlock from the outside. Normally, officers are unfazed when asked for access, but on this day, Maria's request was denied. The officer, she relayed, "made a big fuss about it, not wanting to open the door. That's not part of the punishment, not letting us use the bathroom. Nowhere does it say we shouldn't have the right to use the bathroom. That's a normal human issue." Maria denounced officers' state-sponsored power to control the daily functioning of women's bodies—she concluded it was plain wrong. "This was a moral issue. I'm supposed to be able to use the bathroom when I need to. They treat us like animals," Maria repeated. To her, it felt like once she was found guilty of committing a crime, the world stopped caring how she was treated.[43]

In the face of this callous approach by the boots on the ground, the warden at Mapleside seemed to largely agree with Maria. Warden Davis is a white woman who rose through the ranks after decades working in the correctional system. As she stepped up to the microphone at a volunteer appreciation event I attended, Warden Davis looked out at an audience of about 50 volunteers as she began, "They are women just like you and me, but they made a mistake." A woman sitting beside me, Jeanette, took notice. Jeanette was a white, middle-aged woman with plenty of experience volunteering in other prisons. She knew how unorthodox Warden Davis's humanizing approach was, and she wholeheartedly endorsed it. Like many volunteers, Jeanette had found, upon actually setting foot in a prison, that foreboding warnings about incarcerated men and women as vicious and dangerous were unwarranted. Alongside her comment that the warden sees women in prison as "just like you and me," Jeanette explained that Warden Davis "believes their punishment is coming here. There's no further punishment needed beyond that." The logic had not fully trickled down to all the other state actors at Mapleside, according to Jeanette: "Some of the COs haven't gotten that memo yet, but [the warden is] working on training them in that way."

Officers are used to the old way of doing things. Officer McLean, for instance, a Black woman in her early 30s, was struggling to adopt Warden Davis's approach. When I shadowed her one afternoon, Officer McLean complained, "One thing that bothers me about this prison is that they look at these women as victims, talking about how they [were] battered—they treat 'em different from male inmates." To her, gender-responsive punishment was superfluous. Still, Officer McLean strove to be an effective employee and she indicated that, over time, her outlook had softened: "I just remind myself, 'They're human, and they have good days and bad days, just like I have good days and bad days.'"

Correctional officers are organized in a paramilitary chain of command. As Officer McLean put it, "If it's from above, you gotta do it." I saw this play out firsthand as I sat with her on post in a central artery of the Main Hall. I watched as she had to do her job, whether or not she agreed with the orders from those who outranked her. Officer McLean's task was to inspect passes, making sure everyone who arrived in the Main Hall was supposed to be there and everyone who left was allowed to leave. On that day, it was relatively quiet through the afternoon Count, when Movement was "on hold." Officer McLean confiscated a Dasani water bottle from someone working a custodial job, telling me that it was actually filled with cleaning fluid and therefore could not be taken back to the cellblocks for personal use. Otherwise, her shift was going smoothly.

As dinnertime neared and the housing units were called to the cafeteria, women streamed past in animated conversation. The phone rang—another officer, stationed in a housing unit, was calling to alert Officer McLean that Kiara, a 20-something Black woman in knee-high pink argyle socks, was about to arrive in the Main Hall and she was carrying contraband. The contraband? A pink Hello Kitty fashion scarf, slung over her right shoulder. When Kiara arrived in the Main Hall, Officer McLean approached her: "Step to the side." The woman moved to the right side of the hallway as others continued to file past. Officer McLean fished a plastic Ziploc out from a desk drawer, gesturing for Kiara to forfeit her contraband. "Hand me the handkerchief," Officer McLean commanded.

Kiara protested, "I don't need to give that to you. This is a personal thing! This ain't right." The officer repeated her command: "Hand it over. This is an order from above me."

When Kiara refused, walking toward the cafeteria, she was stopped by Officer Goodson. They exchanged words, and within seconds, the officer handcuffed Kiara. "Take her to lock," Officer Goodson ordered another officer who had since arrived on the scene.

Later, after Kiara was ushered out, Officer McLean chided Officer Goodson: "It's not that big a deal. Now you're gonna have to write a report." Sending Kiara to "lock," Mapleside's version of solitary confinement, meant more paperwork; as Officer Goodson conceded, "I know, but she was getting to me." She cooled down within a few minutes and got on her walkie-talkie. "Okay, you can let her go," Officer Goodson ordered. Kiara was released from lock and allowed to return to the cafeteria.

Watching this interaction in which an officer's discretion escalated the possession of a pink, cartoon-covered handkerchief to an infraction worthy of restraining handcuffs and "lock," I saw a major difference between what Officer McLean had called "good days" and "bad days": On either, an officer can exert discretionary control. But when incarcerated women are deemed to be having "bad days," they can be exposed to physical force, capricious cruelty, and punishment in solitary confinement.

Crucially, the way correctional officers view women in prison is molded by stereotypes around gender. Sociologist Dana Britton has interviewed officers in both men's and women's prisons, finding that although risks of physical violence are greater inside men's prisons, officers strongly prefer to supervise men over women. Incarcerated women are viewed as "manipulative" and "too emotional," and most officers would rather put their lives on the line in men's prisons than deal with what they trivialize as so-called "cat fights." As one female officer in Britton's study put it, "I would much rather work with the [incarcerated] men! . . . I'm just not real good at babying, and the females need a lot more attention. They need a lot more coddling, and that's just kind of our gender."[44] This perspective, which draws on patronizing and paternalistic language of incarcerated women, permeates patrol within prisons, and Mapleside was no different.

I witnessed this myself one evening around 6 o'clock, when Chief Sawyer punished a group of women for using curse words in casual conversation. Chief Sawyer, a Black man in his mid-50s, is the chief of security, second only in the chain of command to Warden Davis. He is a striking figure, typically dressed in a crisp, well-tailored suit, a shaved head evoking his military background. On this particular evening, he took it upon himself to stand outside of the cafeteria and listen in on women's conversations. If anyone cursed, she was penalized with custodial detail. Later, Maria spoke bitterly of the hypocrisy, asking rhetorically, "What's he gonna do about the officers?" She did not dare use the full words, instead telling me, "The officers call us a 'b—' or a 'c—.'" It was, in Asabi's estimation too, an infantilizing rule, particularly given that she and the women around her were "grown women" and, as Asabi declared, "if they want potty mouths, they can have them." As if on cue, the same day I overheard another woman shout at an officer who was reprimanding her, "This isn't a fucking prison, it's a fucking daycare!"

The infantilizing treatment by officers was an especially tough pill for older women to swallow. Ms. Brenda, a woman in her 50s, earned her honorific because others inside respected her age and wisdom. The officers, however, subjected her to the same everyday disregard as everyone else. As Ms. Brenda relayed to me and a group of about ten other women, she had been waiting "at the sliders," the steel doors to her housing unit. This waiting ritual is common—it happens every single time anyone needs to leave the building for work, meals, recreation, medical appointments, or court appearances. Women wait for the officer on post to acknowledge their presence, approve the "movement" as safe, and press a button to open the sliders. But, Ms. Brenda said, the officer "just would not look up to let me out. Meanwhile she'd been opening and closing that door all morning." Although Ms. Brenda had permission to leave her housing unit, she could not do anything until the officer made eye contact from "the bubble." Getting "more and more frustrated," Ms. Brenda said, she finally "let it out . . . dropped the f-bomb." Ms. Brenda's eyes welled as she told the story. She was upset by her own reaction: "I don't want to be like that." Jessi, a younger woman listening with rapt attention, chimed in, "It's because of the lack of freedoms in here. When they lock you in there, like animals." To Jessi, the officer's inattention was only another display of power: "It's all mind games. They see you. The more you bang on the door, [the officer is] not gonna open that." Iris, also in her mid-50s, offered the following words of support to Ms. Brenda: "Everything in here is meant to degrade you. . . . They treat you like a child. It's hard not to get upset."

Even when interactions between officers and incarcerated women go smoothly, it is impossible to forget who is in charge. One young woman warned, for example, "A lot of times the officers mess with you and you want to talk back, but you've got to remember they've got that uniform on, they've got that power." She said she learned the hard way that "talking back" could land her "on lock."

Indeed, I witnessed encounters escalate quickly. Once, when Officer Holt sensed her authority was being questioned, she bellowed, "Let me do what they pay me 40-some thousand a year to do, okay?" These are inescapably asymmetrical interactions, with little recourse for those under the control of the officers. Protocol dictates that incarcerated women can report inappropriate actions by officers, but the women described the grievance paperwork as a futile effort. The rules for officers, they indicated, were unevenly enforced and retaliation was practically inevitable. For instance, Anne told me she understood there might be repercussions, yet she was comfortable reporting officer misconduct. "If an officer does something that I know is wrong, I *will* write them up. And they don't like that. Then they'll treat me like shit for a few weeks, but I don't care. I am going to write them up." Others at Mapleside described similar retaliation, and over my time conducting fieldwork, I heard multiple stories about sexual abuse and use of physical force without recourse, all relayed in hushed tones.

Ultimately, of the arbiters of control, incarcerated women sought "professionalism and respect," in Maria's words. Women understood that being guarded by correctional officers was an inevitable part of their incarceration. As one incarcerated woman told me, they hope that a good officer will just "do his job." Too often, it seemed, the people tasked with manifesting state control intensified diligent enforcement to demeaning and even dangerous discipline.

CONFLICT AND CONNECTION IN CONFINEMENT

"The worst thing about prison is you have to live with other prisoners," one research participant is quoted in criminologist Gresham Sykes's foundational book on men's prison life.[45] Some of the women I interviewed agreed with that assessment. Nevaeh, for instance, had no hesitation when asked what I should know about prison life: "People are weird here. Seriously! I'm the only normal person here," she chuckled. Separately, Estrella gave the same response. "First of all, you know these people are *crazy*." She continued, "It's survival of the fittest in here. . . . It's crazy, so much drama." To her, avoiding conflict felt like an impossible task: "If you sit at a table, you can get caught up easily. You could just be sitting there, but then there's an issue, and someone will come up to you, and say, 'Why you ain't say anything?' Or you could get caught up just because you was there." It was the same complaint levied by Anne: "There's so much crap here. I know they say you're supposed to expect it 'cause you're in jail." She sighed and rattled off her objections, "But there's lying, cheating, stealing . . ." Three women with different ages, racial and ethnic backgrounds, and lengths of time served all shared the sense that nearly every interaction in prison, even with other incarcerated women, was marked by suspicion and fear.

In this environment, simply making a phone call home could be antagonizing. "People who monopolize the phone," Estrella said, would try to bargain and extort money: "If you give me three dollars you can get ten minutes [to make a call] at 6:30." Dorinda corroborated, telling me, "When there are limited resources of something here, it gets horrible." A 60-something white woman, Dorinda described an incident where she was on the phone and "a group of women surrounded me and closed me in a circle so no one could see me." She remembered that she nervously tightened her grip on the phone, but "one woman pulled the phone out of my hand. . . . I don't know what they were going to do." Luckily, another woman stepped in, reportedly admonishing the group, "Oh, leave her alone." The bullies obliged. Although scholars and correctional staff characterize women's prisons by a lack of violence, interactions are not without conflict and potential threat.[46]

At the same time, women's shared struggles with isolation and degradation led many of them to foster supportive, meaningful friendships. The very afternoon I interviewed Estrella, for example, her close friend Honey was being released. Estrella spoke about it philosophically:

A lot of times you say you'll stay in touch and then you never do, because you were only friends because you spent so many years together. It's weird, 'cause you shared so much, but those aren't the people you'd choose to spend time with on the outside.

Still, she was certain it would be different with Honey: "I love her. I'm gonna see her on the outside, I know it."

As we talked, both Estrella and I were keeping an eye out for Honey so we could pause the interview for a goodbye. Soon enough, Honey came walking down the hallway looking prepared for her departure, her hair curled and styled, clutching a clear plastic bag filled with her belongings, the material remnants of her incarceration. Her shaky stance and the look in her eyes betrayed her nerves. "It's going to be an adjustment." Honey gulped. "But it's going to be good. I think I'll be fine this time." Estrella embraced Honey as I retreated to give them space. In an adjacent room, a handful of women crowded the doorway to wish Honey good luck—the officer on duty denied them permission to step into the hallway for a proper farewell, but when the officer was distracted, Honey snuck in for quick, furtive hugs. During one of the hardest times in incarcerated women's lives, many cultivated meaningful connection and forged strong relationships.

Sociologist Erving Goffman wrote of the "fraternization process," in which a neophyte enters an institution believing negative stereotypes about other "inmates," only to learn over time that most incarcerated people "have all the properties of ordinary, . . . decent human beings worthy of sympathy and support."[47] Lexi confirmed, "I was terrified before coming here. I mean *terrified*." She had grown up in a middle class home, earned a bachelor's degree, gotten married, and had a child. She had no prior criminal justice contact until being sentenced to several years in prison for a financial crime. "I thought I would get raped," Lexi smiled sheepishly, embarrassed at what she now viewed as a misguided stereotype. "I didn't know anything. I never knew anyone who had been to prison." Now settled into the rhythms of Mapleside, Lexi's worst fears about the women confined alongside her failed to materialize.

. . . . .

Many women land in prison after lifetimes of hardship and vulnerability. Anthropologist Carolyn Sufrin chronicles this phenomenon in her study of pregnant women caught in the revolving door of jail, writing that a correctional facility can operate as a final safety net, albeit a punitive one: "Economic insecurity and the frayed safety net, coupled with the expansion of carceral institutions, have made jail a safe . . . place."[48] The officers at Mapleside repeatedly invoked the same idea, relying on the idea of prison as providing, at the very least, "three hots and a cot." Officer McLean expounded, for instance, "this is a good place to be, 'cause they got a place to sleep and something to eat every day." But when a correctional facility is the safety net, daily life is "shaded with the knowledge that safety is predicated on criminality."[49] The prison is a chilling reminder of deep layers of poverty and opportunity denied. A world where the prison functions as a safety net is a perverse one, in which some women only get their basic needs met in the context of carceral control. Cloaked in the guise of public safety and correctional security, their punishment may cover the bare minimum human needs, yet the exchange rate is usurious: it comes at the cost of new fears, new insecurities, and new vulnerabilities.

The contours of carceral control map onto the architecture of the prison, the monotony of daily routine, and interactions with officers and among incarcerated women. The next chapter turns to religious programs, showcasing how they can bring moments of vibrancy and joy to this place more commonly marked by anguish and insult. Behind the scenes, religious life is a welcome contrast, acting as a worthy opponent of the state's unyielding efforts of control.

2 *Let There Be Light*

RELIGIOUS LIFE BEHIND BARS

"There is power in the name of Jesus," sings Mapleside's Protestant choir, performing one of their favorite gospel tunes. Churchgoers close their eyes and furrow their brows in pensive contemplation as the choir continues, "to break every chain." In rhythmic syncopation, the choir stomps on the downbeat as each voice lifts the resonant message of breaking chains. So powerful and deeply felt is this song that when Chaplain Harper designed custom T-shirts for Protestant women to wear at Sunday services, she featured an image of a large cross and the words "Break Every Chain" atop a camouflage background, evoking a militant zeal for freedom—both metaphorical and literal. At $10, purchasing the shirt meant exchanging about a day and a half of a woman's labor—a steep cost that many of the incarcerated women deemed a worthwhile addition to their Sunday Best.

Within the bleak, isolating, even threatening environment of prison, religious programs offer a drastic reprieve. The meaningful message of broken chains says it all. The most well-attended religious program—the charismatic Protestant worship service each

Sunday—invites communal ritual, energetic worship, and a notable absence of correctional officers. So, too, Bible and sacred text studies offer fellowship: a chance to learn, confer, and share stories with a close-knit group of people enduring similar struggles. In these spaces, religious activities uplift, inspire, and connect women to a tradition of strength through adversity, a lineage promising freedom through faith.

THE CHAPLAIN'S OFFICE

The chaplain's office is the epicenter of religious activity. Anything related to religion at Mapleside starts and ends with the chaplain. Chaplain Shirley Harper is a Black woman in her mid-50s. She told me that friends and colleagues repeatedly ask her why she left her professional, high-paying position to serve as a full-time prison chaplain for a lower compensation of $50,000 per year. A faithful Baptist, she said she would ask in return, "How much is a soul worth? What's the dollar amount you can put on all the souls I have taught?"

Chaplain Harper's salaried position keeps her working far beyond her full-time hours. The 9-to-5 job stretches into the evenings, even though the part-time chaplain, Chaplain Doris Campbell, is on duty from 5–8 pm. "When I first started," Chaplain Harper explained, "I'd stay late into the night—sometimes 'til midnight. My husband would call me, like 'What are you *doing* all night?'" All of her hours are booked because her list of duties is expansive. Most centrally, she is in charge of administering the constitutionally mandated religious programs at Mapleside. As such, she must ensure that worship services and sacred text studies are available for any group officially deemed a "religion" by the state. This involves all of the administrative and logistical tasks that accompany programming: securing rooms for religious practice, vetting outside volunteers to lead the programs, procuring Bibles and other holy texts, and maintaining current religious affiliation lists to ensure the right people are permitted to attend the right programs (in accordance with their Religious Preference forms).

All of that is plenty for a 40-hour workweek, but Chaplain Harper does far more than the bare minimum. She comes in on weekends, too, attending worship services as a leader of the prison "church." She runs a religious library, officiates any marriages that take place at Mapleside, and performs baptisms for women whose souls are "saved" for the first time, defined in Romans 10:9 as having been delivered from sin through believing and professing Jesus Christ as Lord. She encourages women under her care to initiate new faith-based programs or resources for spiritual growth, entrusting them to lead ministry classes, discipleship classes, scriptural studies, and religious movie screenings without the involvement of outside volunteers. And, most meaningfully to her, she reports, Chaplain Harper provides pastoral counseling for incarcerated Protestant women in crisis.

Incarcerated women see Chaplain Harper as the bigwig in charge, both administratively and spiritually. She is beloved by many, especially the Protestant women in her care, as demonstrated by one woman's remark: "She didn't have to be here. She could be earning six figures somewhere else. For some reason she cares about us." And another's: "I think she's a great leader because she doesn't judge. All are equal in her eyes." Recall the chaplain's weighty words in the epigraph of this book: "I look and see a woman who God loves. I don't see a 'criminal.'"

Thus, in the relative privacy and comfort of Chaplain Harper's office, deep discussions unfold. Not only a space of emotional support, the chaplain's office is an aesthetic reprieve: cozy and carpeted, the room is decorated with religious symbols and scriptural quotes printed on colorful posters. Plush fabric chairs welcome her visitors, and a large banner hangs overhead, reading "Make a joyful noise!" Women use their time with Chaplain Harper to seek guidance on faith, family, disciplinary issues, and personal trauma. Chaplain Harper says the hardest part of her job is delivering sad news, like an illness or a death in the family. Tissues and hard candies sit on the edge of her executive desk, at the ready for tough moments like these. Sometimes, she will allow women to use her personal phone line for a free call, compared to the pricey pay-per-minute calls permitted in the housing units.

Mapleside's non-Protestant laity are assigned to Chaplain Campbell for pastoral care, though she is also a practicing Baptist, and a pair of Catholic volunteers and a Pentecostal volunteer offer counseling to supplement the chaplains' hours. Several women specifically pointed out that it is easier at Mapleside to get an appointment for religious counseling than for psychological counseling.

In the chapters that follow, Chaplain Harper will pop in and out of the storyline. At times, she will have a shadowy presence, a frequent point of reference among COs and incarcerated women, who rarely makes an appearance in the flesh. Chaplain Campbell will be even scarcer. Their apparent disconnection from the daily interactions and religious programs I describe has a structural basis: the chaplains oversee the religious needs of nearly a thousand women, and their time, attention, and resources are stretched thin. On top of organizing programs and offering pastoral care, the chaplains have regular meetings with prison administrators and are responsible for documenting their activities through formal paperwork. As a result, they delegate a lion's share of the on-the-ground execution of religious programs to outside volunteers and hand-selected incarcerated women. Those who volunteer their time, whether outside clergy or devout women confined to Mapleside, make sure religious programs run smoothly as the chaplains work behind the scenes.

THE PREVALENCE OF RELIGIOUS PROGRAMS

Overall, religious programs far outnumber secular programs, not only at Mapleside but in correctional facilities throughout the country (table 3). Consistent with neoliberal state retrenchment in the late twentieth century, support for taxpayer-sponsored secular

Table 3   Voluntary Programs at Mapleside

Meeting Frequency	Secular Programs	Protestant Programs	Other Religious Programs[3]
Weekly or more	12-step programs[1] Anger management Beekeeping[2] Behavioral skills Cat companionship[2] College courses[2] Crocheting Emotional awareness Gardening[2] Service-dog training[2] *Toastmasters International* Yoga Zumba	Adult choir[2] Banner ministry[2] *Battlefield of the Mind* Bible Institute *Celebrate Recovery* Christian witness training Dance ministry[2] Denominational Bible study Discipleship class Drama ministry[2] Equipment set-up[2] Grief counseling Mime ministry[2] Praise and Worship team[2] *Purpose Driven Life* *Recovery in Christ* Religious movie screening *S.H.A.P.E.* class Usher ministry[2] Worship service Youth choir[2]	Study forum Worship service

1. Although 12-step programs refer to a "higher power," they are not classified as Religious Programs by Mapleside Prison officials, nor do they screen participants by official Religious Preference. Thus, they are included with the secular programs.
2. Selective admission.
3. For all other affiliations, including Catholic, Sunni Muslim, Lutheran, Wiccan, Seventh Day Adventist, Jehovah's Witness, NOI, Jewish, Moorish Scientist, and Native American groups.

(Continued)

Table 3   (Continued)

Meeting Frequency	Secular Programs	Protestant Programs	Other Religious Programs
Biweekly or monthly	Book club Legal workshop Girl Scouts[4] Meditation Writing club Storybook project[5]	Christian mentoring *Kairos* religious retreat Life purpose event	

4. Girl Scouts with incarcerated mothers visit for a weekend "sleepover" at Mapleside.
5. Mothers create a voice-recording of themselves reading a book to send to their children.

programming has declined precipitously in American prison policy. Stepping into the void, prison chaplains gained importance as the scope of voluntary activities shifted from secular to religious, addressing everything from idle time to addiction recovery to self-help needs.[1] Religious and faith-based programs do the work of social support, life coaching, and rehabilitation where state funding is limited. Furthermore, as will become apparent, Protestant programs outnumber activities offered by any other religious denomination. Whereas all religious programs are guaranteed a study forum and worship service thanks to religious freedom legislation, there is an extensive list of other voluntary Protestant activities. They run the gamut from outreach programs to Christian-based self-help courses, grief counseling groups, ministry rehearsals, Christian movie screenings, and a multiyear, intensive Bible Institute program.

Religious activities are open to any woman registered to a given denominational affiliation, provided prison officials do not classify her as a security threat. Secular activities, on the other hand, must admit women selectively (fig. 4). There are not enough volunteers or

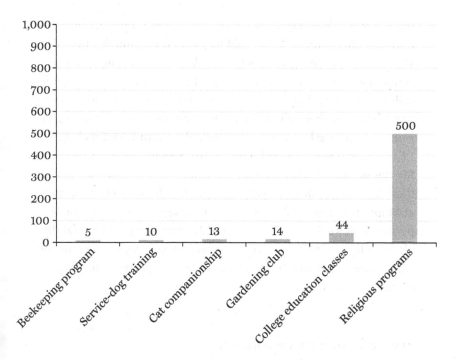

Figure 4. Attendance in secular and religious voluntary programs.

resources for open enrollment. The beekeeping program, for instance, accommodates only five beekeepers-in-training, 10 hopefuls are selected for the service-dog training program, and 13 women can participate in the cat companionship program, which a woman named Dina called "cats on death row." Proudly, she said of the cats, "We saved them. They were gonna be put down." The program was deeply comforting to her: "When I first got [my cat], I was like, 'I can't believe I can have this much comfort in here.' As women, we need to be able to care for something." Yet only a handful of women can participate at any given time. Mapleside's highly coveted college education program admits just 44 students per year—far fewer women than apply (they tirelessly resubmit their applications semester after semester, they told me, until a spot finally opens up). While recovery programs such as Alcoholics Anonymous and Narcotics Anonymous refer to a "higher power," they are not technically considered religious programs since they do not screen participants based on their official Religious Preference forms. Although it is important to acknowledge their baked-in faith-based messaging, 12-step programs are included in the secular category because Mapleside administrators classify them in this way. In contrast to these limited-enrollment secular programs, about half of all women at Mapleside attend voluntary religious programming, totaling 500 participants weekly. Thus, based on sheer capacity and availability alone, religious programs hold a place of key importance in the weekly routine at Mapleside in ways that secular programs simply cannot.

TIME OUT OF THE CELLBLOCK

Voluntary religious and secular programs offer respite from the claustrophobic, cacophonous cellblock. On weekdays, apart from labor, meals, and recreation, Mapleside's incarcerated women are locked into their two-person, 7-by-10-foot cells. Saturdays are even worse, said one woman: "There's literally nothing to do. At least during the week I'm busy with work."

Religious programs offer incarcerated women time out of their cells and a degree of autonomy over their schedules. Most religious activities like study forums and self-help programs are given a wide berth by the prison's officers. Because the Protestant programs are the largest and most frequent, they offer the most opportunities for women to seize the freedom to leave their cellblocks. A religious activity is scheduled almost every day of the week, meaning Protestants effectively have more autonomy than those who select the Catholic, Jewish, or Muslim religious designation.

Table 4	Maria's Thursday Schedule in the Main Hall
Time	Activity
8:30 am–11:00 am	Librarian in religious library
11:00 am–12:00 pm	Reshelve books
12:00 pm–12:45 pm	Pick up lunch tray, eat lunch in library
12:45 pm–1:30 pm	"Piddle"
1:30 pm–3:00 pm	Teach "Discipleship" class
3:00 pm–5:00 pm	"Count"
5:00 pm–6:30 pm	Dinner
6:30 pm–7:00 pm	Arrive early for Bible study
7:00 pm–9:00 pm	Bible study

Maria, a faithful Baptist, cheekily referred to structuring her day with these voluntary activities as "lingering and loitering." To be sure, she found deep meaning in religious programs, but she also noted that she relished the sense of control they gave her over her daily schedule. On a typical Thursday, Maria explained that she could feasibly remain in the Main Hall, out of her cell, participating in religious activities for more than 12 hours. Table 4 chronicles Maria's Thursday schedule.

As usual, Maria's Thursdays started with a 4 o'clock wake-up, followed by breakfast in the cafeteria or time in her cell spent watching television, reading, or praying until she was allowed to report to the Main Hall at 8:30 or 9:00 am. In her position as the designated religious librarian, Maria checked passes against a preprinted attendance list in the religious library from 9 to 11 o'clock. I joined her in this work each Thursday for six months. Another of her duties was to reshelve the books that women returned as they checked in. From the start, Maria rebuffed my efforts to help her and forbade me from reshelving the books, a fact that seemed odd given our congenial relationship. Later, Maria disclosed that if she was reshelving the books at 11 am, most officers would see that she was busy and let her stay in the library until lunchtime. Otherwise, she would be sent back to her cell. I gladly obliged, ceding the reshelving duties to Maria. By noon, Maria would pick up a late lunch tray from the cafeteria and eat it alone in the religious library, savoring a precious moment of peaceful privacy.

Next, when Maria was on good terms with the Main Hall officer, she would "piddle" around, as she put it, until she taught her 90-minute Discipleship class that began at 1:30 pm (described in the book's introduction). Afterward, if Maria stopped by to debrief with Chaplain Harper or chat with her clerks long enough that Count began, she said she was home free. Officers had no choice but to let Maria stay in the Main Hall past 5 o'clock, when Count cleared and "Movement" resumed throughout the compound. If Maria could make it "through Count," she noted, she was set for the day, remaining in the Main Hall for 5:30 pm dinner, then reporting straight to Baptist Bible study, which stretched from 7 pm (when the outside volunteers arrived) to 9 pm.

Thursdays with Maria offer an extreme but demonstrative case, wherein she has curated her day with voluntary religious activities to maximize her time out of her cell. By jockeying among the activities, women can carve out choice in a world defined by constraint. As Maria's schedule demonstrates, religious programs—Protestant programs in particular—are one of the most readily available ways to enact that autonomy.

THE DEMOGRAPHICS OF PARTICIPATION: ATTENDEES AND VOLUNTEERS

Religious programs, then, are notably accessible and frequent, but they stand out for another reason: the ways that they intersect with background characteristics of race and social class. Outside of prison, religious institutions are considered the country's most racially segregated institutions, and 11 o'clock on Sunday morning, "the most segregated hour" in American life.[2] I found this to be true of some religious programs at Mapleside. For instance, both the Sunni Muslim group and the Jewish group are racially homogenous (with roughly 50 Black women and 15 white women, respectively). The Catholic group boasts about 70 adherents, with a rough demographic breakdown of 70 percent white women, 18 percent Black women, and 12 percent Latina women of the 20 or so regular attendees of Sunday services. To some extent, these racial patterns in religious affiliation overlap with what we see outside of prison.[3] The Protestant religious programs are comparatively more racially integrated. Recall that the prison has an even split of white and Black women, reflecting an overrepresentation of Black women relative to their proportion of the total U. S. population. Yet at Protestant Sunday worship services, about 70 percent of attendees are Black and 30 percent are white (only a few Latina women attend).

The racial demographics of religious participation roughly reflect the racial demographics of the outside volunteers and clergy who lead religious programs at Mapleside. Like their adherents, all of the Sunni volunteers I met were Black, and all of the Jewish and Catholic volunteers I encountered were white. The majority of Protestant volunteers were Black women, with a handful of white women and Black men volunteering intermittently.

Volunteers described being motivated by both theology and personal dedication to working against the harms of incarceration. Their intentions were on display when they described what led them to participate in prison ministry. A nondenominational Christian preacher named Ms. J shared her testimony of what convinced her to lead a weekly study session inside prison walls: one night, while preparing dinner, "God spoke to me," Ms. J reported. Hearing God's voice "changed my life," she explained. "I am passionate about teaching to women in prison." Ms. J has been teaching a Protestant self-help class every Wednesday for the past 12 years. "I get up [on] Wednesdays and pop out of bed, like, 'Yay, it's Wednesday!'" Ms. J hopped in place to embody the joy she felt in volunteering. The incarcerated women listening to her testimony chuckled as she continued, "People at work are like, 'You excited to be going to *jail?*'" Ms. J said she responded to this incredulity with an enthusiastic "yes!"

During the calendar year I observed, most Protestant volunteers identified as Baptist (44 percent), followed by nondenominational Christians (26 percent) (table 5). The Protestant umbrella group encompassed a wide range of beliefs, traditions, and customs—primarily focusing on salvation and being "born again," adhering to charismatic, evangelical, and/or historically Black faith communities (like the African Methodist Episcopals). Some sociologists of religion, referring not to political but social leanings, have used the term "conservative Protestants" to distinguish these branches of Christianity marked by Biblical literalism from "mainline Protestants." Others may call them otherworldly or mystical, especially when considering the historically Black denominations that were represented.[4] With this ideologically diverse volunteer pool of lay clergy volunteer, one woman summarized, "We have different groups coming into the pulpit. We get a smorgasbord of religion. We can't expect a consistent Word [of God]; we have to pick and choose what fits."

When I spoke to Dr. Claire Goldstein, a psychologist who works inside nearby prisons, she characterized religious volunteers by saying: "They're always women, always well dressed, and very nice." Indeed, Mapleside's cadre of volunteers largely fit this bill. Most volunteers I encountered dressed in polished pantsuits or fitted dresses, paired with colorful high heels ranging from pumps to strappy leopard-print slingbacks. Compared to incarcerated women's permitted stud earrings, religious necklace, and simple wedding band, volunteers wore sparkling jewelry, dangling earrings, and oversized pearls. "I love my adornment," Reverend Mona confessed one week as she arrived to teach a ministry class. "I love my matching earrings and necklaces." Their hair was dyed and pressed, plaited into up-dos, not a strand out of place. More often than not, volunteers' nails looked freshly manicured, their makeup flawless, and a waft of floral perfume trailed them through the halls. The stark contrast between volunteers'

Table 5 Denominational Affiliation of Protestant Volunteers at Mapleside
         (n = 27)

Denomination	Number Affiliated (%)
Baptist	12 (44%)
Nondenominational	7 (26%)
African Methodist Episcopal	3 (11%)
Pentecostal / Apostolic	2 (8%)
Other	3 (11%)

adornment and prison uniforms was perhaps most apparent at a Christmas Day worship service, when one religious volunteer stood out in a light blue floor-length evening dress, her hair coiffed and crowned with a sparkling tiara. "Where was she *going?*" a woman named Chanel asked a group of her friends, teasing. She and her friends giggled about the "prom dress," as they called it. "Seriously, where was she *going*?" Next to incarcerated women's strict khaki uniforms, volunteers stood in stark contrast, signaling their differences in status and perhaps social class backgrounds.

Indeed, compared to the volunteers, the women confined to Mapleside were more likely to come from socioeconomically disadvantaged backgrounds with limited access to education, roughly reflecting the demographics of incarcerated populations across the country. Nationally, 58 percent of American women have attended some college, but that is true for less than a third of incarcerated women; according to the Bureau of Justice Statistics, only 42 percent of women in U. S. prisons have completed high school or earned a GED.[5] The volunteers, meanwhile, boast of graduate degrees and well-paid jobs. During a Christian self-help class, I heard one volunteer disclose her six-figure income and her half-million-dollar home. Additional social class markers were visible to women at Mapleside. Ja, a Black woman in her early 20s, pointed out a volunteer minister's gold Rolex watch, and Chanel, joining in, chided that Chaplain Harper had looked less-than-polished only once: "The scuff on those shoes! They looked so *old*." Ja added, "It was like a two-inch heel. It wasn't even a kitten heel. It threw the whole outfit off balance." With a dramatic sigh, Chanel declared: "It's so distracting to me, the things they wear." She was restricted to the clothing regulations outlined in the last chapter, and so, like some of my other respondents, Ja and Chanel reacted with quiet derision when volunteers squandered their opportunities to wear stylish clothing, while being keenly aware of the class positions they may have signified.

Chanel's peers expressed additional skepticism about the volunteers and their intentions. Dorinda said coming to the prison "makes them feel important," but pointed out:

> They aren't qualified social workers. Volunteers who come in have their own problems—that's why they are here . . . . They fill a need for these women who are down and out, but it's not genuine. They are taking advantage of a need to feel heard and supported.

Dorinda's mistrust was based in what she saw as volunteers' flakiness. Religious volunteers used to support her regularly at Mapleside, but they would abruptly stop showing up. "They are inconsistent," she charged. This, too, has a structural explanation: pushing against the growing reliance on religious outsiders to lead programs and offer counseling in prisons is the simple fact that unpaid volunteers lack the training, resources, and support to maintain a consistent schedule. Furthermore, volunteers' permissions to enter Mapleside can be rescinded at any moment. The neoliberal turn toward costless correctional programming has induced a lack of continuity in the support available to incarcerated women.

True to the foundations of carceral control, and to Dorinda's point, the administration tightly regulates who volunteers and when they volunteer, and can even filter volunteers based on what they might or might not preach. Every visitor to prison undergoes a form of "secondary prisonization," in which they submit to an array of state mandates that dictate their visits, their dress, and their comportment on the prison compound.[6] Religious volunteers may have more latitude with regard to their outfits and adornments, but their secondary prisonization focuses around paperwork and official imprimaturs. Before they are ever allowed in, prospective volunteers must navigate an extensive screening process, starting with a background check and an application to Chaplain Harper. They are required to submit paperwork documenting baptismal certification and congregational membership, alongside reference letters to endorse their ministerial capabilities. Ms. West, Mapleside's full-time volunteer coordinator, is in charge of conducting background checks and interviewing volunteer hopefuls about their credentials and motivations for joining a prison ministry. Once the assistant warden rubberstamps Ms. West's decisions, volunteers attend a mandatory three-hour orientation. Only then are they issued identification badges. This multilevel process inserts discretion at multiple points, such that volunteers' suitability is evaluated repeatedly, with several exit valves.

Once they are approved, however, the oversight mostly evaporates. There is no training, and volunteers' sermons and programs are minimally monitored. Chaplain Harper occasionally sits in on worship services, but the bulk of the regulation of religious programs is shouldered by incarcerated women themselves. When churchgoers are disappointed with a particular sermon, they speak up. On Pentecost Sunday, after an underwhelming service from Pastor Tamara, numerous attendees complained among themselves and to the chaplain. "I wasn't feeling it," Deanna, a mid-30s Black Baptist, confided. With derision, she marveled, "That preacher? She was all over the place. There was nothing to take from it." A number of "people who faithfully stay in the service" on other days had, she said, gotten up and left. Nevaeh wrapped her arm around Deanna's shoulder and corroborated her point by jokingly imitating Pastor Tamara's way of speaking in tongues. Even Estrella, a longtime Pentecostal who was well acquainted with glossolalia, assured the group that "she was going to say something" about Pastor Tamara's service to Chaplain Harper. In these ways, devout women take an active role in screening and evaluating the religious messages made available to them. They make their concerns known to avert egregious cases of poor preaching. Nevertheless, prison officials always have final say over volunteers' suitability and continued access to the prison. This discretion was made clear when the theater program was canceled for expressing negative sentiments toward Mapleside. As one volunteer reported, sighing, "The warden shut down the theater program. Because they said they didn't like prison." She shrugged, unfazed that women in prison would dislike prison while unsurprised that prison officials would silence any verbalization of dissent.

PROPHECY AND PERSONHOOD

Earlier, I wrote about sociologist Erving Goffman's assessment that prisons can be understood through the lens of "total institutions"; Goffman argues that prison officials strip outside identities away as part of the broader effort to achieve "total control" over prisoners. Markers of personal expression are removed, not only for standardization and efficiency but as part of the package of carceral control. At Mapleside, women are required to wear uniforms, apply only the makeup that is permitted by the prison, and adhere to particular hairstyles. Prison officials regulate their schedules, housing and work assignments, and sexual relationships—the list goes on. This "mortification of the self," as Goffman calls it, seeks to replace an individual's sense of identity with a deep embodiment of the incarcerated role.[7] Although this process operated at Mapleside, it also appeared that religion counteracted the "mortification of the self," allowing women's individuality and personal self-expression to be celebrated.[8]

Mapleside officials' emphasis on self-mortification is perhaps best illustrated by observations from the three-hour volunteer orientation that I attended, led by Sergeant Hodgson. Sergeant Hodgson hammered home the state's goal of erasing individual identities from men and women in prison, viewing them instead in the aggregate. In other words, volunteers should accept incarcerated individuals' self-mortification brought about by prison rules and regulations. "There should be no individualization with any inmate. Nothing about one inmate that should be individualized," she warned the prospective volunteers. "It doesn't matter the security level of an inmate, or their gender; they are all very dangerous. It's not important what they've done," she continued. According to Sergeant Hodgson, volunteers should not differentiate between low-level drug offenders and violent murderers, or between incarcerated men and women—they were all equally manipulative and dangerous. "This is a *prison*," she said menacingly, "Things happen. You want to go home." Her tone threatened the worst. Volunteers seeing prisoners as people, Sergeant Hodgson warned, could be a slippery slope toward their physical assault or even murder.

In practice, despite these dire warnings, the task of de-individualizing the women of Mapleside was impossible—and undesirable—for the religious volunteers. I repeatedly observed their disregard of Sergeant Hodgson's directive. For religious volunteers, individualized attention was the point. It was the work they were called to do. Although this was true across religious traditions, it was even more crucial for Protestants, with their focus on personal salvation.

One night, during a weekly Christian class, Ms. J quoted a line from scripture in which God asks Satan, "Have you considered my servant Job?" (Job 1:18). At this, she strode toward Carla, a Black woman in her late 40s who was a frequent attendee. Placing her hand on Carla's shoulder, Ms. J intoned, "Have you considered my servant Carla?" Carla beamed, submitted by Ms. J as a pillar of faith, as God submitted Job, a faithful believer through his repeated suffering. The volunteer connected with Carla, adding, "You're the best God got. If He don't show [devotion] through you, who [will] He show it through?" Carla and the other attendees were, in this moment, recognized as worthy, "the best God got." If not them, then who?

One of the most individualizing aspects of Protestant religion at Mapleside is the prophetic tradition prevalent in certain branches of the Black Church. Importantly, prophecy in this context is not about predicting the future, but speaking against the status quo.[9] A number of Baptist and nondenominational volunteers prophesy to incarcerated women, delivering what they describe as a personal message from God. Ms. J was among those known for her prophetic abilities. "When I pray for you, when I lay hands on you, it's *done*," Ms. J said with confidence. "Because I have the faith. I was given the gift of the seer, the power of healing."

"I'm going to heal you of a medical issue today. Does that sound good to you?" Ms. J asked Jessalyn, a white woman in her early 20s. Jessalyn nodded, and Ms. J raised her hands toward the young woman's upper body. She prayed for God to heal her headaches and neck pain. Then Ms. J prayed to heal her another woman's "breathing issues" before laying hands on another attendee, telling her, "You're young, but you have high blood pressure." Laying hands is a common practice in certain charismatic Christian circles; at Mapleside, where so many yearn for physical and emotional healing, and for compassionate touch and care, it breaches the norms of de-individualization and interrupts carceral control, if only temporarily.

Prophetic messages ranged from physical health to one's greater purpose in life. Ms. J foresaw, for one woman, a role as "handmaiden," explaining, "Everybody been telling you your whole life you are supposed to serve. This is the last time—the time you'll do it." To another, Ms. J prophesied, "I see you writing. Writing a book, poetry, screenplays. You'll use ink to serve Him." She told a woman named Marcy:

> A lot of times when people look at you, they don't see your intelligence. But you are real smart, and I don't know where down the line you thought you were supposed to hide that from people. But you need to share what you know. There are people who need to hear what you have to say.

Ms. J envisioned Carla as a minister and that Mia would work with children. Of me, she prophesied, "Missions are in store for you." Later, when I shared this prophecy with some others who were not in Ms. J's class, I was struck by Estrella's remark: "You're kind of in a mission right now—coming here. You're outside of your comfort zone, doing something that challenges you." Her words resonated. Although I did not subscribe to their same faith tradition, in that moment, I gained a glimpse into how meaningful these messages could be: it felt significant to take the time to reflect on what Ms. J's prophecy meant for me, considering life's greater purpose.

The women who received Ms. J's prophecies affirmed her abilities. Estrella was a believer: "It was real accurate. She knew a lot of details, and she knew the name of my son. You hear her tell people they getting out—and then they do." As was Vera, who shared with her classmates: "Last week you prayed for my legs, and now I've had so much less pain. All of a sudden I can get my shoes on now—the swelling is down." The room broke into applause at Vera's news. In another prophetic moment, Laura excitedly gestured toward Ms. J as she told me about her upcoming appeal hearing: "She prophesied that [hearing]. A few months ago, she said that a door would open for me." Indeed, several of Ms. J's prophesies came to fruition: Laura was released early on appeal and Coretta testified that her stomach problems went away. Other prophesies appeared not to materialize, including the imminent release of women in her self-help class and certain physical healing that she foresaw. Regardless, the power of these personalized messages, and of the prophetic tradition at Mapleside, was palpable, especially next to the de-individualizing rhetoric of prison officials.

Ms. J was not the only prophet who visited the prison. In fact, I saw the individual nature of prophecy made clearest by Reverend Suraya, an African Methodist Episcopal minister. "God loves all of you," the Reverend began her remarks one evening. "And I don't mean to diminish that, but sometimes His favor isn't fair." She raised her eyebrows to signal that inspiration had struck. "Sometimes, He shows favor to prove His power. And to you, the one sitting right there, what's your name?" Vanessa, suddenly the focus of attention, quietly shared her name. "Well, Vanessa," Reverend Suraya said beatifically, "God is going to show you favor soon. He's going to do something real big for you soon." Vanessa shut her eyes and bowed her head. "I receive that."

Personal salvation, personal relationships with the divine, and personal messages delivered through prophecy all chipped away at the overarching, dehumanizing atmosphere of the prison. These messages stood in stark contrast to prison officials' effort to reduce the incarcerated women to an aggregate group of what they called "dangerous inmates," pushing back against the self-mortification so thoroughly entrenched in prison operations.

THE PROTESTANT WORSHIP SERVICE

Finally, we turn to the main event, the most well-attended religious activity at Mapleside, summoning nearly 260 worshippers each Sunday: the Protestant worship service. The church crowd seems enormous against the 20 or so worshippers at typical Catholic services, let alone the scant handful who attend Jewish and Muslim services on a good week (although I was told the Sunnis' numbers rise when an imam is present). Administration has divided Protestant worship into two separate time slots, a morning and an evening service, with women assigned based on their housing units. The cavernous prison gym comes alive for these services, when the Protestants demonstrate their unparalleled ability to, as one officer put it, "congregate." During this time, worshippers find reprieve from formal surveillance: one or two officers disinterestedly sit in the back of the room or outside in the hallway, leaving the volunteer preachers to lead the service.

The "Equipment Set-Up Ministry" of incarcerated women arrives early to prepare the gym, clearing recreational equipment to make room for seating and religious ritual objects. Positioned on a basketball court, with hoops at either end, six rows of plastic chairs face the central podium, which is outfitted with a microphone and a banner that reads:

Wise men still seek Him
Come and worship the King

In fact, apart from the sermons and prayers delivered by outside volunteers, every aspect of the service is planned, produced, and performed by the women at Mapleside. Ushers wearing golden robes stand at the doorway as worshippers trickle in, handing out printed programs (designed, typed, and printed each week by Chaplain Harper's clerks, incarcerated women Hanna and Asabi). In accordance with "inmate movement" requirements, the ushers also make sure that everyone signs the attendance log to document their whereabouts. On especially hot days, when the industrial fans rattle feebly, ushers distribute cardboard hand fans donated by a local funeral home.

As congregants arrive for the service, they greet each other with hugs: a rare exception to the prison's strict no-contact policy. The atmosphere is chatty and convivial, with popular Christian music blaring and women who serve on the "Banner Ministry" waving colorful flags emblazoned "Amazing Grace" and "Let us crown the King." As Hanna, a Banner Ministry member, explained, "We are waving the banners to open up the gates of Heaven for the Holy Spirit to come in. It's much more serious than people think."

The attendees, working within the confines of the prison's dress code, don their Sunday Best. Some straighten their hair or style intricate braids, and many apply colorful eyeshadow and lipstick, conveying that worship is a special occasion. After a period of socializing and fellowship, the ushers direct the congregants to their seats, and the "Praise and Worship Team" launches into a couple of rousing *a capella* songs to set the tone. A scriptural reading comes next, then an emcee introduces any outside volunteers and guests in attendance.

Next, the choir, cloaked in regal purple robes draped over their khaki prison garb, belts out energetic gospel tunes and popular Christian songs. Then, the atmosphere transforms from festive to contemplative as the "Dance Ministry" takes the floor. A dozen women perform modern and interpretive dance choreography as Christian ballads pipe through the speaker system. On other weeks, the "Drama Ministry" might perform a short play about the life of Christ, or the "Mime Ministry" may express their faith through corporeal storytelling. Worshippers raise their hands in witness, swaying along reverently.

By this time, attendees are ready for the Word of God. The volunteer minister takes the microphone, beginning with a personalized introductory prayer incorporating the handwritten "Prayer Requests" submitted by churchgoers. The sermon follows, lasting about half an hour. As is detailed at great length in the next chapter, sermons range from fire-and-brimstone to messages about God's unconditional love. Some preachers pace around the gym, ramping up energy and enthusiasm, while others promote curative tranquility by "laying hands" on churchgoers in need of healing. Rousing moments elicit cries of "Amen!" "Praise God," and "Preach, preacher!" from worshippers in reverence. In moments when attendees are "moved by the Holy Spirit," they "shout," speak in tongues, cry, or "fall out" as they embrace the hallowed messages.[10] Once each month, Protestant worshippers may receive communion, in which case the minister prays over the prepackaged sacramental "host" and grape juice (as no alcohol is allowed on the premises) before being distributed by ushers to all worshippers.

Acknowledging the fact that not every attendee is a believer, and in response to the Christian imperative to proselytize,[11] the service then continues with an "Altar Call." The preacher encourages anyone wishing to "give their life to Christ" to approach the front of the gym and recite a sinner's prayer in order to be "saved." During one Christian ministry class that I observed, co-teachers Asabi and

Estrella explained that salvation is motivated by Romans 10:9–10, which reads, "If you declare with your mouth, 'Jesus is Lord,' and believe in your heart that God raised him from the dead, you will be saved. For it is with your heart that you believe and are justified, and it is with your mouth that you profess your faith and are saved."[12]

In each of the services I observed, from three to ten women participated in the sinner's prayer portion of "Altar Call," and after the service concluded, more seasoned Christians approached them to suggest they enroll in a weekday afternoon "Follow Up" class to enrich their faith. Another 10 or 15 women would heed the preacher's next appeal, inviting the "backsliders," known as those who moved away from their faith, to approach the front podium to "rededicate their lives to Christ," as they described it, through prayer. Finally, the "Benediction" concludes the service, with the volunteer pastor praying for the health and safety of the congregants. The atmosphere deflates as attendees prepare for "Movement"—the return to their housing units.

Sociologist Randall Collins, building on Durkheimian and Goffmanian interactional theories, writes of rituals as the root of social institutions—and the root of group identity itself.[13] Group identities coalesce around interaction rituals like the Protestant worship service. As individuals gather together in a physical space like the prison gym, religious rituals build solidarity and standards of morality through emotional energy and a shared focus of attention. In this sense, religious activities at Mapleside are valuable not only for their implicit ritual worth, including the freedom and emotional reprieve they offer from everyday life in prison, but also are functionally productive in their ability to galvanize identity, foster a sense of fellowship, and demarcate status and group boundaries, as subsequent chapters will explore.

·   ·   ·   ·   ·

Religious programs provide women an opportunity for connection, physical expressions of faith, and meaningful emotional resonance in an otherwise bleak environment where emotions and bodily movements are highly regulated. Incarcerated women find a space for emotional support and friendship in services and Bible study groups, and they cherish the personalized, humanizing messages delivered by religious volunteers, particularly charismatic Christians. The volunteers' care and concern regarding women's physical and mental health, histories of trauma and abuse, and legal entanglements contrast with prison officials' studied disregard. Moreover, the implications of religious messages and religious community extend beyond the makeshift prison chapel. Religious programs at Mapleside mean more than just a few hours of reprieve.[14]

Take Ms. Lonnie, for instance. After 17 years at Mapleside, Ms. Lonnie had to stop attending worship services. Her "time" in prison seemed to have aged her beyond her 75 years, and she could no longer make it down the set of stairs into the gym. Ms. Lonnie often looked wisely bemused as she gazed beyond the owlish glasses resting on the bridge of her nose. When Maria spotted Ms. Lonnie shuffling past one day, her tall frame curled over her walker, she cried out, "Take me on a ride in that *Cadillac!*" Maria turned to me to explain her smiling exclamation: "You try to uplift. This is their *life*, you know?"

As we see from Maria's playful interaction with Ms. Lonnie, it is not uncommon for devout women to find themselves supporting each other through particularly hard times. Calling on faith helps women bond over shared moral commitments and helps offer answers to life's existential questions. In an environment marked by deprivation, religion provides a source of hope, joy, and autonomy for incarcerated women. Through religion, women gain the ability to make choices about how and where to spend their time, to seek counsel with the chaplains and fellow believers, and to sing, embrace, and express emotion.

At the same time, the freedoms offered by religion are not impervious to carceral control. Religion in prison cannot be mistaken for religion in any other context, no matter how profoundly it shapes incarcerated people's ability to make sense of their lives behind bars. Secondhand carcerality stems from state power and is in conflict with the institutional power of faith. The remainder of this book dives into deeper meanings derived from participation in religious programs, and the tensions they encounter with carceral control.

3 *The Lord Is My Shepherd*

PROTESTANT MESSAGES OF GOD'S
REDEMPTIVE PLAN

God hasn't forgotten you. He knows everything you
do. It's not like a dark cloud came over here and God
can't see in. He still watches over you and loves each
and every one of you.

Chaplain Harper

When it comes to the harms and hardships of a prison sentence, researchers increasingly focus on what it means to be punished.[1] What are the cultural understandings of the meaning of incarceration? How do narratives, logics, and discourses work together to construct how society views people in prison—and how people in prison are encouraged to view themselves? Prison officials and state actors tend to draw on punitive discourses, hinging on themes of retribution and personal responsibility. They describe incarcerated men and women as dangerous "criminals," pathologically flawed, and worthy of harsh punishment.[2] These discourses are underpinned by stereotypes around gender, race, ethnicity, and social class that stoke fears of rampant crime. They insist on a great need to "lock 'em up and throw away the key" to improve public safety. Of course, state-sponsored narratives of crime and logics of punishment not only impact public perceptions but also the self-conceptions of those being punished. Prior research has documented how incarcerated people are encouraged to accept these harsh discourses and embody narratives of redemption and rehabilitation in order to reestablish themselves as "worthy" individuals in the eyes of the state, and in the eyes of society. How people make sense of their time within prisons and how they come to see their identities speak to the forms and functions of carceral control.

This chapter will interrogate how religious narratives and logics seek to challenge carceral discourses, emphasizing the worth of incarcerated persons in the eyes of God, while assessing how narratives of the religious self are constrained by the carceral context. In the entanglement of the two powerful social institutions of prison and religion, we ultimately see that, tempered by secondhand carcerality, religious logics come to align—however uncomfortably—with the state's goals of retribution and personal responsibility.[3]

CARCERAL DISCOURSES OF RESPONSIBILITY AND "DESERVED" PUNISHMENT

Narratives are the stories we tell ourselves *about* ourselves. More than a recounting of past events, narratives shift over time to incorporate new experiences and imbue prior moments with meaning.[4] Narratives shape self-conceptions and cultivate identities. Cultural logics, relatedly, are "shared, internalized, and evaluative cognitive structures" that operate as "organizing principles that guide decision-making."[5] Narratives, thus, are sense-making accounts, while logics direct future decisions. Both are shaped, at least in part, from available institutional discourses like the correctional system, religion, economic and educational institutions, and the family. In the context of prison, the state has the home-field advantage in dictating available discourses.

State-sponsored meanings of incarceration are shaped by the politics of law and order. From the late 1970s through the 1990s, changes to public policy and policing practices brought about a surge in arrests, convictions, and prison sentences of both men and women. This period of rising incarceration, described as the U.S. "prison boom," profoundly altered the landscape of punishment for decades to follow. Policies mandated minimum sentences, implemented "truth in sentencing" guidelines, and converted "tough on crime" rhetoric into legislation, each reducing judicial discretion and increasing the number of people serving time behind bars. As we saw in chapter 1, these policies disproportionately impacted low-income populations and Black and Latinx communities. Fear-based narratives about a "new dangerous class" helped Americans accept these political moves.[6] Malcolm Feeley and Jonathan Simon coined the term "new penology" to describe how, in this period, the discourse "shifts away from a concern with punishing individuals to managing aggregates of dangerous groups."[7] Rehabilitation was for individuals, but with public safety in the zeitgeist, incapacitation became the group-level solution to foster retribution and "keep criminals off the streets."[8] Notably, these dominant carceral discourses had little to say about the structural factors that led to greater police surveillance or criminalized activity in the first place.

Today, we have entered an era we might call late-stage mass incarceration. It appears that incarceration rates have peaked, sloping downward for the first time in decades. Carceral control, however, has not waned. Instead, it has pivoted, replacing imprisonment with a growing reliance on sentences of community supervision, leading sociologist Michelle Phelps to describe "mass probation" as heir to mass incarceration.[9] Accordingly, carceral discourses have shifted to accommodate the political and economic interests of the day. Now, legislators refer to prison as being reserved for the "worst of the worst" of society, as determined by a host of "risk assessment" tools.[10] Risk assessment tools use quantifiable metrics, codifying past patterns and stereotypes into calculations. Supposedly neutral numbers and big data practices guide decision-making and give punishment determinations a scientific sheen.[11] State actors can use these tools to evaluate people deemed "worthy" of punishment. If a person is declared capable of sufficient transformation, they may receive less restrictive punishment, like probation or intermediate sanctions.[12] By contrast, prison sentences are meted out to those viewed as flawed beyond repair—and the state encourages them to see *themselves* that way. After all, "the production of a subject . . . is one means of its regulation."[13] Thus, criminologists look to the narratives and logics of incarcerated people to better understand what prison "means" to them as one key mechanism of control.

Within today's neoliberal framework of punishment, discourses of accountability and self-determination are paramount. Incarcerated men and women find themselves required to accept culpability, to tell the "right story" and even "perform a flagellant self" to be considered capable of rehabilitation.[14] Often, to be granted parole requires admitting guilt: a "willingness to 'own up' to [one's] misdeeds—to acknowledge culpability and express remorse."[15] Criminologist Ebony Ruhland's interviews with parole board members show how narratives of remorse figure centrally into their parole calculus. As one board member said, "If they come to the hearing and they start making excuses for their behavior or blaming the victim, then I feel like . . . they're not at that point where they're willing to change and take responsibility because they're not even taking responsibility for past behavior . . . . I'm hitting defer as soon as I hear that." Another board member asked, "Isn't that the heart of the matter? . . . that the inmate . . . takes remorse for what they did so that they can use that to repair themselves."[16] Alongside remorse, carceral discourses go as far as encouraging incarcerated men and women to view prison as a positive turning point in their lives. Despite scant evidence that imprisonment actually leads to deterrence or desistance, prison officials seek discursive compliance, encouraging incarcerated persons to describe their time as "life-changing," laying the foundation for viewing prison as a "reinventive institution."[17]

RELIGIOUS DISCOURSES OF REDEMPTION
AND SUFFERING

Enter religion. Specifically for our case, Protestant Christianity. There is reason to believe that religion could be a powerful competing institution when it comes to adopting or rejecting state discourses. We know that incarcerated individuals negotiate dominant discourses by culling a wide array of available messages from peers, culture, and competing institutions—including their faith traditions.[18]

In the world at large, scholars refer to religion's "double function" as both a liberating and suppressing force.[19] When it comes to prison, the former function—religion's liberating potential—makes intuitive sense. Not only does religion serve the practical functions outlined in chapter 2—fellowship, resources, a ticket to greater control over one's daily schedule—it can, as numerous studies document, serve an oppositional function, pushing back against punitive state discourses and instilling a sense of intrinsic worth. In the 1970s, criminologist James Jacobs writes of the "considerable success" of what he calls "unconventional religions," referring to the Nation of Islam and Jehovah's Witnesses within prisons, "in providing an ideological shield to the assaults on self conceptions that attend imprisonment"—they helped incarcerated people "reject [their] rejectors."[20] Indeed, teachings from the Nation of Islam promote resistance against structural anti-Black racism and the criminal legal system.[21] Even Goffman, who theorizes prisons as all-encompassing institutions that strip away identities and all forms of self-expression, suggests religion as a potential antidote: "Strong religious and political convictions may also serve perhaps to immunize the true believer against the assaults of a total institution."[22] In contemporary prisons, studies of faith-based Protestant initiatives highlight their redemptive function, contrasting with the dominant state discourses denying the moral worthiness of those behind bars.[23] In this way, Protestant religion can afford a sense of hope and greater purpose—what religion scholar Tanya Erzen names a "heart change"—although they remain within an institution designed to degrade.[24] Incarcerated women find an additional comfort as Protestant religion informs discourses around motherhood.[25]

On the other hand, a spate of scholarship reminds us that, for all its liberating potential, religion's "double function" means it also supports the latter function, as a suppressing force. Religion has famously supported and promoted dominant power structures throughout history. Recent empirical research suggests that religion might quell sociopolitical resistance by promoting "traditional" and "family" values that support the status quo. In such congregations, the faithful are encouraged to focus on otherworldly paradise rather than on the here-and-now.[26] In prisons specifically, Protestant language of self-help and "individual transformation" may underscore the correctional rehabilitative goals of the neoliberal state.[27] As Irene Becci and Joshua Dubler argue, the prevalence of "religious discourses that favor individual salvation and individual rehabilitation" in U. S. prisons is no accident. Mirroring the responsibilization rhetoric of state discourses, religion suggests it is up "to incarcerated people to rehabilitate themselves. This neoliberal drift ... has severely disincentivized politically minded religious organizing."[28] If religious organizations promote discourses of personal transformation deemed necessary by the state before freedom is granted, then it means, to some extent, accepting the systems of racism, classism, and sexism that structure justice-involvement.[29]

Whether challenging or supporting dominant state discourses, the remainder of this chapter will introduce readers to women's descriptions of God's role in their crime and punishment.[30] I will present four women's stories, intended as case studies, with each woman's narrative representing a prevalent pattern among the devout serving time at Mapleside. Throughout are examples and vignettes from other women, adding evidence of the greater range of people behind these patterned ideologies. Geraldine and Kimmie are among the women who use a Protestant lens to see religion as offering freedom from carceral control, much like Asabi in this book's introduction. Meanwhile, much like Maria in the introduction, Geneva and Laurelle demonstrate how discourses become logics, moving from sense-making to guiding principles, as religion can urge carceral compliance in the name of godly self-control and personal improvement. As freedom and constraint parry in these stories, readers will see more clearly how religion and the state compete for institutional primacy.

GERALDINE: GOD'S ROLE IN PATHWAYS TO INCARCERATION

Geraldine is well liked in the prison compound. Her sunny disposition lifts the mood whenever she enters a room. "I like to smile and make people laugh," she confirmed, "but I'm hurting on the inside. People don't know how unhappy I am." A Black woman nearing 50, her tall, slender frame stands hunched and her neck craned forward, suggesting all the years she might have had to literally keep her head down. Geraldine styles her curly hair in a tightly wound bun, a holdover from her military days. A couple of missing teeth give her trouble pronouncing fricatives, the "th" in words like "this" and "that." She told me with evident relief, "I'm getting my teeth fixed soon because I'm sick of people saying they can't understand me when I talk."

Geraldine "gave her life to Christ" in the prison gym on her very first Sunday at Mapleside. Two years later, I met her at the Thursday evening Baptist Bible study, which she attended weekly to deepen her faith. "That's my little friend. I always look for her on Thursdays," Geraldine told another woman as she gestured toward me. "I tell her she look like a kindergarten teacher." I laughed sheepishly at her seemingly accurate characterization.

Geraldine had recently started attending another voluntary Christian program, a Wednesday night self-help course on Rick Warren's bestselling book, *The Purpose Driven Life*. It was taught by

Ms. J, the prophetic volunteer introduced earlier. One night, before class began, Geraldine raised her hand to tell Ms. J she felt conflicted because she was struggling with her sobriety that day. "I was talking to the officer, 'cause this class meets at the same time as AA. And my case manager said I have to go to AA for parole. I'm 16 months clean, but today I really wanted to drink. The warden had to come down and talk to me, 'cause for some reason today I wanted to drink."

Ms. J has volunteered at Mapleside for over a decade, devoting several hours per week to prison ministry. She cares deeply about incarcerated women and their everyday challenges, a sense of care made visible in her religious classroom. As mentioned previously, Ms. J says she "get[s] up [on] Wednesdays" with excitement over volunteering at Mapleside, exclaiming, "Yay, it's Wednesday!" Ms. J elsewhere demonstrated her compassion and commitment when she offered herself as a caring visitor for women who otherwise had none: "Some of y'all haven't had a visitor this year. . . . Well I'll be your visitor for the next [few] weeks [during our class]."

Thus, it seemed to emerge out of her dedication to prison ministry that Ms. J advised Geraldine, "Well, you should pray and ask God where you should go. No one is forcing you to be here. But I will say they got [Alcoholics Anonymous] every day of the week." Geraldine stayed put.

Ms. J turned to rest of the class, asking, "Who in here struggles with addiction?" Almost 40 hands shot into the air. Ms. J was familiar with addressing the challenges of substance abuse in her religious classroom.

For the next hour, Ms. J led a discussion on finding your "purpose in Christ." Then, as the clock neared half-past 8, it was time for prophecies—Ms. J's signature close to each session, which she understood as the Holy Spirit providing insights to share with incarcerated women: reflecting on their pasts, predicting their future, or prescribing a change of course in their behavior. On this night, prophecies began when Ms. J called Geraldine to stand with her at the front of the room.

"You have free choice and free will. I can't help you unless you're ready. Are you ready?"

Geraldine nodded. Ms. J continued, asking why she wanted to stay clean. Geraldine paused before turning to look Ms. J squarely in the eyes. "I want to be a right mother for my grandkids, and my kids." The class broke into supportive applause, but Ms. J interrupted.

"Don't tell me, tell Him!" she commanded. "Tell God you don't want to drink anymore!"

Timidly, Geraldine lifted her gaze and said, "I don't want to drink no more."

"Say it like you mean it!" Ms. J urged with a preacherly zeal. Geraldine tried again. A little louder, she stated, "I don't want to drink no more."

"Now say it to your body. Put your hand on your heart."

Following orders, Geraldine rested her hand over her heart. She lowered her eyes. Again, she said, "I don't want to drink no more."

"Now tell Hell you don't want to drink no more," Ms. J instructed, pointing down toward the floor. Geraldine mirrored her, pointing and peering down as she repeated, "I don't want to drink no more."

"Good! One more time: tell God, your body, and the Devil!"

As Geraldine obliged, another student in the front row, Carla, widened her eyes and murmured, "I never heard her say that."

Ms. J pivoted in place, directing her attention now toward Carla. "What'd you say?"

Evenly, Carla responded, "I never heard her say that, all the years I've known her." At that, Geraldine nodded, confirming for Ms. J: "She and I go way back. We're from the same part of town."

"Put your hands up," Ms. J instructed the class. "We're gonna pray for her." Heeding Ms. J's instructions, I glanced around, taking in a sea of empathetic expressions as hands rose around the room, arms outstretched toward Geraldine.

Ms. J closed her eyes in contemplation. "I'm hearing the words, 'Why? Why do you drink?' I see you in a dark room. I see hands. Someone abused you." Geraldine stood stock-still, her arms crossed in front of her body and her head bowed. Though she remained quiet, several women in the room began to audibly cry. Ms. J told Geraldine, "Rid your mind of depression. Take away all suicidal thoughts." She continued praying aloud for several minutes.

After concluding her prayer, Ms. J asked Geraldine, "Did any of that make sense to you?" Then she added a caveat, "You don't have to share if you're not comfortable."

Geraldine lifted her chin. Leveling her gaze at Ms. J again, she was firm: "I don't care if they know—it was my father." The volunteer shook her head sympathetically. Self-consciously pulling at her collar and fanning herself, Geraldine broke the silence to say, "My body feels on fire."

"Your cells are changing! They're hard at work. That's why you feel like you're on fire." Ms. J sounded satisfied as she explained that Geraldine's cells were changing: it was part of the process of healing from alcoholism and trauma.

"Come on, Carla, come give her a hug," Ms. J enjoined Geraldine's longtime friend. Carla rose to hug her and to tell her, "I love you."

"You too, give her a hug," Ms. J said to another woman in the front row, teary-eyed Sasha. One by one, without further instruction, nearly all of the remaining women formed a line, queuing up to console Geraldine. Some pulled Geraldine close and whispered into her ear, while others embraced her in silent support. Ms. J transformed her typically energetic, vibrant class into a somber space intended for healing. Although others may have sought counsel in AA or resented the public nature of the self-disclosure, on this evening, Geraldine seemed to find comfort in her religious community.

·   ·   ·   ·   ·

Geraldine was not alone in the remarkable challenges she faced prior to her incarceration. Even more so than men in prison, women face demonstrably high rates of mental illness, drug and alcohol abuse, trauma, and economic marginalization.[31] The numbers say it all. One 2018 study in Boston found nearly two-thirds of formerly incarcerated women experienced addiction or mental illness, compared to just under one in three formerly incarcerated men.[32] A nationally representative sample specified that more than half of all women in state prison have a diagnosable substance use disorder, while over two in three women tested positive for illicit drugs at the time of their arrest.[33] More than 50 percent of incarcerated women in Texas reported having experienced childhood abuse or neglect, and a full three-quarters reported victimization in adulthood, including emotional, physical, and sexual abuse.[34] Nationwide, a startling four in five women in state prison were survivors of intimate partner violence according to the Bureau of Justice Statistics.[35] The ACLU of Virginia found that women were twice as likely as men to cite "economic need" as a motive for their crime.[36]

Feminist criminologists argue that these factors of social and structural vulnerability have important implications for women's contact with the justice system. They are often described as "pathways" to incarceration: each can lead to arrest and eventual imprisonment.[37] These vulnerabilities, scholar Beth Richie writes, "compel" women to commit crime in order to secure their survival, whether by supporting themselves and feeding their families, facilitating their addiction, or escaping the abuse of an intimate partner.[38] In short, women's responses to high-risk backgrounds and situationally oppressive circumstances often trace a pathway that ends in correctional contact. Given these pathways, psychological treatment and recovery support services in women's facilities are in high demand, outpacing the dwindling supply. Shrinking correctional spending means vanishing resources to address the underlying traumas, addictions, and mental illnesses that can lead to incarceration. Religious voluntary programs, not wanting to leave a high-needs population out to sea, has waded in as a replacement. This has involved not only addressing existential needs of the incarcerated, but also speaking to their disproportionately shouldered social and psychological challenges, including the life events that led to their incarceration and the traumas of incarceration itself.

As they did for Geraldine, religious messages across denominational divides encourage women to consider the role of God in their narratives of pathways to incarceration. For instance, during Sister Victoria's sermon at the Catholic worship service one Sunday, I observed her tell the congregation, "I know it's hard for us to believe sometimes. But remember, Christ died for *all* of our sins." Raising her index finger for emphasis, she stipulated, "Even the one that got you here." Likewise, at a Protestant worship service, Pastor Young told the crowd, "God does not care what you did. If you asked for forgiveness, He cast it into the sea of forgetfulness. [God] gave you a clean slate!" Energized by applause for his allusion to Micah 7:19, he cried out, "You're not serving time, you're serving Christ!" In a world defined by blame and retribution, messages of forgiveness are especially powerful. The promise of a "clean slate" contrasts with the imperatives of responsibilization and stigma found in state discourses.

A number of devout women narrated religious interpretations of their pathways to incarceration. In one ministry class, for instance, Bev, a white woman in her early 30s, linked her difficult past to her previous lack of faith. "I was raised with an abusive father, and that's all I knew," Bev shared. "So that's what I chose when I grew up. . . . I was in another abusive relationship. . . . For my codefendant—my boyfriend—God was the furthest thing from him. He thought God was dumb. That's why I'm here." In large part, Bev attributed her trauma and her subsequent incarceration to the godlessness of her personal relationships.

Anne also connected her previous lack of religious conviction with the abuse that led to her incarceration. In an interview, she recalled, "I remember a few years ago, my husband was beating me pretty bad, and I was angry at God. My husband wanted me to kill this man who he found out I was having a relationship with." Anne's extramarital affair with a man named Carl had become a life-or-death situation—kill or be killed. "I remember being in my kitchen, on my hands and knees, praying to God: 'Please let me find another way out of this.'" Reenacting the moment, Anne clasped her hands together as if begging for mercy. But God, she said, had not given her any answers. "Two days later, I killed Carl. And I was angry with God. I was *mad*. I don't know why He didn't find another way for me." Her unanswered prayer in a moment of crisis, Anne suggested, led her to commit a crime she deeply regrets. In the early days of her incarceration, Anne leaned on God to make it through her life sentence. Eyes downcast, Anne said she would talk to people on the outside, and "Some of my friends made fun of me, like, 'Oh, you went to jail and found religion.' But it's *true*. When else in your life does everything stop and you have time to think?" Her religious devotion grew as the years progressed. "So yes," she said assuredly, "I *did* find religion in here."

For Geraldine, Bev, Anne, and many other women, religion offered a framework through which to make sense of past challenges. Religious discourses replaced condemnation with God's love. As we will see next, they additionally gained poignancy when it came to redefining the meaning of incarceration itself.

KIMMIE: INCARCERATION AS PART OF GOD'S PLAN

Kimmie was a few years younger than Asabi, but the two were friends back home. They ran in the same social circles, and they experienced many of the same hardships as kids. Kimmie had fled her childhood home, unable to put an end to the interminable physical and sexual abuse she suffered at the hands of her own family members. To numb her pain, Kimmie began to rely on drugs and alcohol.

Kimmie and Asabi were teenagers when they plotted the robbery that opened this book. Kimmie, age 15 the night of their crime, maintains that she was so drunk that she has no memory of it. Unlike Asabi, Kimmie *was* the person who pulled the trigger. She *was* the person who killed the bartender in their botched robbery. Kimmie was sentenced to 50 years for homicide, a score longer than Asabi's 30-year sentence as a co-conspirator. Their friendship was fractured by resentment from the events of that fateful night, and the two women kept apart at Mapleside.

"When I first got here, I felt distant [from God]," Kimmie recalled. "God, where are you? Where are you?" she would ask. Finding the answers was a slower process for Kimmie than for Asabi. Soft-spoken Kimmie was too shy to take a front-and-center role in worship activities, but her faith grew over time. Kimmie explained that she participated in weekly Protestant programs and made space to process her emotions by writing music. As she explained it, she had come to see prison as God's way of getting her to make a change in her life: "I know He's always been with me. I realized He brought me here to get my attention."

I heard narratives about God's greater purpose similar to Kimmie's from many women as they spoke about their incarceration. Ja sounded grateful as she told me, "You don't know yourself until you come to a place like this, stripped of everything you have." In fact, she insisted, "God saved me . . . putting me here." A Black woman several decades older, Hollis shared Ja's assessment. Despite her chronic health issues and her 10-year sentence, Hollis told me she woke each day with a smile, happy to be alive. She noted, "Some people thank God for saving them. I thank God for *rescuing* me." By sending her to prison, she reckoned, God had saved her from a dangerous path.

Religion also transformed how Rosemary, a white woman in her late 40s, saw herself and told her story. She was not a woman who wore her heart on her sleeve. But one night, the Baptist Bible study group was discussing the books of James and 1 John. Rosemary decided to participate, telling the group, "These scriptures reinforced who I am in God's eyes." Her own eyes welled. She believed, now, that she was more than her crime, more than her 15-year sentence. "I have been chosen by God and He loves me tremendously.

I've used this as affirmation that I am not what I used to be because I've accepted Him as my Lord and Savior."

Viewing prison as part of God's plan was not unique to Mapleside's Protestants. Tati, a 40-year-old Black woman and devout Muslim, said, "I used to think it was bad to be here, but now I'm happy to be here. I *know* that God saved my life by putting me here. He saved all of us from something; we might not know what that is." Even in the darkest of places, Tati trusted God's divine plan: "There's a blessing in everything—even being here. What we think is bad is not bad. There's always something good that comes out of it."

In such statements about God's constant presence and preor-dained plans, we see how religion can be profoundly meaningful in the prison context. Prison's meaning is transformed from deserved retribution to divine intervention as religious discourses supersede carceral ones. Religion, in other words, helps many make sense of one of the hardest, most vulnerable times in their lives by declaring it has a purpose greater than pure punishment, just as it converts past traumas into tests of faith.

.   .   .   .   .

Religious volunteers took these ideas a step further when they defined imprisonment itself as a righteous trial. On a stiflingly hot Sunday in June, a Black Pentecostal volunteer named Pastor O'Neill epitomized this approach. The 40-something preacher delivered a charismatic service in the windowless gym, ramping up the energy even over the din of the industrial-sized fans that attempted to cool down the sweltering room. Pastor O'Neill shouted over the fans' humming, "Eighty-two percent of people in the Bible went to jail! Jesus *Himself* went to jail!" Applause erupted at his interpretation of Acts 4:1–13, in which apostles Peter and John are jailed for preach-ing the gospel. In this reformulation of punitive discourses, impris-onment should not be a source of stigma but a sign of righteousness. Sweat clinging to his brow, the preacher grinned at the attendees:

"*You* know why the caged bird sings." Maya Angelou's metaphor struck a chord, rousing the notion of personal dignity against the affronts of structural injustice.

In my observations, countless Protestant volunteers preached similar messages. Ms. J, for one, described incarceration as "an assignment, a test," qualifying her statement by adding, "Your assignment is not always good." Construing everything as spiritual, including imprisonment and even my research project, Ms. J encouraged the participants in her self-help course to see everything as part of God's plan. "Good, bad, or indifferent, everything is spiritual." She ticked through examples: "Your judges, the court? Spiritual. Who's in this room this week, who was in the room last week? Spiritual. Rachel's here? That's spiritual."

Pentecostal minister Reverend Mona repeatedly told her own weekly ministry class that prison was "a necessary struggle" for them. "You are exiled," she said succinctly, drawing on religious language to interpret incarceration. "That's why you're here. Some of it is what you did, but some of it is because [God] wants you to be here." Reverend Mona acknowledged that crime played a role, but emphasized an equal measure of divine providence. "In Christianity, we believe God uses us *through* suffering. We have no worth outside of God. Anybody and everybody can suffer." Another time, Reverend Mona instructed her students, "God wouldn't give you the assignment if He didn't trust your heart." As women nodded in agreement, she cupped her hands around her mouth and whispered, as if letting them in on a secret: "He believes in you even more than you believe in Him." In Reverend Mona's view, prison was a form of suffering within a divine plan. Importantly for Reverend Mona, there was a distinction between a divine "assignment" and a "deserved" punishment. She made sure to praise her students rather than condemn them:

> You are some of the strongest women I have ever met, did you know that? If no one ever told you that, I'm telling you today. Some of you

are wondering if you could have avoided things or done things different that got you here. But you know what? Some things are preordained, and God put you in those situations for growth and maturity.

Language regarding divine "assignment" also came out in Pastor O'Neill's Young Adult Bible study session for women under 25. "God is not concerned about your crime," he began, apparently contradicting punitive carceral discourses, but then he continued: "He's concerned about what you're going to do *next*. He wants you to get out of a criminal mentality." That meant the women had to take action. "When God allows time-outs in your life, He's giving you the opportunity ... for your soul to grow. It's all about motivation." Crucially, although affirming women's worth by de-emphasizing their former criminalized activity, Pastor O'Neill's message also dovetailed with dominant carceral discourses. According to him, godly women should view prison as an "opportunity" to engage in self-directed transformation, despite the way it obviously limited their autonomy.

Pastor O'Neill went on to provide a vignette to illustrate his point. He started out by describing his own son "winging it" through school. He chided, "You can't just 'wing it' ... You got to get out of that Nintendo mentality." Pastor O'Neill's message reinforced neoliberal notions of personal transformation through the suffering of imprisonment, and could also be construed as paternalistic. Between the choice to characterize incarceration as a "time-out," alongside his comparison between incarcerated women and his own son's "Nintendo mentality," Pastor O'Neill's infantilizing tone was all too familiar among women at Mapleside. Even if Pastor O'Neill sought to upend carceral discourses, he equally doubled down on many of the same themes of responsibilization and paternalism that prison officials promoted.[39]

Apostle Kendra echoed similar themes. A Black nondenominational Christian in her 50s, she was charged with delivering a sermon on Mother's Day, one of the most dismal days at Mapleside. The holiday made many incarcerated women most viscerally carry the heartbreak of being separated from their children. Some mothers have gone years without seeing their kids. Others' relationships are totally severed. Thus, Apostle Kendra seemed to try her best to be as inclusive as possible when she began her sermon on "spiritual motherhood," a term she used to refer to a religious calling to nurture fellow Christians in their growing faith. This theme deliberately incorporated congregants who were not mothers, as anyone could be a spiritual "mother," or nurturer, to others. According to Apostle Kendra, the calling of spiritual motherhood is one possible "birth assignment," what God destined as their life's mission:

> We *all* have a birth assignment . . . a *spiritual* birth assignment. We might not ever give birth to a physical child, but we all have [one]. . . . We were not just born for no reason. God put us here for a reason. I'm talking about a birth assignment *you might not want.*

Here, the sermon turned from general to specific, from God's plan, broadly construed, to Mapleside incarceration as part of God's plan. She continued, emphatically:

> You have an assignment down here, at Mapleside. You might not like it, but you [are] here for a reason. Perpetrating brought you here, but you're here for a reason. And you're wondering, "I'm doing everything I can, I'm praying, why am I still here?"

According to Apostle Kendra, the answer was simple: "It's because you haven't completed your birth assignment." Incarceration, from this perspective, should be viewed as a divine intervention to steer women toward their greater purpose. Congregants stomped their feet and applauded at her message. Seemingly energized by the worshippers' enthusiasm, Apostle Kendra declared in a booming voice, "You have to *accept* that you supposed to be here."

Trying to relate to the women confined to months, years, or decades at Mapleside, Apostle Kendra reflected, "We've all been through things . . . . No matter what you done, you ended up here for a reason that you haven't fulfilled yet." Incarceration had a spiritual purpose. "You need to stay here, that's your assignment."

The importance of offering dignity and moral worth cannot be understated. Protestant messages of forgiveness and God's greater plan offer a powerful counterpoint to punitive state discourses. At the same time, we must interrogate the implications of these messages. What does it mean when Apostle Kendra encouraged women to "accept" that women are "supposed" to be incarcerated? Supposed to be locked into a 70-square-foot double-occupancy cell. Supposed to be inundated with constant noise and clamor, artificial lighting flickering above, without a scrap of privacy. Supposed to be separated from their children for years on end. When we consider this message from a critical lens of structural inequality, we see that it reinforces dominant carceral discourses of deserved punishment in the name of rehabilitation promulgated by the state.

So, too, when we reexamine Geraldine's story: we see that religious programs in prisons work to fill voids left by diminishing state-funded social service programs. Ministers volunteer their time in order to help women as best they can, holding their protégées in high esteem. For instance, Reverend Mona once extolled her ministry class students by saying, "They're hungry [to learn]. And they're *genuine.*" However well-intentioned, though, Mapleside's religious volunteers were not professionally trained in trauma-informed psychology, nor were they certified in best practices with regard to treatment for substance abuse. It is possible that their unregulated religious interventions could do more harm than good for women like Geraldine. As Estrella later remarked, religion was "taking the place of therapy." She said that, in her view, volunteers come in with the best intentions, but "there's a danger to it. They aren't licensed therapists. They [give] us the best that they could."

Looking to Kimmie's story, we can likewise see how religious-based rehabilitative programming offers a great deal of meaning but also reinforces the neoliberal rhetoric of self-directed transformation. Kimmie says that God used incarceration to get her attention.

Her religious narratives do not describe the social safety nets that failed her when she weathered childhood abuse, when she was homeless, or when she struggled with addiction as a teenager. As researchers Becci and Dubler argue, "Whether by buttressing such organizational goals and promoting ideologies of personal transformation, religious volunteers and professional[s] help to perpetuate a system that blames the poor and the dispossessed for their poverty and dispossession."[40] In this way, religious carceral discourses may bolster punitive state goals when they maintain the notion of prison as a positive turning point or a "life-changing" institution.[41]

At Mapleside, this tension was made plainest in Chaplain Harper's language. Her opening prayer at an interfaith Thanksgiving service encapsulated her preaching on the subject. I observed as she instructed the worshippers to bow their heads, readying them to pray. She began, "Even if you were surprised you got here, God wasn't. Believe me, God knew you were coming here before you did." Under an omniscient God, incarceration was not a surprise. It was an opportunity to seek religious transformation, Chaplain Harper asserted. "View your time here as a training, [as] time to strengthen your spiritual muscles. . . . I always say, if you can make it here at Mapleside, you can make it anywhere." With a state employee suggesting they make their incarceration a spiritually "productive" period, we now turn to the second major way that religious discourses inflected women's interpretive experiences of prison: helping them make sense of constraint, they undergirded logics that endorsed submission to carceral authority as itself a godly act.

GENEVA: PAROLE AS PART OF GOD'S PLAN?

The shelves of Mapleside's religious library are stocked with donated books on faith, spirituality, self-help, theology, and religious history—ranging from evangelical Christian bestsellers to Wiccan resources on homeopathic remedies. Because Chief Sawyer would not allow Maria, the unpaid head librarian appointed by Chaplain Harper, to oversee the library alone, I was asked to join her each week. One brisk March morning, while checking patrons in and inspecting their passes to be sure they had permission from the chaplain to peruse the stacks, I met Geneva, a 45-year-old Black woman who was serving time as a repeat offender.

Geneva looked crestfallen as she told Maria and me how her week was going: "I went up for parole last week. The [Holy] Spirit was telling me 'immediate release,' but the parole board said something different. I was really torn up about it." After faithful prayer, Geneva said she heard the Holy Spirit speak to her, assuring her that God would intervene in her parole hearing.

This is a common point of discussion in Mapleside's Protestant circles. If incarceration is part of God's plan, so, too, should release from prison be under God's purview. In a legal sense, women's release dates are defined by sentencing guidelines, mandatory minimums, and risk-averse parole boards. But, in line with the ways religious messages challenge carceral ones, I repeatedly heard God described as the "ultimate judge." Religious volunteers drew on concepts of divine omnipotence to pray for imminent release and overturned convictions. As Ms. J prayed, "God's got you. I don't care what the court papers say." Likewise, Chaplain Harper told the faithful attendees at a Sunday worship service, "I stand in agreeance with your prayers about parole, sentencing, reconciliation with your families ... I declare many of you will be out by your next birthday." Whether or not these prayers and prophecies were ultimately fulfilled, they offered a great deal of hope to the devout women whose legal options were finite, and a reminder that their religious framework superseded the judicial here-and-now.

Geneva finished her story by saying that Minister Patrice, a Pentecostal volunteer from a well-regarded local church, had comforted her after the devastating parole board rejection. The minister reportedly told her, "You don't know what [God's] plan is for you," and that "You don't know how many lives you touch in here. He might *need* you in here."

I heard Geneva's story again the following week in Reverend Mona's ministry class, with about two dozen other women in attendance. "I had my parole hearing two weeks ago," she shared with the group of women who had been rooting for her. "They told me no, that I would have to go up again next year. I was down, I was real down. I was about to go in my room and hang myself right now." She gulped, remembering her intense sorrow. Geneva gestured to some women sitting near her: "The sisters behind me prayed on me, they 'covered' me [with protection in prayer]. Now I know . . . God wanted me to be here." With the support of her fellow Christians, Geneva described taking solace in her faith. She said she felt sure there was a divine reason for her remaining at Mapleside. Reverend Mona affirmed this message by saying, "No parole board can get in the way of God's will."

Ceding parole decisions to godly authority offers a sense of control. It also allows for the possibility that the parole board is acting in a manner consistent with divine fate. "I'll get out in God's time," commented one woman serving a 25-year sentence. Another woman, Sabina, told me when she returned to Mapleside on a parole violation, "I left before God's time. I wasn't ready—that's why I'm back." Where others might blame an inflexible parole officer, outsized consequences, or even their own actions that violated some stringent rule or another, Sabina viewed God as controlling her freedom or lack thereof. Back inside, Sabina planned to deepen her religious commitments: "I'm trying to take in as much Bible study as I can while I'm here. This time I want to leave on God's time." Unlike the penitence and quiet self-reflection promoted by religious reformers of the past, the current iteration of faith-based rehabilitation programs seems to be an active engagement in "bootstraps" reformation, mirroring the state's discourses of personal responsibility and retribution.

.   .   .   .   .

To learn more about religion's role in parole decisions, I interviewed Dale, a white man in his late 50s who is a former attorney turned parole board member. I met with Dale in the first-floor lobby of a DOC building. He pulled an overstuffed folder from his briefcase and began leafing through parole calculation forms. Getting right down to business, he explained the parole board's decision-making rubric:

> It's supposed to be scientific. We calculate "How likely are they to reoffend?" The factors are their criminal record, education, work experience, whether they completed drug programs [in prison]. One big factor is age. The older they are, they less likely they are to mess around anymore. And we look at if they're getting in a lot of fights in prison, then they're likely to be trouble wherever they go.

Dale and I reviewed the forms line by line, so that I could see a "risk assessment" tool in action. In this calculation, personal attributes become numbers on a scale. Score high enough and qualify for parole. Score low and stay in prison. As Dale explained, the variables included the incarcerated person's age, offense seriousness, institutional misconduct records, and so on—the same sorts of "risk factors" included in prosecutors' sentencing recommendations and other points of evaluation. Despite the scientific gloss of these scales and metrics, Dale admitted, "It's all bullshit though. We have leeway in what we decide."

Dale was firm when I asked whether the parole board considers religious faith: "No, not at all."

I tried another angle: "What about if they have certificates from religious programs? Doesn't that show participation in prison?" Countless television shows and films depicting parole hearings had made me believe that showing remorse, especially through religious redemption, helps sway parole boards. Again, Dale shook his head. Himself a Catholic, he took the same matter-of-fact tone as he answered, "Not really. We really look at if they complete drug programs and work training, not religious programs at all. 'Cause what else do they have to do all day? They can sit in those classes but it doesn't mean anything."

It doesn't mean anything? Cynics like Dale focused on factors like Maria's schedule, described in the second chapter, trying to maximize time out of their cells by leveraging the relative availability of religious activities. Yet that does not preclude religion from being more than merely utilitarian. Maria herself found deep meaning in religious narratives. She said her entire life's purpose is bound up in her faith, taking seriously her evocative words in the book's introduction: "I don't care if they carry me out or if I walk out of here. All I want is that eternal life."

Contradicting those who dismissed religious participation as solely performative or strategic, the observations and interviews I had already completed told a different story. In the course of 12 months studying religious life at Mapleside, I met only one woman out of several hundred who, adhering to the idea that "parole looks at that stuff," told me she participated in religious activities because "I just want the certificate." Religion seemed to mean a great deal to the preponderance of women I met. Religious volunteers agreed: "If jailhouse religion is what it takes for you to get your relationship with God, so be it!" one volunteer quipped.

Estrella's outlook on religion and parole adds nuance to this story. A devout Pentecostal, Estrella believed in God's active role in her daily life, but rejected the idea that incarceration was part of God's plan: "God put you here? *You* put you here," she chortled dismissively. Her smile faded as she continued: "It's true that I wouldn't have been alive if I didn't come here. But I don't think God was like, 'This is my child and I want her to end up in jail.'" In fact, she said of her drug-dealing, "God was talking to me the whole time, I just wasn't listening." In other words, God did not put her in prison, her criminalized actions did. This mirrored a caveat Ms. J once made in light of viewing prison as a "test" from God: "Before you got here, He said 'Don't do it.' He put blocks up, gave you a way out, but you ignored it. God is talking to you, but are you listening?"

Furthermore, Estrella pointed to well-documented inequalities that affected her sentencing—ones she did not attribute to God: "The whole system is harder on women. I've only been here [in prison] once before, but the father of my son has four convictions for the same type of crime, in close time proximity, and we both got the same sentence: ten years." Estrella was correct regarding the empirical evidence: women—especially Black and Latina women and especially for drug crimes—are receiving harsher sentences than ever before, even exceeding those handed down to their male counterparts.[42]

In light of her skepticism, it surprised me when Estrella shared that she did believe God could intervene with the parole board on her behalf. "[A] few months ago, [God] told me I was going home, but I didn't know how," Estrella said with an air of mystery, describing hearing God's voice while she prayed. Estrella received a 10-year mandatory sentence without the possibility of parole. That did not leave much wiggle room. However, as she told it, Estrella received a call from her prison case manager several months later. She was going up for parole. Relaying her astonishment, she murmured in awe, "I'm thinking, 'No, I'm not.'" But, she continued with a laugh, "The Holy Spirit says, 'Shut up!' So I shut up and listened." Estrella completed the necessary paperwork and readied herself for a parole hearing. A few weeks later, Estrella learned the whole thing had been a mistake. She was denied parole. But the disappointment could not shake her faith. She continued to attend Bible study weekly and pray daily, curious but at peace with the mysterious revelation when God, via the Holy Spirit, told her she "was going home."

Months later at a Sunday worship service, Estrella bounded toward me, arms outstretched. She shared the good news: she went to court and the judge reduced her sentence. Estrella was cleared to leave prison two months later, having served three of her 10-year sentence. For devout women like Estrella, Sabina, Geneva, and others, religious discourses help make sense of the unpredictable and sometimes capricious decisions of judges and parole boards. With little clarity into the opaque process of sentencing and parole decisions, devout incarcerated women lean on their faith and rely on God to intervene in what the state views as largely preordained risk assessment scores. Women recognize the inherent tensions and competing sense-making frameworks amidst religion and the state's continual jockeying for discursive primacy.

LAURELLE: THE SECONDHAND CARCERALITY OF RELIGIOUS LOGICS

If religious narratives and discourses are subject to secondhand carcerality, so are religious logics. (Recall that narratives curate past experiences to construct identities, whereas logics are organizing principles that direct decisions and actions.)

Sociologist Robert Bellah defines religion as "a control system linking meaning and motivation."[43] Religious messages at Mapleside teach women to search for sacred meaning in all the details of their lives, simultaneously shifting their perspectives on what it means to be in prison and motivating them to specific courses of action. In a similar vein, Émile Durkheim theorizes: "Religious conceptions aim above all to express and explain not what is exceptional and abnormal but, on the contrary, what is constant and regular."[44] In other words, religious beliefs can help people process both miracles and atrocities, but their primary purpose is to explain the innerworkings of everyday life. It may come as no surprise, then, that devout Protestant women at Mapleside applied their beliefs about God's active role in daily life to a variety of "constant" and "regular" features of the prison environment.[45] Secondhand carcerality was evident in how religious logics served to naturalize the prison's rules and affirm the authority of state actors, no matter how fickle or unfair they might appear.

"When I first got [to prison], I was so different," Laurelle said one evening at a nondenominational Christian event. Laurelle, a biracial woman in her mid-40s, was in the sixth year of her sentence for robbery and assault. Her history of aggression haunted her first years at Mapleside. "But He transformed me. It's all God," Laurelle shared with a beatific smile. A few weeks later, at a Bible study session, she reiterated the same point: "When I got here, I was real violent. But once I got saved [through Christ], I realized my expectations needed to be on God."

Laurelle's transformed sense of self through Christian salvation was not mere lip service—her religious logics linked her narratives with action. A month after her self-disclosure at the Bible study session, she recounted an incident where her commitment to avoiding contentious conflict was tested. That afternoon, after a full day's work, Laurelle could choose to stay locked in her cell or participate in a voluntary religious program in the Main Hall. Around this time of day, some women would scurry off to the visiting room to meet with loved ones, but not Laurelle. Her family relationships had long since strained, she explained, and few visitors ever came knocking. Instead, she intended to go to the religious program using the attendance pass she had procured in advance. She just had to show it to Officer McClintock, the officer on duty, who would open the sliding metal doors to allow her to leave the housing unit and head over to the Main Hall.

The problem was that Officer McClintock's attention was diverted by a group of raucous women in the housing unit. As Laurelle described it, each time she requested to leave her cellblock, Officer McClintock raised her index finger and directed Laurelle to "Hold on." Finally, the officer turned to her with exasperation: "I'm gonna need you to come back later. I can't sign you out right now."

Laurelle was upset. She said she replied, "Really?" and stomped back to her cell. She was going to be late to class or miss it altogether. Plus, the officer's dismissal was infantilizing, further limiting her autonomy to leave the housing unit despite having the required "hall pass" to move from building to building. Yet Laurelle restrained herself. "It took a lot.... It took everything to humble myself," she reflected later, deciding to avoid escalating conflict with the staff member. Instead, she marched back to the command desk to apologize to Officer McClintock. "I am a Christian woman, and that is not how I behave." Laurelle told me her anger subsided when she remembered the behavioral expectations of her religious identity— in her words, she did not "want to blow my [Christian] witness" with insubordinate behavior. Evangelical Christianity extols proselytization through conduct. For her, the concept of "witness" meant expanding the kingdom of God by example.[46] Cultivating a Christian identity—at least in this case—meant acquiescing to the status quo even amidst frustration.

Accepting the authority of prison staff helped Laurelle avoid a disciplinary infraction, and her religious logics helped her follow the rules to survive prison unscathed. But secondhand carcerality meant that this conclusion was almost inevitable—a reissuing of prison rules and regulations in a new way, through the lens of her Protestant faith. Her sentiments mirrored the responsibilization logics of the state, justified as religious practice. Importantly, Laurelle did not come to these conclusions on her own. She was surrounded by religious messages supporting adherence to prison authority from religious volunteers and fellow churchgoers.

Ms. J was typical in extolling the benefits of obedience to authority: "First it's the CO, then it's the PO, then it's your boss," she would say, listing the stages toward a respectable life on the outside. Incarcerated women should respect the authority of corrections officers now, their parole officers upon release, and their workplace supervisors in the future. "The structure of authority in the kingdom [of God] is set up for a reason," Ms. J reasoned. "If you're rebelling now, you'll never get anywhere." Adherence to the dominant authority structures was apparently going to be a lifelong project, part of living a devout life at every stage. If, as Foucault argues, prisons seek to construct "docile bodies," then religious logics like these do a great deal of the legwork.[47] After all, prison authority seeks "not so much to make prisoners . . . merely obedient," argues criminologist Ben

Crewe, "but to inculcate in them a kind of enthusiastic engagement with the terms of the regime."[48] In certain circumstances, infected by secondhand carcerality, religion can fulfill that goal.[49]

. . . . .

Rashida's story further illuminates the secondhand carcerality of religious logics. Rashida is an Apostolic adherent and Black woman in her mid-40s who is active in Protestant programs. She has absorbed many of the same religious lessons as Laurelle. She is also an avid writer, and one day hopes to publish her book manuscript about her difficult childhood, impressively perfected over months of one-hour-a-day computer lab reservations at Mapleside. To that end, Rashida identified 13 publishers, planning to send a printed copy to each in order to cast a wide net. At two stamps per envelope, she needed 26 stamps—an expense she could not afford on her prison wages. So, Rashida devised a workaround to come up with the postage.

As she recounted it, the very day she planned to pilfer some stamps, Rashida said she stopped herself. "I heard God say, 'I cannot bless this book out of thievery.'" The mailing would have to wait, even if it took several months to save up the money for her 26 stamps. Moreover, she said she was rewarded for this conscious decision to follow the rules. "I was telling this [other woman] about it," Rashida reported, and the fellow Christian woman returned later with a fresh book of stamps. "'God told me to keep two and give you the rest.' So, I got eight stamps right then and there," Rashida remembered, clasping her hands to her heart as she felt gratitude anew. Maria, sitting nearby as Rashida shared the story, recited a lesson she gleaned from Luke 11:28: "Obedience is a sure favor."

Rashida's decision not to steal the stamps helped her avoid the risk of a disciplinary penalty that could send her to solitary confinement, prevent her from working on her book, and potentially thwart her chances at making parole on good behavior. "We [are] trying to do the right thing, trying to stay out of trouble," another woman remarked, on using religious logics to follow the rules. In casting this decision in religious language, we see that the behavioral transformation promoted by Protestant leaders at Mapleside was ultimately one in line with obedience to prison rules and state authority.

Heather was another incarcerated woman whose ideas about deserved punishment were redefined by religion. A white woman in her 50s, her story began with getting caught sneaking a new pair of shoes—contraband—into Mapleside. If she had purchased these shoes through the private vendor, as noted in chapter 1, there would have been no problem with having new sneakers. As it was, Heather could not afford them through the commissary, where there is no room for shopping around for price comparison, and nothing ever goes "on sale." As punishment for sneaking in the shoes, Heather was immediately sent to solitary confinement, where the only human contact came in the form of a thrice-daily meal-tray thrust through the slat in the cell's metal door. Being locked alone in that spartan room was harrowing enough to challenge even the soundest of minds. As she sat in solitary, awaiting the administrative hearing that would decide her fate, Heather devised a plan to defend her actions and potentially avoid further punishment.

"I found a loophole," Heather explained in our interview. Heather prided herself on being what they call a "public defender" in prison, someone who angles to "get out of things" and find any sort of workaround. "I was going to tell them something so that I wouldn't have to go on lock." But the night before her administrative hearing, Heather, a lifelong Catholic, said she heard God's voice whisper to her while she prayed. "That's when I was saved," she said somberly, believing that God told her how to proceed. "I went into my hearing the next day and I told the truth." A convert to evangelical Christianity in the space of that prayer, Heather surmised that God intervened to prevent her from lying. She owned up to the shoe-smuggling attempt, and calmly accepted the penalty for this offense: 200 days in solitary confinement. She bided her time by memorizing one scripture each day as almost half a year passed. Heather's perspective shifted dramatically. Once a wily "public defender," she was clear, "Now I think if you do something wrong you should be punished for it."

Given this logic, helping incarcerated women like Heather submit to the rules and authority of the officers, it may come as no surprise that prison staff and officials saw religion as beneficial. For one, the DOC director of religious services suggested during our interview that religion fosters a "tranquil, calm mood in the facility." Officer McLean likewise remarked that, in her experience, when women participate in religious activities, "they calm down." In fact, every now and then, some officers were known to reward the religious women on the compound. As Nevaeh put it, paraphrasing James 4:10, "If you humble yourself before God and man, God and man will show you favor."

Asabi benefitted from this association, being "shown favor" when a pair of scissors went missing at Mapleside. Scissors are a security risk, since they can be weapons as well as tools. Officers immediately undertook a "shakedown" in the cellblocks, ransacking every bed, desk, and drawer, leaving no room unturned. It was several hours before the scissors were located; they were in a cell whose occupant is said to have taken them to give the other women haircuts.

The shakedown turned up more than the scissors, though. Asabi was distressed when officers found contraband in her cell. They confiscated a few items, like a fashion scarf (reminiscent of Kiara's notable Hello Kitty kerchief) and books in excess of the 20-per-person limit. For two days, Asabi sulked, ruminating on the loss of her cherished possessions. On the third day, however, Asabi was grinning ear to ear when she waltzed into Chaplain Harper's office, boasting, "Lieutenant Turner gave me all my stuff back—even stuff I wasn't supposed to have!" Then she asked tantalizingly, "And you know why she did?" She answered herself, saying that Lieutenant Turner told her, "It's not *who* you are, it's *whose* you are." Asabi spelled it out for me: Lieutenant Turner, like many officers at Mapleside, was

Christian. Thus, Asabi, being a child of God, "saw favor." Were she a nonbeliever, Asabi insinuated, the lieutenant would not have given her contraband back.

Religious logics working in this way—in line with the goals of the prison institution—are evidence of what Foucault calls "disciplinary power" in action.[50] Disciplinary power is the way that state governance controls individuals by shaping their everyday behavior and eventually transforming their belief systems. In this chapter, we see how religion unfolds in such a way that bolsters prison's disciplinary power. Mired in the mechanisms of carceral control created by state authority, particular religious messages proliferate while others fall by the wayside. It is likely that the prison administration, having sieved and sorted prospective religious volunteers before allowing them to enter the guarded gates, would filter out messages that extol resistance to prison rules. One final vignette showcases how religious logics come to life in supporting the everyday inner workings of carceral power.

One month out of the year, Mapleside's Protestant adherents host a "fast": a common conservative Protestant practice that involves collectively abstaining from certain foods. "I'm not good at fasting," Maria laughed as she told her Discipleship students. "I'ma keep it real." The fast required her to avoid meat and bread, "and I did fine for the first few days." She was careful not to partake of tempting meals in the cafeteria. "But then Wednesday was Chicken Night, so I had that." Maria adjusted her fasting plan. "I thought I would just give up bread, because I thought it would be easier," she admitted, pinching her forearm. "That's my flesh." Smiling sheepishly, Maria pointed out that she was only human. She equivocated when her craving won out over her spiritual goals.

"Then they had turkey," she sighed, continuing the story. "And I really wanted to make a turkey sandwich. So I went into the dining hall and brought out some bread to take back to my room." On the cusp of sneaking a few slices of bread back to her cell, in defiance of prison rules, Maria told the women, God intervened: "As I was standing there waiting to leave, the CO asks me, 'Where's the food you wrapped up?'"

Maria doubled over to laugh at how quickly she got caught. She reenacted the scene, patting her left shoulder: "Of course, it was right there. That wasn't nothing but God." Rather than viewing the interaction as an officer's choice to employ punitive austerity, Maria attributed the moment to God preventing her from breaking her fast. When the officer enforced the prison rule, Maria viewed it as an act of divine intervention. Maria finished the story by noting that she surrendered the slices of bread to the officer, averting an infraction but more importantly sticking with her religious commitment. Viewing this situation through a Protestant lens of God's active role in daily life emphasized her dedication to her Baptist faith. At the same time, Maria's religious logic downplayed the role of second-hand carcerality, wherein religiosity supported the state's goals of compliance and personal responsibility.

.   .   .   .   .

This chapter dug into how individuals adopt discourses and apply logics provided through one institution, religion, to meaningfully challenge or justify discourses pushed by another institution, the state. As we have seen, religious discourses shape women's perspectives on the meaning of incarceration and religious logics motivate women to certain courses of action, while steering them away from others. One reason that religion might be so powerful in a discursive sense is its ability to speak to existential questions of the kind common in prison: what is fair, what is right, and what is human. Another is its offer of forgiveness. Even if chain-link fences render women invisible to the surrounding community, their faith community is steadfast in its belief that God is still watching over them.

The criminological concept of the "redemption script" is useful here to explore the persistent tensions in how religious discourses come to bear on carceral discourses. Shadd Maruna defines redemption scripts as a narrative mechanism in which narrators link "negative past experiences to the present in such a way that the present good seems an almost inevitable outcome."[51] As discussed in this chapter, devout women draw on religious narratives to describe incarceration as part of God's plan, such that they decide to surrender to the penal environment as a "test" or "lesson" in service of a greater personal "good." In this context, redemption scripts are quite literal, offering both religious redemption and a criminological "making good," marked by rule-following and transformed behavior. Whether intentional or inadvertent, in tying together these two forms of redemption within the confines of prison, Protestant practice ends up reinforcing the aims of carceral control and the legitimacy of prison authority as a sort of conduit for divine instruction. If incarceration is part of God's plan, and if women accept that incarceration may have "rescued" them from their previous lives, then state authority is necessarily implicated as part of that plan. As such, religious narratives and logics, shaped by secondhand carcerality, can simultaneously challenge carceral sense-making while promoting the embrace of individual responsibility and the adherence to prison rules and authority.[52]

4 *Blessed Is The Fruit Of Thy Womb*

GENDER, RELIGION, AND IDEOLOGIES
OF THE FAMILY

"A lot of 'em try to use kids as a reason they want to get out," Dale insisted. A parole board member introduced in the previous chapter, Dale told me he was skeptical when incarcerated women invoked their children while petitioning for early release. "Now's not the time to think about your kids. While you were in the streets committing the crime is when you should've been thinking about 'em."

By now, it should be apparent that the correctional system does not punish crimes—it punishes people. As we saw in chapter 3, when someone is convicted of a crime, state actors' words and actions deem them fundamentally "bad," collapsing their multifaceted identities into a singular label: "criminal." We also know from prior research that when it comes to gender, state agents judge women in prison not only as "criminals" but also as *women* and as *mothers*, punishing them on all three counts.[1] This chapter will examine gender and ideologies of the family when it comes to the rhetorical punishment of women in prison by state and religious actors.

As they evaluate and regulate justice-involved women, state actors like judges, correctional officers, and parole board members draw on stereotypes related to gender, contrasting those deployed against their male counterparts. Women are described with long-standing misogynist tropes: they are labeled manipulative, hysterical, or untrustworthy.[2] Black and Latina women are further stereotyped as "real criminals" in contrast to their white women counterparts, with prison officials more likely to use language like "aggressive," "predatory," and "manipulative" to describe them.[3] When women are criticized *as women*, an "empowerment paradox" is apparent: they are simultaneously exhorted to take responsibility, while also being expected to submit to the state's normative prescriptions.[4]

Empowerment discourses ignore the well-trod pathways to incarceration discussed in the last chapter, relying instead on an individualistic understanding of women's participation in crime (i.e., bad people doing bad things).[5] Contrary to the assumptions embedded in state-sponsored discourses around crime, extant research bears out what I heard from women serving time at Mapleside: "It was them or me." In other words, the crimes that land women in prison are often about survival.[6] One woman told me she and her cousin, both 15, had gotten into a fight with each other: "One had a baseball bat, the other had a gun," she remembered, indicating that she was the one with the gun—the one who survived. Another woman explained that she was charged as a co-conspirator when her uncle, learning she had been raped, took vengeance into his own hands; she was sentenced to incarceration for failing to inform the police of her uncle's plans. A mother described being roped into her son's drug distribution scheme, and a young woman who had turned to sex work for survival disclosed that she was offered money to serve as a distraction for a robbery—when it went awry, she was arrested and charged right alongside the robbers.[7] When we consider the circumstances of each woman's story, the lines between "victim" and "offender" muddle and blur. When we look for the places where safety nets failed women before their criminal justice involvement, the label "criminal" loses its cachet.

Recent prison reform efforts have tended to focus on nonviolent offenses. Indeed, that is a big driver of incarceration: at Mapleside, one in three women is serving time for a nonviolent property crime or drug offense. Yet setting up a moral distinction between nonviolent and violent criminal convictions allows for the idea the latter are less deserving, and if not outside the sphere of social obligation, nearer its edges. What of the one in two women at Mapleside who have been convicted of a violent crime including homicide, assault, sexual assault, or robbery? As sociologist Bruce Western argues:

> Trying to divide the prison population into good people and bad, between violent and nonviolent, fundamentally misunderstands the nature of violence in poor family and neighborhood contexts. The division between the violent and the nonviolent is a moral distortion of a complex social environment in which victims, witnesses, participants, and offenders are often *one and the same individuals* who suffer harm from each part they play in episodes of violence.[8]

Among justice-involved women, empowerment discourses of dual imperatives of culpability and submission have no room for such nuance.

Embedded in gendered carceral discourses, many women are also criticized *as mothers*. Across the country, more than half of women held in state prisons are mothers to children under the age of 18, and four in ten women report they were single-parent heads of household prior to their incarceration.[9] Locking up mothers, it almost goes without saying, can cause an enormous disruption in childcare. Most often, children whose mothers are incarcerated go on to live with a grandmother (42 percent) or other extended family member (23 percent), but 10 percent will be placed in the foster care system (along with 2 percent of the minor children of incarcerated men).[10] Legal scholar Dorothy Roberts aptly identifies the overlap of the foster care and criminal legal systems as "evidence of a form of punitive governance that perpetuates social inequality" to which Black mothers are particularly subjected.[11]

The forced separation of mothers and their children is only one way the prison system punishes women's perceived failure as caregivers. Long have mothers (especially low-income minoritized mothers) carried the blame for the delinquency of their children, attributed to so-called broken homes in the late twentieth-century crime scare.[12] When mothers themselves become justice-involved, they draw a particular kind of discursive scorn. State actors describe them as aberrant mothers, "irresponsible" or "out of control" and thus "dangerous" to their children.[13] Their parenting is on trial as much as their crime. Anthropologist Carolyn Sufrin traces the fundamental entanglement of incarceration and motherhood within broader governmental paternalism, noting "the state's deep and persistent involvement in regulating women's reproduction . . . controlling and valuing (or devaluing) women's reproductive behaviors along differentials stratified by race, poverty, and addiction."[14] Mothers, especially low-income mothers and historically marginalized mothers, face shame, judgment, and cruelty, their motherhood weaponized against them by dominant institutions including the criminal justice system.

Through punitive discourses around gender and motherhood, prison officials seek to produce not only "docile bodies," as Michel Foucault argues, but, as Jill McCorkel specifies, "docile girls."[15] Gendered state control manifests not only in narrative but also in practice. In the name of security, prison officers may restrain, strip, and search any incarcerated woman and, in most states, they are allowed to handcuff or shackle pregnant women during and immediately after childbirth.[16] Though it is illegal, COs perpetuate sexual assaults against incarcerated women, inspiring a looming sense of threat among women who understand they will have little recourse if they are victimized. Coercive control is gendered through the state's governance over women's bodies. Femininity, motherhood, and sexualization are all pieces of the puzzle.[17]

This is the carceral environment in which religious programs operate, attempting to counter the punitive narratives that castigate incarcerated women as calculating criminals, deviant women, and unfit mothers. Religious messages seek to confer humanity, defining the devout as inherently worthy "women of God." Protestant volunteers additionally emphasize women's special value as mothers.[18] At the same time, tainted by the toxicity of secondhand carcerality, Protestant messages replicate and reproduce rather than undermine many state discourses: women of God should rely on men of God to secure their paths; state authority represents divine authority and must be obeyed; and mothers, simply by being incarcerated, are understood as flawed and must learn a new way to parent.

BECOMING A WOMAN OF GOD

It may sound like a truism: being a woman in a women's prison means being evaluated on stereotypical measures of cisgender femininity. This type of gendered judgment is overt. For instance, before I started my fieldwork at Mapleside, I met with the assistant warden to sort out some logistics. As she reviewed my research plan, she passed along what sounded like an offhanded criticism of the people incarcerated in her facility: "You'll see women—and some women who look like men." Her remark was among the first times, but nowhere near the last time, I would hear a variation of a state agent scrutinizing the gender expression of the woman incarcerated there. Clearly, the women were exposed to far more of this commentary than I was, yet I was struck on one visit to hear one woman tell another that an officer who passed by her in the hallway "told me I need to get my hair and nails done because she said, 'You're too beautiful to be dressing like a boy.'"

Similar policing of masculinity occurs in men's prisons, where studies confirm that staff securitize incarcerated men's gender expression, promoting cisgender and heteronormative manifestations while penalizing and punishing transgender, nonbinary, and gender nonconforming expressions.[19] This sets up another point of contrast between institutional discourses: religious leaders pointedly and unequivocally embraced the women at Mapleside *as women*.

Where women's gender expression is subject to criticism by the prison administration, religious programs offer a redemptive salve. In one of Pastor Tamara's Sunday sermons, I noted that she invoked Rahab, a Biblical figure who is described as a faithful woman and ancestor of Jesus in Matthew 1:5. Pastor Tamara gestured to an inconsistency, in which Rahab was described in scripture such as Joshua 2:1 as a prostitute, while other biblical scholars indicate that she was an innkeeper. Pastor Tamara landed on the side of Joshua when she declared of Rahab, "She was a prostitute. Some modern-day philosophers want to say that maybe she was an innkeeper or tavern lady, but she was a prostitute. A sure enough harlot!" Pastor Tamara used this as a point of connection to her congregants: "You might say to me, 'Well, prostituting isn't my thing. I do drugs, or I murdered somebody.' Who cares? Only one that remembers that is you! Rahab was a prostitute and she is in the Bible. The *holy* Bible. *God* put her in the Bible." Her pitch escalating with enthusiasm, Pastor Tamara concluded, "That means there's hope for you and me . . . . She was a lady of the night. A madam. We all make mistakes. [God] wanted to make sure we would not lose heart—that's why He included her in the Bible." Far from condemning Rahab, the volunteer suggested she was an example for all godly women. Despite the "mistakes" they had made, the women at Mapleside had the potential to live righteously and in God's favor.

Reverend Mona used scripture to a similar end in her ministry class. As she explained it, John 4 described Jesus revealing himself as the messiah to a Samaritan woman he met at a well. Why? Because this particular Samaritan woman would tell the men of her town about the revelation. Reverend Mona was among the Christians who interpreted the woman at the well as a prostitute. "The woman who *knew* all the men in town, and knew *how to talk* to all the men

in town," Reverend Mona said with a coy smile. "Show me a prostitute, and I'll show you an evangelist!" The students gasped in delight,
a woman sitting next to me remarking, "Wow!" Prostitution is the
only crime that women commit more often than men,[20] and so,
although only a small fraction were serving time for a sex work conviction at Mapleside, the point was well taken. Protestant messages
that recast women engaged in prostitution as righteous doubled as a
way to prove that faithful women matter to God—not in *spite* of, but
because of their pasts. We might interpret these discourses as a gendered "making good," as mentioned in the previous chapter, where
prior acts of deviance are a necessary step toward women's
redemption.[21]

In my observations, religious messages celebrated incarcerated
women for their feminine traits instead of critiquing their perceived
failures of femininity as the state so often did. In her Sunday message for Catholics, Sister Victoria reminded the congregants, "Ladies,
I've said this before: You are prisoners here on earth." Then pointing
her finger upward, she continued, "But to God, you are precious
gems; worthy, important, beautiful daughters of God." The worshipper seated beside me brushed away a tear.

In another instance, while I was making small talk with Kathy, a
Methodist volunteer, she commented that every beige uniform we
saw was stamped with the letters "DOC" (for the Department of
Corrections). Smiling warmly, she shared, "I call 'em Daughters of
Christ." Her linguistic rejection may be small, but it is symbolic,
overturning the state's efforts to control their charges' identities by
lifting up their standing as women of God.

When Protestant messages of God's love elevate women's humanity over their carceral status, it can impact how the women see themselves. Esther, for example, found deep meaning in the idea of a
personal, faithful relationship with God, beaming as she shared, "I
wake up every day with joy, with God telling me 'Wake up, baby girl.'"

While sidestepping the rhetoric of insufficient femininity, religious volunteers nonetheless represented and spread faith traditions

that drew on a gender-essentialist framework. The socially conservative and evangelical traditions prevalent at Mapleside were especially wrapped up in stereotypical measures of feminine expression
and heteronormative ideals about marriage and the family.[22] In
another of Reverend Mona's classes, she said plainly, "God set up the
order in this world, for men to have dominion." She did not, she clarified, mean "man" as a synonym for "mankind" or "humanity." Rather,
the happily married Reverend Mona told the 20 or so students that
she did not desire equality in her own matrimony. "God set a natural
order," she explained during another session: "First it's man, then
woman, then family. You're not *partners*, it's not *equality*." This "natural" hierarchy ultimately benefitted women, she contended: "I like
that, because if something goes wrong in a marriage, God goes after
the husband first. I'm happy with it that way. I'm glad the bills are in
my husband's name. If there's a problem? Talk to him." Reverend
Mona flicked her hand, shooing away the problem in her scenario,
signaling that her husband's authority offered her welcome respite
from worry.

To Reverend Mona, submission was actually an act of feminine
agency. It may sound like men are in control, she told her ministry
students, but "women have power over men." She straightened her
spine to sit upright in her chair, then clarified: "The stronger one is
strong enough to be submissive. The most powerful person is the
wife . . . . It's the natural order." Lessons like these were impactful for
Oaklynn, a regular participant in Reverend Mona's classes. In fact, I
observed her sharing some of the reverend's teachings with a group
of fellow Protestants several weeks later: "Women are made from
bone. We are not made from dust like man. And we actually run the
world, we actually control everything, we're just taught by society
not to believe that." Though it reinforced gender traditionalism, the
message had an empowering tone. "Why would you want to be dust
instead of bone?" Oaklynn asked provocatively, repeating a question
she said Reverend Mona posed. "I don't mean no offense to the *doms*
in here," Oaklynn added, careful to clarify that her critique might

offend the gender nonconforming and sexually dominant individuals in the room who did not identify as cis women. Gender traditionalism and the emphasis on submissiveness as the truest form of feminine power repackaged the empowerment paradox: women should take responsibility for their actions by submitting to a male authority, be it a spouse or the state.

Key to being a woman of God, it seemed, was the search for a "man of God" to marry. Ministry students heard from Reverend Mona that they should seek "someone who gives wisdom" because "God never meant for women to be making decisions by themselves." Then she took a beat to add a laugh line: "We *can*, but look at Eve!" In the Bible, Eve, the first woman, succumbed to temptation, eating forbidden fruit from the tree of knowledge of good and evil. She and Adam, the first man, were cast out of Paradise as a result. If the first woman, made by God, could not make wise decisions, Reverend Mona implied, that meant all women required the guidance of men. They could not be trusted to make good choices as autonomous agents.

The advice continued, covering what women needed to do in order to remain desirable to a male partner once they found him. "Remember, you're *his* helpmeet," Reverend Mona reminded her class, citing Genesis 2:18. She used another Biblical story, about Esther and her preparations to meet her husband, the king, as a launching point for rather specific instructions: "There is a way to prepare your body for a man to enter you. It involves fasting, a certain amount of oils, and a certain amount of bathing. I don't care if you been with 19 men, that will make it feel like he is entering a virgin." With a chortle, a woman called out from the back row, "Say what oil it was again?" Reverend Mona was unruffled: "It was the oils that Jesus Christ used to anoint himself: myrrh, frankincense, and certain kinds of bath salts. And if you feel like a virgin every time, he is going to give you everything you ask for." This received several audible "Amens." According to Reverend Mona, if a woman hoped to influence her husband's decisions and keep him around, she needed to bring him sexual satisfaction.

The advice that women must find a "man of God" when they leave prison stirred a variety of reactions among the faithful at Mapleside. Coretta, for one, embraced it wholeheartedly. "I don't know about you, but I'm looking for a real man who will be the head of the house and all that," she insisted, a statement made all the more powerful by her own past. Coretta was serving 40 years for her part in a violent crime masterminded by her then-boyfriend. Other women were more skeptical, like Iris. "They say you should marry a Christian," she ventured, "but you could be with someone who learns by observing you." Iris, in other words, thought her own faith might influence a future partner's beliefs—if he was not already a Christian, he could become one. Supporting this idea, she cited scripture from 1 Peter 3:1, then continued on to interpret it: "I was struck by the discussion about a husband and wife, and how the person you marry can change just from how you act." Still other women rejected the premise that they need a "man of God," at least right away, if they are to be success-ful in reentry. Felicia, a 30-year-old woman, declared, "I want to be celibate when I go home." She might want a partner at some point, but at the moment, she craved a romantic connection replete with "walks in the park, [we'll] go out dancing." A friend, she said, was courting her from the outside, hoping to date once she is released, but she has refused his advances. "I know he's not good for me," she explained succinctly. No matter if religious messages were conveyed as imperatives, incarcerated women took an active role in evaluating the worth and relevance of each message preached to them.

Protestant volunteers' focus on heterosexual marriage and femi-nine submission was surprising given that, by virtue of their incar-ceration, the women to whom they minister are largely isolated from the marriage market. Their capacity to "submit" to men, at least in terms of marriage, is on hold. So why preach to incarcerated women about finding and submitting to a man of God? Whether or not the parallels were intended, the practices of submission and dependence align with the empowerment paradox that pervades the gendered carceral regime.

REGULATING SEXUAL RELATIONSHIPS

Protestant messages around sexuality fit tidily with official prison rules and regulations, too. The faith traditions most prevalent at Mapleside reject relationships between women. This is no different from the stance of conservative and fundamentalist-leaning religious groups outside prisons; one study reports that 55 percent of evangelical Protestant respondents and 40 percent of respondents from historically Black Protestant churches agree that "homosexuality should be discouraged."[23] It is also the official policy within U. S. jails and prisons, where *all* sexual relationships are prohibited.

The Prison Rape Elimination Act of 2003 (PREA) defined all sex inside prison as nonconsensual, regardless of whether it occurs between incarcerated persons or involves staff members.[24] Between officers and incarcerated women, coercion obviates consent. Among incarcerated women themselves, penal paternalism, as described earlier, reduces women's bodily autonomy and seeks to rescind their ability to make decisions about their own sex lives. Of course, PREA eliminated neither rape nor sexual activity behind bars. The punishments for incarcerated women engaging in sexual relationships start with disciplinary tickets, which can be raised in parole hearings as evidence of bad behavior, and can escalate to isolation in solitary confinement. Still, though reliable statistics are nearly impossible to obtain, scholars suggest between 30 to 60 percent of all women have a romantic or sexual relationship while incarcerated.[25] To hear Officer McLean tell it, the numbers at Mapleside are far higher—in the neighborhood of 80 or 85 percent. "Some women won't wear their wedding ring except for when they have visits, then they'll put it on," the officer ventured. A couple women I spoke with gave even higher estimates, figuring closer to 90 percent of their peers are partnered with each other. "They call it 'gay for the stay,'" Bernadette declared of the couples that formed around her. Of the women who abstain, Anne chortled, "We're the minority here—they call us 'strictly dickly.'"

In the mid-twentieth century, a number of studies on incarceration seized on the idea that women's intimate and family-like relationships within prisons were a gendered form of adjustment to the hardships of incarceration.[26] Yet "pseudo-families" and "fictive kinship" were presented by academics in ways that may have ultimately replicated normative heterosexual family values and sensationalized women's sexual expression. Where women's relationships were characterized as a form of resistance at best, or utilitarian at worst, it trivialized them and suggested they were, for various reasons, inauthentic.[27] Turning now to the dynamics of incarcerated women's sexuality and relationships through the lens of religious programming, I ask whether and how religious and carceral narratives align regarding the regulation of women's bodies and their intimate relationships. My goal is to avoid reproducing the historical objectification of women's sexuality in prisons, although this topic necessarily does entail sharing quotes and vignettes that describe how these relationships played out within the prison.

Couples who live in different housing units must be creative in finding ways to spend time together. At Mapleside, women in relationships are able to spend time together at work, in the cafeteria, during recreation in the yard, and in voluntary programs. Religious programs are among the best venues, as anyone affiliated with a particular faith is permitted to attend.[28] Especially on Sundays, without any other work assignments or voluntary programs, worship services "can be a place where girlfriends meet," Sister Harris observed, based on a decade of her volunteering at Mapleside.

Estrella, active in the Protestant programs, corroborated this point. She suggested that "really it's just the first three rows" who were attending for worship, while "everyone else uses it to sit down with their girlfriend." Estrella reckoned that when "people on the outside go to church, [they] have to wake up, get in their cars ... because they *want* to be there. Here, it's different. People come [to services] for something to do, or to meet their girlfriends." A number of worshippers like Estrella indicated their discomfort with women who used religious programs as a space to connect with romantic partners. One woman I interviewed complained, "There's a lot of lesbianism here" and some women went to church only "to meet partners." Another woman groused, "I know you see a lot of girlfriends in here, girls sitting together real close. That really bothers me."

The socially conservative Protestant preachers were equally displeased. During a Sunday worship service, I observed Chaplain Harper scolding, "Don't just be one of those people who goes to church to hook up. Be who God wants you to be." To the chaplain, anyone using worship services to "hook up" was the antithesis of "who God wants you to be." Once, she told me, she actually banned from Protestant programs a churchgoer who was "being inappropriate with another woman during the service." Pastor O'Neill went further, preaching from the pulpit that the women of Mapleside should, upon release, "come to my church and find a *real* man." He wrinkled his nose as he began to spell out his assessment that, at Mapleside, "Your church is 60 percent women and 40 percent—." Cutting himself off, he shrugged: the point was made. In his eyes, the 40 percent remainder were *not women*, nor were they "real men" either. Chaplain Harper was not amused by Pastor O'Neill's transphobic derision, and warned Pastor O'Neill off the topic of gender nonconformity. "You better start your sermon," she chided curtly.

Many Protestants at Mapleside echoed the religious teachings they received regarding sexual deviance. Time and again, they told me they rejected sexual relationships with women. A number of the churchgoers I interviewed shared what sociologist Dawne Moon calls "conversion narratives," in which "conversion to God meant conversion away from homosexual 'practice.'"[29] That conversion, like other behavioral changes in line with the prevalent Protestant teachings, happened to align with the rules of the prison prohibiting romantic and sexual relationships.

The afternoon before Thanksgiving, I sat down with a Black woman in her 30s named Giselle in one of the Main Hall classrooms. We enjoyed an uncharacteristic degree of privacy thanks to treacherous wintry road conditions—most of Mapleside's voluntary activities were cancelled for the day. I sat perched on a heater in the corner of the room as the brisk November air crept in through old window panes.

"I used to engage in homosexual activity," Giselle began. "I was a lesbian before I got here, and I never thought there was anything wrong with that." She paused to collect her thoughts, then backtracked: "Or, I knew it was wrong, but I didn't think I had to change anything. When I first came to Christ, I thought I could keep doing it." She laughed dismissively at her former belief that she could be both a lesbian and a "saved" Christian. Giselle had jumped into her faith, both feet first, and I knew her as a regular participant in Protestant programs, ready to quote scripture in almost any situation.

As her testimony continued, the smile disappeared from her face. "One day, I was sitting on the floor in my room reading my Bible when my fingertips started to feel like they was on fire." Wiggling her fingers as if to demonstrate, she said, "I threw my Bible on the ground. I was scared; I didn't know what was happening." She continued to mime the scene as she described the fateful moment in her cell. "I picked [the Bible] up again, and my hands felt hot. That's deliverance. I was delivered." When I asked her to elaborate, Giselle clarified, "It's when you're released from a stronghold, released from your demons." The transformation was sudden and absolute. "It was like a light switch," Giselle snapped her fingers for emphasis. "I don't do that no more. It just stopped." From that moment on, the narrative of "deliverance" from her sexual orientation was central to Giselle's testimony of Protestant redemption and practice.

Lucille, too, experienced inner strife about her sexual orientation long before she was arrested. In our one-on-one interview, she recalled, "Every day for thirty years, I would pray the same prayer." Then she recited her prayer from memory: "If it's wrong [to be gay], God, make me right." When God did not intervene, Lucille figured her sexual orientation must not be "wrong," so she continued dating women. When she began her 25-year sentence at Mapleside, Lucille explained, she "played around a little," initiating romantic relationships with other incarcerated women. But as the years progressed, Lucille became an active participant in Protestant programs, attending a Bible study or ministry class nearly every day of the week. This is where her "conversion narrative" picked up: "It was midnight. It had just become my birthday. I was alone in my cell." As she recalled the moment, Lucille clasped her hands together in prayer. Her eyes traveled to the ceiling, remembering her thoughts from that transformative night. "There has to be more. This isn't it for me." Lucille's quest for greater purpose, she believed, required not being gay.

"I used to be a homosexual," Lucille shared with a frown. "I'm not anymore."

In her memory, the change was immediate and definitive. Lucille placed both hands over her heart, attesting, "After that night, I never engaged in homosexuality again. I didn't want it anymore." Leafing through her Bible, she paged over to Leviticus 20:13, reading a passage to me in which being gay is identified as a "detestable" sin. Then she spelled out that the issue was not about "loving women" but engaging in a "sexual sin." "You [are] not supposed to have sex outside of marriage, no matter what. And the only real marriage is between a man and a woman."

Several years had passed since Lucille's conversion, and she told me she had become a mentor to several other incarcerated women as they tried to reject their sexual orientation for religious reasons. "Ironically, I ended up here around a thousand women for it to be relinquished," Lucille remarked. She also planned to start a "Same Sex Attraction Ministry" to help her pious peers achieve what she described as "deliverance from homosexuality."

Oaklynn, for one, came to rely on the support of Lucille and others to help change her sexual orientation. The more time she spent in Baptist Bible study and worship services, the more certain she believed that her previous "lifestyle" conflicted with being a good Christian. "I can't have *eternal life* if I practice that lifestyle," she said as she traced her finger down the spine of her leather-bound Bible.

Looking at me intently, she acknowledged the alternative: "I don't want to go to Hell, for real." She shook her head to underscore the point.

Oaklynn was fervent about what she called "stay[ing] away" from relationships with women. "I used to think that as long as I was a good person, it didn't matter if I was a lesbian. I could still go to Heaven." Now, she said she believed there would be no redemption without a rejection of "that lifestyle." When an ex-girlfriend tried to rekindle their relationship, Oaklynn reported, she demurred. "I wouldn't want to start up a relationship with her again." Certainly, this took effort. When "God told me to give up homosexuality," Oaklynn said, "it was hard as Hell. That's all I've ever known." She managed to live out her intention by relying on the support of her fellow Protestant women: "I couldn't have done it on my own. It helps to have a group of people here going through the same thing."

Among the devout Protestant women at Mapleside, I also encountered many who did not conform to this imperative prohibiting sexual relationships. Seneca and Ginger were one such couple. They attended Bible study and worship services together every week. At a Youth Bible Study Session, among 15 other attendees, the two spoke about their relationship and their faith, trying to impress upon the others that the former did not preclude the latter. "I go to church with my girlfriend, and we really pay attention," Seneca insisted, while Ginger told the group: "We go [to church services] together, but she really listen. Seneca is humble. She's always listening to the preacher." The couple sounded acutely aware of others' scrutiny. They perceived that fellow Protestants doubted their religious devotion because of their relationship. Her voice growing adamant, Ginger pointed out that Seneca "listens to the Word," and "I do, too." In fact, "If we're talking" during the worship services, it was a sign of their participation: "we'll talk about what we're hearing in the sermon."

That sort of judgmental surveillance had proven too much for some religious women I spoke to, like Rebecca, a Latina woman in her 40s. For the first few months of her incarceration, Rebecca attended Catholic worship services. Though she was raised Catholic, she told me she stopped attending those services when the volunteer priest criticized her sexual orientation. "The priest turned me off immediately when I said I was married to a woman. I'm *legally* married to a woman. . . . He said he didn't even recognize my divorce [from a man] since it wasn't an annulment." Rebecca was not interested in hearing criticism of her marriage, so she changed her religious affiliation. She began attending Lutheran worship services "because one of the volunteers who comes in is a lesbian. I didn't want to go to services where they condemn homosexuality." Lutheran services meet separately from the Protestant worship services since they do not adhere to an evangelical or charismatic tradition. Rebecca was steadfast: "I'm not gonna be told not to be a lesbian."

The fact that women like Seneca, Ginger, and Rebecca had to spell out the sincerity of their beliefs demonstrates the persistent idea that the forms of Christianity most prevalent at Mapleside were incompatible with romantic relationships between women. Their experiences grappling with this incompatibility highlighted how the religious proscriptions created a parallel set of normative behavioral expectations that remained tethered to formal institutional discipline. Based on these particular messages, being a "Daughter of Christ" in the "DOC" seemed to mean, to most, that they must embody a particular form of feminine expression, embrace gendered hierarchies, and participate only in heterosexual relationships. Again, these norms align with the very same ideals espoused by prison officials as they regulate incarcerated women's gender expression and sexual practices. The parallels between religious logics and carceral logics around gender and sexuality need not be intentional to be consequential: certainly, the administration's discretionary power in sorting religious volunteers may filter out prospective religious messages that lead to friction, and whether this process is deliberate or happenstance does not alter its implications.

MOTHERING BEHIND PRISON WALLS

As we saw with Dale, and corroborated by countless studies of women's prisons, state agents are intensely critical not only of women's sexuality but also of their role as mothers, condemning them as "out of control" or "unfit" parents.[30] To those who see womanhood's fullest expression in motherhood, this meant a mother who became justice-involved had rejected her highest duty and calling—an affront that only amplified the crime in their eyes. Briefly setting aside how religious discourses jockey with carceral discourses around the meaning of motherhood, we will first explore how women describe and manifest their identities as mothers at Mapleside.

Contra Dale's presuppositions described at the beginning of this chapter, incarcerated women give no indication that they have ignored or rejected their role as mothers. Instead, they describe the separation from their children as one of the cruelest aspects of imprisonment.[31] This was certainly true for Isadora, a Honduran woman in her early 40s who was serving a 20-month sentence. "It's so hard for me to be away from them," Isadora said of her four children, aged two to 15 years old. "My mother tells them that 'mommy is in school'—that she is not in jail, she's in school." Because her children have been shielded from this truth, they have never visited Mapleside. The separation is palpable.

Lexi, a white woman in her late 30s, was another mother who had gone without seeing her child since the day she became incarcerated. Her ex-husband gained custody of their young son, and because their divorce was marked by friction, he withheld visits. "I have to look at pictures," Lexi said sadly as she showed me photos of her six-year-old. "That's the only thing that gets me through." Many women keep such photographs close at hand, carrying the reminders of their children, even taping them to the backs of their DOC ID badges so that they can look at them at all times.

Custody is a topic that looms large for many women. Like Lexi, Hanna lost custody of her two young children. The kids live with their father and they have no contact with Hanna—not even phone calls. Cracking open a carefully organized binder, Hanna produced a stack of neatly typed poems and letters she had written over the years. She began to read a poem to me: "Mommy loves you and she's trying to get better for you. I want you to know I love you, even if I can only tell you through a letter." I noticed there were glossy photographs of her children tucked into the binder's plastic cover when she handed it to me. I also noticed there were tears in her eyes, but I was not sure she wanted me to see that part.

One day, I was present as normally ebullient Felicia burst into tears, too. She was in the hallway, distraught that her daughter's father had gained custody, when Chief Sawyer, Mapleside's chief of security, overheard her lament. Unsolicited, he chimed in: "You should be grateful that your child isn't being put in foster care." The callous comment threatened a worse outcome—the involvement of Child Protective Services and a potentially more embattled process of regaining custody after Felicia's eventual release.

More than two decades since finishing her sentence, Petunia was still nursing the pain of separation from her children. She was once incarcerated at Mapleside, and she now returned as a Protestant volunteer. "Not everybody has an aunt or grandmother or a cousin," she reasoned. "Not everybody has someone who can take the kids." Petunia gulped hard. "So, I lost my kids; the state took them. I was fortunate enough to be able to get my son back later. But that was hard. And my daughter, it has taken some time for our relationship to be rebuilt." Petunia could not be grateful, as Chief Sawyer had suggested to Felicia—her kids had entered the foster care system.

Nor could Anne, who had been incarcerated since her daughter was two years old. Now five, she was going to be adopted by another family. Anne was finishing up the adoption paperwork for this incredibly difficult decision when we spoke a week after Mother's Day. "Mother's Day here is just horrible." Wrinkling her nose, Anne said, "I decided I wasn't celebrating Mother's Day this year. No matter where you are and how good a relationship you have with your mother or your daughter, it can be a tough day." She averted her gaze before adding, "My daughter is getting adopted and I was just thinking about how she was celebrating with her new mom." Anne shared that not only did she have a life sentence to serve, she had struggled with addiction prior to her incarceration and had since been diagnosed with a serious mental illness. "It would not have been a good situation for my daughter," she granted, to remain in her care, even if that was possible—but that reality was no cure for the deep and visceral pain of their separation.

Pregnant women in prison anticipate this pain acutely. In the U. S. as of the 2010s, about 5 percent of women in state prisons are pregnant during their incarceration—1 in every 20.[32] As mentioned previously, some will labor while shackled to their hospital beds. None will get to spend more than a couple of days with their newborn after giving birth. They will be returned to their housing units, and their babies handed over to substitute caregivers. Often this is the child's father, aunt, or grandmother. Like other children, infants can come to Mapleside to visit their mothers. Not all women's prisons specifically try to help mothers interact with newborns and toddlers, but Mapleside designates a space for extended visits with young children, from newborn to toddler age. In the Main Hall, there is a large room painted in pastels, boasting a cheerful cartoon mural, the floor covered in toys, children's books, baby dolls, and colorful blocks. Although they can spend no more than 10 hours a month in this space, new mothers cherish it; they know many incarcerated women make do without.

Laura was one mother who was pregnant when she became incarcerated. I met her a couple years after her baby was born. Laura considered herself "lucky" because she was allowed three days with her newborn after delivery in custody. "Most people get 24 hours," she explained, but because she gave birth on a Friday, "and the social worker wasn't in over the weekend," 40-something Laura, a white woman with a four-year sentence, got extra time. She also felt lucky that two of her four children were young enough to spend time with her in the special space in the Main Hall. When her son aged-out at three years old, she shared, it was "hard." "He's like, 'Why can't I play with Mommy anymore?' " Behind her plastic-framed glasses, Laura's eyes welled. "He sees that his sisters can still come in," she pointed out with a sniffle.

Returning to her relative good luck, Laura described her husband's willingness to coordinate visits and make a four-hour round-trip drive to bring their children to visit her. By the time they arrive, the kids "are all wet" and so, "First I hug 'em real good, then I change 'em." Administrators will not abide dirty diapers in the trash. Thus, she added with chagrin, "He can't throw 'em away on the property, so he has to take 'em to a McDonalds nearby." It meant a lot to Laura to have a partner on the outside who has the time, resources, and dedication to care for their children, let alone travel long distances and invest significant effort in navigating prison visits. "I am lucky that I have him to take care of them. I know he's struggling—he has his hands full with four kids . . . . But they stole his heart. The little one especially." Laura paused, and her voice caught. "And it breaks my heart a little because she *loves* [her father]. She's so happy to see him. I hope she will feel that way about me, too."

The raw emotion of these portions of my interviews and observations bristled against my knowledge that state agents are disparaging of incarcerated women's motherhood. They routinely dismiss the idea that women who commit crimes can also be devoted mothers. In none of my conversations did I sit with an uncaring mother. "I only know him through phone calls," said Tati of her nearly 19-year-old son. The youngest of her four children, he was "nine months old when I got locked up." He had never visited Mapleside in all those years, Tati shared, "And I don't blame him." With a sharp inhale, she continued, "He's not ready to accept who his mother is, what his mother did." Serving a life sentence, Tati hoped to cultivate a stronger relationship with her son—with all of her children—as best she could from behind bars.

Vanessa, who was sentenced to a 25-year prison term, was a few years into her sentence when we met, and she was still wracked with guilt. Her guilt as a mother was double-edged: "Every time I see my child," Vanessa reflected, "I remember that my victim had children." She squinted, and her words came pouring out: "I hate visits. I hate phone calls. I hate children's day. I hate family day. Because while I love the time I get to spend with my son, I hate that he has to leave. And that gives me a glimpse, just a glimpse"—Vanessa pinched her forefinger and thumb together to show how small the glimpse— "into what the mother of my victim feels." Repairing the harms done seemed insurmountable, tying the pain of separation from her son to the tragedy that befell her victim's mother.

Where they wish for closeness and connection, most incarcerated mothers' relationships with their children are painfully character- ized by distance and separation. Less than half of the mothers in state prisons (42 percent) ever receive a single visit from their chil- dren. Fifteen percent have no contact with their children—no letters, phone calls, or visits.[33] This is not merely the case if relationships are frayed, but also because prisons are often geographically distant from major residential areas. Caregivers with already-strained schedules, transportation challenges, and financial hardships strug- gle to make visits work, especially given that nearly two-thirds of people held in state prisons are incarcerated more than 100 miles from their children.[34] This is even harder for women. There are fewer women's prisons in every state—sometimes only one— suggesting incarcerated women are even likelier than their male peers to be confined at prohibitive distances from their families. Furthermore, parents and caregivers may wish to limit children's exposure to the hostile environment of a correctional facility,[35] and the cost of setting up phone calls through the private companies that control communications makes even that a tough alternative. One study pinpoints the financial burden of visits and phone calls to incarcerated relatives at one-third of a low-income family's monthly budget.[36] When mothers are punished, their children and relatives are punished, too. Far from indifferent, the mothers I met at Mapleside battled guilt at every turn: guilt over their crimes, guilt over their victims, guilt over relying on relatives as surrogate guardians, and most of all, guilt over separation from their children.

PARENTING UNDER RELIGIOUS PATERNALISM

One way religious programs intervene in gendered carceral discourses is in offering a less punitive space in which women's motherhood is explicitly elevated (one such example of Christian theology's respect toward motherhood is in this chapter's title, from Luke 1:42 and repeated in the Catholic tradition's Hail Mary prayer: "Blessed art thou among women, and blessed is the fruit of thy womb"[37]). Secondhand carcerality, however, infects the efforts of elevating motherhood, ultimately bending toward a reproduction of state paternalism and the scarcity that defines parenting behind bars.

Hanna's experience is illustrative. With almost 15 years remaining in her prison sentence, Hanna told me it was her sixth Christmas apart from her two young children. Like Mother's Day, the holiday season is especially hard on mothers carrying the heartbreak of family separation. Chaplain Harper, in an effort to rouse Christmas cheer, papered her office door with poinsettia giftwrap and lined the door's trim with tinsel. Two large Christmas trees crowded her office, weighed down by red and gold ornaments, along with a set of reindeer figurines and a third, sparser "Charlie Brown" Christmas tree, as she called it (Asabi was taking great care to revive the third tree to fuller abundance, but it remained spindly).

The décor might not have lifted Hanna's spirits, but Chaplain Harper had another way: a baby doll named Bonquesha.[38] The chaplain brought Bonquesha into Mapleside as a therapeutic tool.

Perhaps the women could nurture the doll, she figured, mothering by proxy when they missed their children. Sure enough, in the weeks that followed, I witnessed numerous Protestant women stopping by Chaplain Harper's office to fuss over Bonquesha. Hanna, who connected with the doll right away, offered to wash Bonquesha's onesie in the bathroom sink: "It looks like real spit-up. See?" Maria fretted that Bonquesha's feet might get cold because she was not wearing socks. Ruby, who works as a custodian in the Main Hall, checked in often and professed to be Bonquesha's "real mother."

Hearing this, Hanna teased back, "We're gonna have a problem then. That's my baby, but I let you name her." She scooped up Bonquesha and patted her bottom. Then, her smile fading, she revealed to Ruby, "I would only trust a few people to say this to, but it's really helping me." She rocked Bonquesha in her arms. Ruby retorted, "You're spoiling that baby!" at which Hanna grinned, "Yes, I am."

About a week later, Ruby, Hanna, and a number of other Protestant women gathered in the chaplain's office to help with a big project. Eyeing Bonquesha in the corner of the office, Ruby prodded Hanna, "She needs to know who her real mother is. With that skin and a name like Bonquesha?" The doll had dark brown skin and dark eyes, much like Ruby's, compared to Hanna's white skin and blue eyes.

At first, the therapeutic baby doll seemed effective. I even noticed that someone had composed a lullaby, scrawled on the chalkboard of one of the Main Hall Bible study classrooms:

Bonquesha
Hush little baby
Don't you cry . . .
Mommy loves you!

She was so beloved, in fact, that Chaplain Harper purchased two more dolls from Walmart. The baby dolls, one white and one Black, were named Gracie and Sherrell. Because the chaplain knew they would be considered contraband by prison officials, she warned the doting women not to take Gracie or Sherrell out of her office: "It's gonna get snatched!" Perhaps for my sake, Chaplain Harper clarified, "It'll get confiscated probably."

Things went fine for about a month, until Reverend Donna, the volunteer teaching the weekly Baptist Bible study, spotted Hanna cradling Gracie, one of the new dolls. (Now that there were two dolls of two different races, Hanna opted for the white baby doll.) Concerned, Reverend Donna reported straight to the chaplain. As Hanna summed it up later, Reverend Donna "wanted to make sure I was comforted by Christ and not by an object."

After mulling it over for a few days, the chaplain came to agree with Reverend Donna. She would no longer allow Hanna and the other women to nurture the toy dolls. The afternoon that Chaplain Harper tossed Gracie and Sherrell into a plastic bag and carried them through the sliding metal doors toward the prison gates, Hanna lay on the floor wailing. Hanna surmised of her initial remonstration, "If [Chaplain Harper] had come back, I'd have clung to her leg and not let go." Ultimately, Hanna said dejectedly, "I was relying on them too much. It's easy to make an idol of an object." She said she eventually came to peace with the chaplain's decision, based on the Abrahamic tenet to not worship false idols—in this case the dolls intended to comfort lonesome mothers.

Caregiving emerged as a constant, deep-rooted component of women's narratives about motherhood. Being separated from their children, many of the incarcerated women I spoke to ruminated on how they might have done better by their children. Jessica, a mother of four, shared, "My one regret is that I wasn't as good of a mother when I was an addict." It sometimes seemed administrators' narratives of maternal condemnation were superfluous atop the women's internal monologues of regret and longing. They were part of the pervasive paternalism scholars have repeatedly documented in women's prisons. Incarcerated women are treated as less-than-competent adults. Just as prison rules dictate they cannot consent to sexual relationships, prison discourses dictate they cannot be viewed as good mothers. Their autonomy is stripped away, and their parenting practices are examined with intense scrutiny. Mothers are relentlessly reminded that their parenting styles are unacceptable and that they lack the final say in matters related to their children.[39] In McCorkel's study of a state women's prison, referenced earlier, she captures a rehabilitation counselor lambasting an incarcerated woman by screaming, "What kind of woman, what kind of mother, would choose—if she had *control*—would choose to be in prison?"[40]

That question can be flipped in a curious way: What kind of state, what kind of criminal legal system would choose—if they truly aim at rehabilitation—to weaponize motherhood and deny caregiving opportunities? After Chaplain Harper took away Gracie and Sherrell, Warden Davis went further, ruling that no baby dolls would be permitted outside the designated space for mothers and newborns in the Main Hall. Hanna, Ruby, and the other women who found comfort in the therapeutic dolls were accustomed to policies that sought to wrench their children—as well as their autonomy in parenting—away. The dolls seemed a useful replacement, but they were paltry substitutes for actual connection with their own children. They were playthings, meant for children, and in giving them to bereft mothers, Chaplain Harper had infantilized the women like prison officials did. Describing the women in her pastoral care, the chaplain once mused, "Sometimes you can't tell if they're babies or grown women." Adding to this cruel tug-of-war was the paternalistic decision to remove the dolls, dictating "what is best" for women's religious devotion.

The attempts made by the chaplaincy at Mapleside to comfort mothers ended up reproducing some of the very regulation, condemnation, and infantilization they sought to undermine. The prevailing religious discourse described the baby dolls as a false idol, while the prison discourse described them as contraband. Although the interpretive meanings differed, the outcome was the same. Tainted by secondhand carcerality, religion tried to give but, like the prison, kept on taking.

.   .   .   .   .

In contemporary U. S. prisons, women are punished not only for their crime but also for their deviance from norms of motherhood, femininity, and heterosexuality. Parole board member Dale accused incarcerated women of trying to "use" motherhood to secure early release, without ever mentioning the tangible, documented harms born out of separating mothers and children. Mapleside's assistant warden scrutinized the gender expression of her wards. Nationwide legislation prohibits all sex in prisons, which ends up outlawing meaningful gay and lesbian relationships among confined populations.

By contrast, many religious messages at Mapleside affirm women *as women*. They use theological and religio-cultural notions of gender to reframe what it means to be an incarcerated woman, mother, and wife. However, as much as they offer a counterpoint to punitive prison messages, religious messages—Protestant ones specifically—ultimately contribute to penal discourses constructing normative womanhood and ideologies of the family. Drawing on scripture to affirm tenets of gender traditionalism, religious volunteers engage in many of the same narratives about how they believe incarcerated women *should* act and what they *should* desire. They shore up the infantilizing rhetoric that regulates incarcerated women. They call on their identities as mothers and as women, while also knee-capping autonomy by promoting feminine submission to prison authorities and to the "man of God" they are encouraged to find, marry, and serve after release. None of the preachers, Bible study groups, or religiously affiliated self-help programs broached gender inequality, or how, together with poverty and racial inequality, it can propel women onto well-trod pathways that lead to crime and incarceration. Instead, through secondhand carcerality, religious messages reinforced the prison's normative prescriptions of womanhood through feminine reliance on men, heterosexual orientation, and a paternalistic approach to motherhood.

The next chapter turns to the social organization of religious activities at Mapleside to interrogate the practical, day-to-day implications of freedom and constraint that we have seen thus far borne out in religious rhetoric.

5 *For Many Are Called, But Few Are Chosen*

STATUS AND DIGNITY IN THE PRISON CHURCH

When it comes to the day-to-day operations of religious life in prison, congregations in the "big house" rely on the volunteer labor of their parishioners to keep things running smoothly. They operate much like houses of worship outside of prison, where lay leaders oversee services, attend to the organizational needs of their religious community, and promote engagement beyond it.[1] At Mapleside, religious volunteers come and go when they lead worship services and Bible studies. Meanwhile, it is the task of incarcerated acolytes to plan, set up, clean up, and otherwise carry out the details of religious programs. These women are called "church officials," deputized by Chaplain Harper, to voluntarily run the logistics of religious programs at Mapleside. The system of church officials has both religious and social implications. Gina's story demonstrates how important the church official system can be in governing social status and hierarchy among devout women at Mapleside.

Gina was a Protestant church official before she had a stroke. She attended worship services and Bible study, week in and week out. On

Sundays, she donned a golden robe atop her prison-issue khakis to serve as an usher. I remember the Tuesday in October when Hanna told Asabi and me the news of Gina's stroke. Our focus on the copious paperwork in Chaplain Harper's office came to an abrupt halt as Hanna explained that Gina was now confined to the infirmary. We worried over the prognosis and Gina's possible road to recovery. Then Hanna raised an additional concern. "We gotta tell her she's not an usher no more," Hanna ventured carefully, "to avoid an awkward situation."

Knitting her brow, Asabi wondered why Gina could not remain an usher until she recovered. Why demote her now? Hanna explained: "She became Lutheran. Or I should say, on November 1st, she'll *become* Lutheran." Gina was converting. That meant she would no longer be allowed to attend Protestant worship services. In the wider world, Lutherans are considered Protestant Christians, but at Mapleside, they worship in their own, smaller group, separate from the larger, charismatic, and historically Black denominational Protestant services (see chapter 2). By extension, Gina was set to lose her status as a Protestant church official.

Because even religious conversion is beholden to bureaucracy in prison, Gina's Change of Religious Preference Form was in process when she had her stroke—hence Hanna's specificity. Gina would "become" Lutheran on the first of November, and with that, she would forfeit her position as a church official in two weeks' time. Through her religious conversion, she was withdrawing from one of the major organizing forces of social structure at Mapleside.

As sociologist Elijah Anderson tells us, local cultures generate unspoken norms of interaction and signals of social status.[2] This chapter draws on Anderson's theories of culture and interaction to examine the local culture of the prison church, with attention to the interplay of race and the cultivation of dignity.[3] In a carceral environment, where women are intentionally de-individualized, stripped of social status, and thwarted in their collective organizing, the role of "church official" affords personal dignity, social status, and a sense of community. Inasmuch as the previous chapter focused on gender, this chapter speaks to race.[4] Lay leadership is an important source of personal dignity and mode of collective organizing across American religious congregations, and especially in the Black Church, where the structure can "confer titles of honor and respect . . . [and] a sense of achievement and worth" against the affronts of racism and socio-economic precarity.[5] Put simply, service among the lay leadership can be a political act as much as an act of community building. Lay leaders may foster collective organizing, and they have a long history of working alongside clergy toward major, transformative causes: the abolition of slavery, the achievement of civil rights milestones, and today's activism fighting against key issues like environmental inequality and persistent poverty.[6]

Nurturing communal life and unsettling the status quo are just as important to the Protestant women incarcerated at Mapleside. Here, as we will see, the lay leaders are most often Black women serving long-term prison sentences. Their status as church officials inverts the hierarchical, interlocking systems of racism, classism, and sexism that more often relegate financially precarious Black women to the lowest rungs; by contrast, at Mapleside, the chaplain's so-called "chosen ones" rise to the top. The opportunity to organize within religious identity groups allows for collective efforts, communities of emotional support, and even moments in which church officials are able to revise and resist prison rules.

At the same time, W. E. B. Du Bois and scholars following his theoretical tradition have recognized religion's dual capacity as a liberating *and* a suppressing force—it has the potential to challenge and to maintain the status quo, sometimes in the same moments.[7] Gina's demotion was a clear example: any internal hierarchy risks leaving people out. By building a hierarchy among congregants, engagement that fosters collective efficacy also sows further division. Where state control dominates and seeks to suppress, competition over scarce resources means those who are less involved in Protestant programs, those who participate in non-Protestant faith traditions, and those who are not religious feel the sting of inequality keenly as they see the tangible resources available to "church officials." In what follows, we will see congregants draw on Protestant religion to nurture personal dignity and build supportive community networks within a highly punitive institution—and we will also see how lay leadership becomes a site of competition through the divisive spread of secondhand carcerality.

COMMUNITY AND CONNECTION

By now, we have established that religious programs throughout the week are more than a place to learn scripture and discuss religious practices. They provide a modicum of autonomy and personal identity. They also serve a crucial function as caring environments in which women facing hard times can share stories, console each other, and even physically embrace. Adelaide's harrowing experience demonstrates the extent to which religion can offer a strong sense of social support.

Adelaide has chin-length braids and a warm smile, though I most often see her sitting quietly in the back of a Main Hall classroom during Baptist Bible study or gazing upward prayerfully during Sunday worship services. She serves on the "Dance Ministry" and values her position as a church official. In her early 40s, Adelaide has served nearly 18 years at Mapleside so far. She was in her 20s when she began her life sentence.

Although some women openly discussed the details of their cases, Adelaide never did. All she shared was that her mother had served time at Mapleside, too, until she passed away a few years prior, and that she is now estranged from her 20-something daughter, Kelli, who was a toddler when Adelaide was arrested. After years of unreturned phone calls and unanswered letters, Adelaide prays to God that she will one day reconnect with her daughter. Later, Hanna would tell me, a Saturday night tragedy would transform into a

Sunday afternoon miracle for Adelaide and her daughter, Kelli. To me, the story also revealed the strength of a religious community to support its members in the darkest moments.

As Hanna told it, it was about 9 o'clock on Saturday night when Chaplain Harper's cell phone rang. The chaplain was at home, and the caller was her colleague, the chaplain at a nearby men's prison, where Marcus—Kelli's father—was incarcerated. He was calling to inform Chaplain Harper that Kelli had died. Delivering news like this is a chaplain's responsibility, no matter how difficult. So, Chaplain Harper drove straight to Mapleside, marched to her office, and requested that Adelaide be escorted to the Main Hall. She would share the heartbreaking news and comfort Adelaide however she could.

After their unspeakably difficult meeting, Adelaide had no choice but to return to her housing unit. She lived on the "honor pod"—a building reserved for women who have decades-long sentences and maintain records of "good behavior" with the administration in exchange for relative "privileges" like unrestricted telephone hours and cells that stay unlocked during the day. Hanna explained that she, Estrella, and several other women were waiting for her: "We didn't know what happened, but we started preparing because we knew it couldn't be good." There was never any good news awaiting someone called to the chaplain's office after hours, late on a weekend evening.

"The officers gave us grace, and we stayed up all night in a vigil for Adelaide," Hanna reported, drawing on the religious language of "grace" to characterize this official permission as an act of mercy or special favor. The women prayed together until morning.

As Sunday dawned, Chaplain Harper logged into Facebook to post a message about Adelaide's daughter, soliciting information from anyone in her virtual social network. By afternoon, Chaplain Harper had received a truly unexpected phone call—from Kelli herself. Kelli, very much alive, asked to speak to her mother, Adelaide, for the first time in seven years.

"I don't know *why* it had to be something like this, but maybe that's what it took to reunite them," Chaplain Harper reflected in her sermon during that day's Protestant worship service. Hanna, too, was convinced that this was God's handiwork. Smiling wryly, she described something that happened during the women's all-night prayer vigil. "Estrella doesn't remember saying this, but at one point ... she came in and said, 'Why are you looking for the living among the dead?'" Estrella, Hanna recalled, had quoted a line of scripture from Luke 24:5. "She doesn't remember because she was channeling the word of God," Hanna interpreted. During Adelaide's darkest moments, her fellow Christians and the prison chaplain provided care and succor.

The roots of Adelaide's family tree are deeply entwined with the American penal system. Her mother died in prison. Adelaide expected she would, too. Kelli's father was incarcerated. Aside from prison, Adelaide had never known a safety net. Now within this *de facto* safety net of last resort, Protestant religion and congregation offered up the support that state institutions had repeatedly failed to provide. It would be hard to overstate its profound importance to Adelaide.

STATUS AND HIERARCHY

As cherished as this sense of community could be for women like Adelaide, not everyone was able to access the same degree of companionship. Secondhand carcerality shapes the ways in which religion is able to subvert insidious state control. Its introduction of social hierarchy merits consideration. Scholars of men's correctional facilities have shown how state officials weaponize group identities to this end, as incarcerated men are enlisted to enforce prison rules and manage their own internal hierarchy.[8] Status derived from religion is not immune, as those designated as church officials gain social and material resources that are perceived by others as unfair advantages. In an environment as highly punitive as a prison, which forces women to compete for scarce resources, the attention and support among church officials do not escape notice. Others are necessarily left out. Examined in light of the carceral context, we can hold up religion as a protected space to connect and commune, while at the same time interrogating its implications for those shut out of the inner circle.

For instance, Heather raised the specter of inequality when she talked with me about her conversion from Catholicism to evangelical Christianity (described in chapter 4). "Like when they thought Adelaide's daughter had died," Heather theorized, "they all gathered around to support her. But what about if someone *else's* daughter died?" Heather was skeptical that others in an equally traumatic situation could count on the same level of support available to the women who were most active in Protestant programs. Absent a counterfactual, it is difficult to know. However, as Durkheimian theorists argue, the creation of group cohesion functionally excludes others.[9] In Heather's words, "A lot of times they leave people out. They're such a group, that they forget that there are other people around."

Kifa agreed. Although she dabbled in religious programs here and there, Kifa, a Black woman in her early 40s, identified as agnostic. In fact, that is how we met. After I put out the word that I wanted to include nonreligious women in my study, I was introduced to Kifa by Esther, a white woman who was active in the Baptist programs as a church official. Esther escorted me to the computer lab, where Kifa was typing up an essay for one of her college classes. When Kifa spotted me, however, she buried her head in her hands, protesting to Esther, "You're setting me up!" Kifa bristled because she assumed I was a religious volunteer, there to convert her. This was not an uncommon assumption, given all the time I spent observing Mapleside's religious programs and volunteering in Chaplain Harper's office—plenty of people I met were surprised to learn I was actually a researcher when I explained my study and consent procedure. Esther assured Kifa, "No, she ain't like that. She has no religion. She grew up—Jewish?" Esther turned toward me, raising her eyebrows to confirm. For Esther, being Jewish meant being a nonbeliever, thus her characterization that I had "no religion."

Kifa consented to the interview, growing increasingly candid as she saw my genuine interest in her perspective. It was hard, she shared, to reconcile the suffering around her with a belief in a merciful God. "You see how we live in here?" she asked rhetorically. "There can't be no God." Kifa elaborated, explaining that her skepticism had as much to do with others' interactions with the penal system as her own incarceration:

> I'm in here for armed robbery. That's why I'm here. I robbed someone. I ain't never killed anybody or hurt anybody, and some people who have [are] walking out of here before me, they're out there on the street doing the same things or even worse. And I'm still here. That's why I don't believe in God. If there was a God, He wouldn't let that be.

And so, Kifa rejected religious affiliation.

The problem, in her view, was that not practicing religion in prison seemed to mean being relegated to a lesser social status. She used a story to illustrate her frustration: "Like for instance, I went up to the chaplain, and she was talking to someone, one of her 'church people.' I asked her for five minutes to talk. And she kind of brushed me aside." Kifa flicked her wrist, reenacting Chaplain Harper's dismissal. "That was two weeks ago; I still haven't heard from her." With a hint of dismay, Kifa raised her hands as if surrendering to the inequality. "I see mass murderers in here who are *blessed*," she said in a mocking tone.

Resentment toward the chaplain's "church people" was commonplace among nonbelievers as well as non-Protestant believers. Lexi and Dorinda, both Jewish, expressed a similar degree of irritation with the church officials. "They feel like they get more," Lexi posited, with Dorinda adding, "They also do it to feel important. They get to boss other inmates around and tell them to sign in." Kifa's words raced through my mind as Dorinda lamented, "Religion teaches that the righteous are rewarded, but it's not true. The righteous are punished and the wicked walk free." These comments reflect a downside of any system set up to distribute limited resources, be they material or social, in a world defined by scarcity. Forms of authority and privilege take on immense meaning in a space that deprives women of autonomy and power by design.

Mapleside's Church Officials

In granting the title of "church official," Chaplain Harper designates a leadership role that tasks women with running worship services and programs. To be sure, every religious group at Mapleside has its acolytes, but when women remark on "church officials," it is unspoken that they mean the *Protestant* church officials—the prison's largest and most visible group of highly devout women who serve within its best-resourced religious group.

Becoming a Protestant church official requires joining a ministry: Adult Choir, Young Adult Choir, the Praise and Worship Team, Dance Ministry, Drama Ministry, Mime Ministry, Banner Ministry, a team of Ushers, or the Equipment Set-Up Ministry. Church officials exchange the monotony of their khaki uniforms for satin purple, floor-length robes as members of the choir. Members of the Dance Ministry don flowy Spandex costumes in an array of colors: royal blue, deep purple, bright white, and a pink Hibiscus pattern. Mime and Drama Ministries have access to special makeup and costumes for their performances.

As a measure to ensure active participation in religious programs, Chaplain Harper requires all church officials to attend at least one Bible study class per week. They prove their attendance on a special sign-in sheet designated for church officials only. If anyone misses Bible study four weeks in a row, Chaplain Harper sends a warning letter; future absences risk demotion. Switching religious affiliations, like Gina had done, results in the instant revocation of church official status (though it may be conferred in their new denomination).

Church officials are tasked with specific jobs during the Sunday church services. They can serve as emcees, introducing outside guests, reciting an opening prayer, or reading introductory scripture. They can serve as ushers, who direct churchgoers to the official sign-in sheet and to their seats among the congregation, distribute communion, and offer Styrofoam cups filled with ice water to outside volunteers. Others set up the gym before church, powering up the sound system, staging the podium, and arranging 200 plastic chairs in orderly rows. Still others work as the clean-up crew, stacking chairs after the service, ensuring the sound system is returned to the locked closet, and restoring the worship space to its role as the recreational gym. Church officials are issued a special ID badge, printed and laminated by Chaplain Harper's clerks, to be worn clipped to their official DOC ID at all times. Flashing a church official ID badge allows its owner to leave her cell 30 minutes early for the religious program and return to her cell 30 minutes late after clean-up.

Jessica, a mid-40s Latina woman who identifies as spiritual but not religious, conveyed her cynicism about church officials' religious devotion when describing the material advantages that come with the status. "People want to get out of their pod," she asserted. "Church officials can do anything. They get early feed, [those] baby privileges that we care about." When she was first incarcerated, Jessica told me, she was motivated by such "privileges" to become a church official. "It was nice—got me out of my room," she conceded. "But I felt bad about it, like I was being false. So I wrote into the chaplain about it, telling her to take me off the list."

As was becoming evident, many of the women incarcerated at Mapleside harbored at least some degree of resentment toward the church officials. Bernadette, for instance, is a mid-60s white woman and Catholic church official who is one of only three who sing in their Sunday choir. She was typical in taking umbrage at the way Protestant church officials felt entitled to cut in line at mealtimes: the "early feed" that Jessica mentioned. Their rationale was that church officials must eat early in order to help with setting up worship services and Bible study activities. "Last Monday, four of them cut in line," Bernadette huffed, bristling at her recollection of the moment in the cafeteria. "'Church official!'" she said imperiously, raising her arms and puffing out her chest to mimic the way they butted ahead. "And I said to them, 'Have you ever read Matthew 16 that says "The last shall be the first and the first shall be last"?'" With that quip, she brazenly cut in, taking her place before the Protestant church officials. Anne, sitting with Bernadette and me as we spoke, laughed at Bernadette's bravado.

I witnessed another mockery of the line-cutters when I stood among a large group of women who were bottlenecked outside the gym for a Good Friday worship service. A young Black woman named Harriet, unamused by the wait, flung her arms in the air and cried out, "Church official! Church official coming through!" Harriet was not actually a church official, but she pushed her way through. The other women waiting in line must have been amused or nonplussed, such that they allowed Harriet to pass ahead of them into the gym without incident.

The conferral of authority bred contention among the incarcerated women in all sorts of ways. Tensions sometimes cut across racial lines, as in the case of Bernadette, and sometimes did not, as in the case of Harriet. Those who were not church officials resented the latter's privileges; those who were tended to feel unfairly maligned. In one such incident, I was working alongside Maria, the church official who volunteered as head librarian in the religious library. It was a Thursday morning, past 11 o'clock—time for the religious library to close. Maria shut off the lights in the library. We sat in the library's antechamber, writing up a list of the women who checked out books that day. Half an hour passed, and Maria went to the cafeteria to pick up a late lunch tray. She would bring it back to eat in the library and relish a rare moment of privacy.

I was using this time to talk with Officer Abell, the CO on post in the hallway outside the library, when Sandee approached. Sandee is a Black woman in her mid-40s, and although she is a regular worshipper who attends weekly Baptist Bible study, she is not a church official. Sandee had a pass to visit the religious library that day, but explained that the officer on duty in her housing unit was late in buzzing her out. I waved her in to the technically closed room.

Returning with her lunch tray, Maria frowned when she spotted Sandee browsing the shelves. She seemed upset that I had bent the rules. "You got three minutes, then we're closed," Maria called out. Sandee looked up, eyebrows raised, but said nothing. Maria did not notice, because Officer Abell was laughing at the encounter. "You sound like us!" she scoffed at Maria, comparing her authoritative rebuke to that of a correctional officer.

Maria, for her part, felt that church officials were held to an unreasonable standard. "People are watching church officials all the time," she complained. "And it's not just us—anyone who follows the rules in here, anyone who does what they're supposed to do, gets persecuted." Maria's use of the verbiage of persecution drove home her point that the church official role was both righteous and maligned. The status differentials created by the church official system, it seemed, could go both ways, with each group sensing that the other was allowed more leeway than their own.

Social order emerges even where expressions of identity are stripped away and markers of status are limited. Sister Harris, the white woman and Catholic nun who has volunteered at Mapleside for nearly a decade, was well aware: "You give women a little power here, and they run with it," she commented. "You have lifers who have been running things for years." A while back, Sister Harris reported, she witnessed the hierarchy firsthand. "There was one woman in a class I taught who was the sweetest, kindest girl. And I gave her the job of running the attendance list, and she became a *bear*." Sister Harris lurched forward, demonstrating the woman's animalistic aggression in fulfilling her role. Without knowing the person to whom she referred, I wondered whether Sister Harris's interpretation drew on coded language of race, gender, or both, in embodying a position of authority. Although Sister Harris's tone was critical of the women who "run with" their "little power," the women given that power certainly held it dear. With few alternative avenues for status and respect, the church official system was a coveted source of social status at the same time that it bred contention. The church official system is yet another byproduct of the deprivation of material and social resources endemic to secular prison life.

The Chaplain's "Chosen Ones"

Tangible effects of the religious social hierarchy surrounding church officials reverberated through daily interactions at Mapleside. It was perhaps no more apparent than on the day of the annual Christmas gift bag distribution, when every woman at Mapleside, regardless of her faith, receives a goodie bag stuffed with items donated by local religious organizations. "That was the best thing that happened all year long," Estrella commented later. December at Mapleside was oriented around the Christmas spirit, overt and palpable. The Christmas gift bags were for all, but I noticed there were no menorahs on display. Not a kinara in sight.

Chaplain Harper ran the annual gift program, and on this day, she had recruited eight outside volunteers, including myself, to assist her and a dozen church officials who were authorized to skip their work assignments for the day. We all congregated in the prison gym to distribute the Christmas gift bags. Violet, a church official in her early 50s, said she was pleased to be selected as part of this privileged few: "I was real glad when I got called up here this morning [to the Main Hall]." Bending closer to whisper, she added, "I wasn't sure I was gonna be one of her *chosen ones.*"

Although an imperfect measure, the chaplain's "chosen ones" are one indication of the background characteristics of church officials compared to the general population at Mapleside. The chaplain's "chosen ones" skew, on average, five years older than the total prison population. They are serving longer sentences on average, too, on the order of about two decades more. They are much more likely to have been convicted of homicide, and less likely to have been convicted of a drug-related offense. These patterns suggest that church officials rise through the ranks by an investment of time. Or, perhaps, there is a greater draw toward religious participation among those who seek to build meaningful lives to fill the decades of incarceration that stretch ahead.

On the day of the gift bag distribution, the atmosphere in the gym was jolly. Outside volunteers replaced their typical business casual and "Sunday best" attire with Christmas sweaters, blue jeans, and Santa Claus hats. A few wore elf ears, and Chaplain Harper's jingle bell necklace chimed as she dashed around the room in high spirits. Around half past 9 o'clock, we formed what some called a "North Pole" assembly line. Our job as volunteers and "chosen ones" was to stuff each of the thousand clear plastic bags with goodies including a colorful notebook, a pencil, a toothbrush and toothpaste, makeup, a calendar, body lotion, a bar of soap, chenille winter gloves, and a handful of Protestant pamphlets and gospel tracts. We worked quickly, assembling and methodically packing the bags. Chaplain Harper returned from her lunch bearing a bevy of oatmeal cookies—a treat for our preparatory efforts—and a warning: chaos was coming.

Sure enough, a thousand women funneled into the gym after lunchtime. At tables organized alphabetically by last name, volunteers and church officials checked the official DOC roster, crossing the names off one by one. The goal was to make sure each person picked up one and only one gift bag. "No ID, no bag," Chaplain Harper cautioned. Her other caveat was against exchanges. Each bag varied by the color of the winter gloves—purple, pink, brown, black, or white—and by makeup product. Based on her past experiences, she anticipated the women may try to get volunteers to swap if they preferred one of the other bags' contents. We were to hold firm. "No exchanges," Chaplain Harper instructed. "What you get is what you get."

The chaplain's "chosen ones" got to claim their gift bags first, before the other women arrived. "Do you want [eye] pencils, do you want shadow? What do you want?" Adelaide asked a younger church official named Jojo as she rummaged through a box of the gift bags, looking for one with her desired glove color and makeup product. Of course, we could not do this with each person. Once the crowds arrived, Chaplain Harper had explained, it was all we could do to hand out the bags, check off names, and keep the commotion to a minimum.

I sat beside Esther and Adelaide at the N–Q table, with Hanna stepping in to help when they scurried across the hall to pick up their own lunch trays during a lull around 1 o'clock. Hanna crossed the names off the list while I examined the IDs. I heard other volunteers calling out "Merry Christmas," but I turned over the gift bags with a cheery "Happy holidays!" knowing that nearly one in three women at Mapleside identified as neither Protestant nor Catholic. At one point, a woman I had never met approached the table.

As I reached for the next available gift bag in the pile, she interjected: "Can I get the pink gloves?" I had been reaching for a bag with brown gloves, though I spotted another bag, visibly containing the coveted bright pink gloves, inches away. I grabbed the bag with pink gloves and the woman grinned appreciatively. It was not exactly an exchange—more of a preemptive request, I reasoned. And why not make someone happy? In a sea of khaki uniforms, I understood that pink gloves were a welcome change.

When Adelaide and Esther returned with their Styrofoam lunch trays, they grabbed a spot on the bleachers, a few feet behind the N–Q table, to eat their subs and chips. From there, they could watch as Blanche, an elderly white woman who walked with a cane, approached the table. They could also witness as Blanche frowned, taking a bag containing black gloves from Hanna. "Can I get the purple gloves instead?" Blanche asked. Hanna complied, reaching for a nearby bag with purple gloves. That is when Esther intervened, jumping up from the bleachers to race toward the table, choking down a bite of her hoagie.

"No exchanges!"

Esther turned to Hanna, saying, "Don't let them use you." Then, to Blanche, who must have been 20 years her senior, she added, "Sorry, no exchanges. Those are the rules. I'm just being obedient." "But it would have been just as easy for her to hand me that other bag," Blanche protested. Esther was unmoved, repeating: "No exchanges, sorry." Blanche muttered, "I'm sure you're doing it all the time, but okay . . . ," suggesting that favoritism in the church officials' clique was at play. I watched as Blanche slunk away, face flushed. She lingered near the gym's entrance, eyeing other women's bags to see whether they contained purple gloves and asking if anyone would trade. Disappointed, she gave up after a few minutes. No one wanted her black gloves, and she had to return to her housing unit for afternoon count.

AND YE SHALL RECEIVE

As Blanche's dismay suggests, the material resources offered by religious programs at Mapleside figured centrally in the lived experience of incarceration. After all, material deprivations are a hallmark of prison life, while religious programs are comparatively resource-rich. Take it from Rashida: "The Religious Department is the best organized department in this institution, and not just the spiritual side. If you need counseling, hygiene—whatever—you go to the Religious Department *first*, because it's quicker and better quality." Rashida had served multiple stints in prison, and she knew not only that she had to ask for what she needed but exactly who to ask.[10]

Certainly, as a matter of constitutional protection of religious freedom, administrators provide for different ritual items (see fig. 5 for a DOC memorandum stipulating these provisions in the state of Tennessee). What is more, some resources flow through the Religious Department regardless of denominational affiliation. For instance, when Chaplain Harper conducts her weekly rounds to visit women in solitary confinement, she brings crossword puzzles and Bibles for

Correction

MEMO

BUDDHISTS
1. Plastic prayer beads (1) solid color.
2. Scapular (Traditional image inside a plastic casing)
3. Polar fleece prayer rug (1) no larger than 30 x 40 inches, does not require a fire retardant label attached; the rug may be used exclusively for prayer and placed on the floor only during prayer.
4. Yoga Mat (must be donated and kept in the Recreation Office). Used for religious gatherings only.

CATHOLICS
1. Plastic rosary with crucifix (1), solid color.
2. Scapular

JEWISH, HOUSE OF YAHWEH, AND HEBREW ISRAELITES
1. Yarmulke or kippah (2), solid black, white or gray.
2. Prayer Shawl (tallit) may have TZITZIT.
3. Tefilin (Phylactery).

MUSLIMS
1. Hijab (2) solid white head covering (female Muslims).
2. Kufi (2), solid white, black or gray.
3. Miswak sticks, up to 10 sticks.
4. Plastic prayer beads (1), solid color.
5. Prayer rug (1), no larger than 27 inches x 44 inches, does not require a fire retardant label attached; the rug must be used exclusively for prayer and placed on the floor only during prayer.

WICCANS/ASATRU/ODINIST/PAGANS
1. Triquetra pendant (1).
2. Tarot cards, must comply with all policies, including but not limited to Policy 507.02.
3. Chakra bracelet of seven (1) with a maximum replacement value of $30.00.
4. Necklace (1) pentagram/5-point star enclosed in a circle, and not an open star, with a maximum replacement value of $30.00.
5. Earth/soil (up to 1 tablespoon).
6. Tap water (up to ¼ cup).
7. Flat stone (1) up to 1 x 1 inch which may have a hole in the center.
8. Book of shadows/personal journal (1).
9. Ring (1) with a maximum replacement value of $25.00.
10. Oak Sacred feather (1), uncut, no more than 8 inches in length. Must be kept in the cell and removed only for group gatherings.

ALL: Single battery powered plastic candle.

Figure 5. Tennessee DOC Inmate Religious Property Memorandum, May 2017.

all who request them, as well as hygiene kits containing toothpaste, toothbrushes, soap, and shampoo for women deemed "indigent" by the prison (those with under five dollars in their accounts). I also watched the chaplain secure an HIV test from the medical ward for a woman on lock, and I heard her call the cable company to request a service repair when the television reception was spotty in the cell-blocks. In short, the Religious Department, and the chaplain's personal dedication, maintained women's well-being and quality of life in ways that extended beyond the theological.

Yet neither the official "religious property" nor the items provided to all by the chaplain were the central source of concern among women at Mapleside. Rather, because state funding has dried up and outside congregations have intervened in their stead, it is the uneven distribution of resources based on religious affiliation that was impossible for many women to ignore. Due to the greater number of Protestant volunteers and the greater flow of financial donations to Protestant programs, women who participated in Protestant programs gained more access to certain material resources, a fact that others noted with evident irritation. For instance, anyone who participated in a nondenominational Christian weekend retreat received a bag of nine cookies to take back to her cell: three oatmeal, three sugar cookies, and three chocolate chip. Leftover cookies were distributed by Chaplain Harper to the participants in her own ministry class. Additionally, while women otherwise had limited access to literature, a massive amount of Christian reading material was available *gratis,* from weekly newsletters to informational pamphlets, graphic novels, scriptural analyses, and poetry. Moreover, Christian literature did not count toward the 20-book limit per person, and those who attended Bible study received free copies of self-help books, prayer guides, textbooks, and even decorative journals. As another example, a full year after it happened, I heard Protestant women fondly reminiscing over the Victoria's Secret body lotions distributed by a big-name Pentecostal preacher who visited one Sunday. The women who did not attend

that Sunday evening's worship service, including those whose housing units were assigned to the morning service, bemoaned that they
unfairly missed out.

Through secondhand carcerality, the competition for limited
resources becomes a defining feature of religious participation at
Mapleside. Discussions in prior literature of material resources tied to
religious participation often end up denouncing religious affiliation in
prison as "utilitarian" rather than "sincere," or questioning the motivations of those who participate.[11] But we can move beyond the individual-level lens. Here I take a structural approach, demonstrating
how unequal access by religious affiliation reflects the core problem:
that religion, however unwittingly, reinforces carceral control through
secondhand carcerality. In other words, by facilitating a resource-
deprived environment, the prison sets up a system in which religious
volunteerism is tied to resource provision. Because Protestant volunteers donate vastly more time and goods compared to other religious
groups, volunteerism is further tied to resource inequality.

Women at Mapleside who were not Protestant described a sense
that they "go without" because of their religious beliefs. Maya, a mid-
40s Black woman and Muslim religious official, pointed out the disparities in available programming and support across the religions.
"The Christians have the dance ministry, the theater ministry, three
kinds of choir—youth, middle, and adult choir," she rattled off, with
the unspoken follow-up that Muslims at Mapleside have no ministries at all. More to the point, Maya lamented that unlike Muslims,
Protestant adherents can rely on a network of material supports:
"[Chaplain Harper] can write to anybody and ask for something . . .
and they will send it in. She could type an email today." Maya wig-
gled her fingers as if typing an email. "But we don't have someone
like that for us. Chaplain Campbell won't go out on a limb for us."

Part of the problem was logistical: Chaplain Campbell worked
limited hours, in the evenings. She was responsible for the so-called
minority religions at Mapleside, leading Maya to say, "It's her *job* to
provide us with what we need." She admonished, "But we'll order

stuff—I wrote requests to Muslim communities outside who donated $40 or $50 worth of books and they sent them—but she keeps them in her office." These items were technically available, but because Muslim services convened on Fridays at noon and Quranic study on Saturdays at noon—hours in which Chaplain Campbell was not present—the donated books were effectively unusable, stored behind her locked office door.

Maya pointed to a related problem, in which Protestant churches sent donations of new DVD releases of megachurch preachers and Christian movies, while Muslim women had to make do with outdated VHS tapes. "I blame the prison," Maya said. "It shouldn't be like this. Our TVs shouldn't play only VHS." She speculated, "I think it's a political issue," and suggested the prison's Religious Department "shouldn't use all their finances towards the Christian programs when we're left without."

Suggesting an even deeper issue, Maya and several other Muslim women described feeling misunderstood since Chaplain Campbell is a Baptist, as is Chaplain Harper. "The chaplains are both Christians," said Brigit, a Muslim woman, who ascribed that fact as evidence of what she termed "active discrimination." Ronnie corroborated: "They don't give us what we need." Indeed, compared to Protestant programs, which drew dozens of outside volunteers weekly, Muslim women relied on one or two outside volunteers every few weeks. The local imam almost never visited, instead volunteering his time in the state men's prison. As Maya explained from a religious perspective, "A formal service is required for men, but it's not required for women . . . . We don't need to get together to pray, but men need to come together in brotherhood to pray. When women are at home, it's more important for them to take care of the house." However, Maya continued, "We need him to worship correctly." Muslim worshippers described a lack of support not only from the prison administrator but also from the paucity of outside volunteers and donated goods.

Catholic women described much the same. "We get treated like we are lesser," Bernadette summed. "It's because Chaplain Harper is

Protestant." She went on to mention a petition lodged by Catholics to be allowed vegetarian meals on Fridays during Lent. It was denied, which felt like a major affront. "And every other group gets their things, like the Muslims have their special meals for Ramadan and even the Wiccans have their lavish feasts," Bernadette compared. Anne, listening to Bernadette's grievances, agreed: "We go without."

With prison officials responsible for administering constitutionally protected religious freedoms, the disconnect between religious requirements and the realities of practice was a problematic and persistent issue. The Catholic, Muslim, and Jewish women I interviewed at Mapleside told me they felt misunderstood by the Protestant chaplaincy. The Jewish "high holidays" were one instance of the cultural mismatches made obvious. A local synagogue donated a traditional *challah* for Rosh Hashanah, the Jewish New Year celebration: a round baked loaf of braided dough, speckled with raisins to represent the sweetness of the year to come. "It didn't arrive on time," Dorinda recalled, "so Chaplain Harper set it out for Yom Kippur," a day of atonement through fasting that comes ten days after Rosh Hashanah. Dorinda was horrified, remembering how she cried out as Chaplain Harper began to slice the *challah*, "No, you can't slice it now. We can't eat it now!" The blunder was significant to the Jewish faithful, for whom it was inconceivable to eat *challah* during a holy day requiring abstinence from food and drink. Jewish volunteers who might mediate these misunderstandings were few and far between, not simply because their faith has fewer adherents in the U. S. and inside its prisons but also because a religious prohibition against driving on Shabbat (the Sabbath) and on high holidays meant that only the least observant volunteers could feasibly visit—hardly any did. Instead, the onus landed on Dorinda and a handful of other Jewish worshippers to regulate their own practice.

A lack of clear instructions from the chaplaincy on how to administer religious practices led to routine limitations on the Jewish women's ability to exercise their faith. Outside of prison, Jewish practitioners light candles to signify the beginning of Shabbat starting at dusk on Friday—the most observant Jews schedule this carefully, given that Jewish law prohibits the lighting of the candles after sundown. At Mapleside, however, regardless of seasonal shifts in the time of sunset, the Jewish Friday night worship service runs from 7 to 9 o'clock. Women are permitted to perform a ritual candle-lighting and a prayer, so they must light their prison-issue tea lights at 7 pm if they wish to light them at all. As another accommodation, their ceremonial Shabbat meal replaces wine with grape juice and the traditional *challah* with *matzah* (unleavened bread traditionally consumed during Passover).

Each week, I watched as the women attending the Jewish worship service prepared for their ritual Shabbat practice. I could see that, like the resources for the Muslim women, the Jewish worship items were kept in a locked closet in a separate room, presumably to prevent them from being stolen. The women needed the officer on post to unlock the closet so they could procure their ritual objects. Moreover, to light the candles, they needed the officer to secure a lighter by venturing past the metal sliders that separate the Main Hall from the warden's administrative wing, where all objects deemed potential weapons are stored and inventoried. Furthermore, since incarcerated women are not allowed to handle open flames, they must ask the officer to light the candles on their behalf. Then the Jewish practitioners would recite a prayer. If, by the end of the worship service, the candles had not burned out, the women had to make yet another request, calling on the officer to abandon their post to come blow out the Sabbath candles—Jewish women were religiously prohibited from doing so, meanwhile letting them burn after 9 pm was forbidden by the prison.

One Friday, I watched Dorinda approach Officer McLean, on post at the central desk in the Main Hall. Officer McLean agreed to accompany her to the locked closet where the ceremonial objects were stored. All the way to the end of the hall, inside a locked room, Officer McLean unlocked the closet. My peek inside revealed the victuals: a half-empty plastic bottle of grape juice, a cardboard box of *matzah* stamped with an expiration date two years prior, and a stash of tea light candles.

As we returned to the classroom where Jewish services are held, arms full with ritual objects, it dawned on Dorinda that she had forgotten to ask: "Could we get the lighter for these candles?" Officer McLean demurred: "Uh huh. No way. I'm not going back up there." There would be no negotiation. Officer McLean had already gone out of her way, and she was not about to do it again. The Jewish service pressed on without the ceremonial lighting of the Shabbat candles.

Later that night, after Dorinda returned to her housing unit, Officer McLean gave me her side of the story, unintentionally revealing that she did not know the prison guidelines. In accordance with both Jewish law and the prison's policies, Jewish women light candles each week on Friday night. Yet Officer McLean insisted that Dorinda does not "get that lighter every week. She only gets it on—what's that holiday—Rosh . . . Hashanah?" Apparently the officer had never been instructed to this effect, nor was there oversight or recourse.

Although procuring their ceremonial materials should have been automatic and without obstacle, in practice, it was quite the opposite for Jewish and Muslim women. On another Friday night, only three women attended the Jewish service, which I learned was typical. There was no outside volunteer. I caught up with the women for a few minutes, then asked, "Do you want to light Shabbat candles?" Dorinda responded, "I don't know if I feel like it," then laughed self-consciously. "You're going to write 'The Jewish inmates didn't even want to get the candles from the closet.'"

.   .   .   .   .

In my observations, Mapleside's social world was governed, at least in part, by the structure of religious programs. Whereas prior studies on prison society have identified religious participation as a protective barrier to *avoid* the social hierarchy,[12] at Mapleside it was a pathway *into* that social organization. Religious programs could not operate without the volunteer staffing of incarcerated women, mobilized by Chaplain Harper's system of church officials. Church officials handled planning and logistics, offering a consistent and reliable source of labor, and they ascribed great value to the sense of dignity and autonomy their roles provided. This was especially meaningful in light of racial dynamics, in which Black and Latina women achieved positions of status and authority in the prison church. At the same time, the hierarchy generated in service of dignity created conflict in this low-resource environment. Prisons that rely on religious programs to fill the gaps where secular programs once flourished end up allowing for informal status systems that disadvantage Jews and Catholics, who were predominately white, Sunni Muslims, who were predominately Black, and the nonreligious of all racial backgrounds. These "others" describe having to "go without," the deprivations of prison amplified by what they described as preferential treatment for the Protestant faithful, especially among the church officials endorsed by the chaplaincy.

The interplay between material resources and social status is by no means unique to Mapleside Prison. Local cultures generate unwritten rules that govern interaction and hierarchy.[13] Furthermore, in all environments with "competition for scarce goods," social theorist Peter Blau asserts, "status differences emerge."[14] Competition for resources crystallizes into a relatively stable social hierarchy, reinforced over time through interaction, exchange, and exercises of authority. The ethical problem arises when those social and material inequalities hinge on religious affiliation, and are amplified in an environment devoid of alternate avenues to those resources. For those "left without," as Maya put it, differential access to status and resources can start to feel like part of the punishment. The question is not whether this is unexpected or unusual, but rather whether it is unconscionable in light of the constitutional protection of religious freedom. What does religious freedom look like when there are material and practical obstacles for some religious groups and not others? What does the uneven distribution of social status and material objects mean for the freedom of religious practice in an environment otherwise defined by deprivation? The growing reliance on volunteerism rather than state-sponsored resources leads to tangible inequalities, privileging Christians at the expense of non-Christian groups.

Importantly, Mapleside does not appear to be an outlier in the dominance of Protestant resources or in the relative scarcity of resources for other religions. Other studies have noted the prevalence of evangelical Christianity in men's and women's prisons across the country.[15] Ultimately, while religious practice promises dignity and provisions where they are otherwise stripped away, an undeniable tension emerges when we ask *which religion*, and *for whom*. In a place where status, social support, and material resources are painfully limited, the access facilitated by religion—despite the best intentions—becomes warped into a carceral trap: it fosters a system of social and material inequality defined by religious group membership and participation.

Conclusion

When I first embarked on this project, I planned to observe both secular and sacred programming at Mapleside. After all, as my academic mentors advised, programs like crocheting club, Toastmasters International classes, college education courses, and the service-dog training program might shape incarcerated women's lives in ways that were as important as religion. Indeed, months of ethnographic study confirmed that many women derived a great deal of meaning from participation in the prison's secular programs. Heather, for instance, spent six years petitioning the warden for a honeybee-keeping program. Her labors were rewarded the day 45,000 bees were delivered to the prison complex. Along with four other incarcerated women, Heather learned to tend the hives, finding it incomparably rewarding. She told me, "I want to do my part to save the environment. There's a real danger with the bee population. It's my way to help the world, my way to help my family from in here." Like the women who were active and consistent in their religious participation, Heather described a sense of freedom and social connection

165

derived from the program she helped establish. But it was equally apparent that secular activities were fundamentally different than religious ones.

Religion is much more than a hobby. Pilates, gardening, and beekeeping—although deeply fulfilling—do not compete with the state for institutional primacy. Religion, however, is an elemental feature of society. Religion shapes culture, rituals, and social hierarchy. It shapes attitudes, values, and systems of power. Religion is so entrenched that the United States committed to the separation of church and state from its outset. Those creating the founding documents of their new nation believed the state should not have the legal authority to endorse, impose, or deny anyone's religious affiliation. The constitutional protection of religious freedom inside correctional facilities sets religion apart. Leaving aside for the moment the uneven accommodations of different faith traditions, religion is decidedly unlike other activities, whether in the halls of government or the Main Hall of Mapleside.

Whereas the state formally relinquished control over religion, it has never given up the power to control its inhabitants who come into contact with the correctional system. The prison remains a brick-and-mortar expression of state authority over society's most marginalized. Mounting evidence shows that prisons do not effectively deter criminal behavior or make "our streets" any safer.[1] Incarceration rates have only recently begun to dip in the U. S., but the carceral population is high and will remain so for many years to come. Judges have handed down sentences of decades or longer to hundreds of thousands of people, and for more than 200,000 people serving life sentences in prison, decelerating incarceration rates has not parlayed into decarceration.[2]

Amidst debates over reforms and policy change, prisons have steadfastly accomplished the goal of retributive confinement. Austerity measures have made prisons more punishing, as state-funded programs aimed at education, addiction treatment, and personal improvement of all kinds have been cut. Prisons have supplemented meager budgets by entering into partnerships with private corporations, monetizing the provision of communications and personal hygiene products, and profiting from the labor of the incarcerated. Moreover, they have leaned on outside volunteers and religious organizations to fill the gaps that remain: faith-based rehabilitative programming prime among them.

Many women at Mapleside turned to religion in their search to "make something" out of their incarceration—a refrain I heard repeatedly throughout my year-long ethnographic study. This owes, in part, to theological imperatives that inspire prison ministry and situate the prison as a space for contending with existential questions. The prevalence of religious programs also stems from the confluence of three contextual realities: the historical linkages between religion and punishment, contemporary constitutional protections of religious practice in U. S. correctional facilities, and the aforementioned need to secure voluntary programming when state funds are tight.

For those who drew on faith traditions for answers to their most pressing questions, religion was often paramount to their experience of punishment. It seemed a worthy opponent for carceral control. Evangelical and historically Black Christian traditions in particular challenged carceral control by putting God above the authority of state actors. Religion also confronted carceral control by fostering moral worth and dignity among people deemed damaged, flawed, or wrong by prison officials. It celebrated womanhood and motherhood, and fostered comfort and community. Religion operated as an alternate source of social status and pushed back against carceral control by offering a sliver of access to material resources and an abundance of emotional support in a place devoid of both.

Religion at Mapleside also proved to be necessarily enmeshed in state regulations and state aims. Although religious accommodation is a constitutional right, religious provisions are strictly circumscribed by the rules, procedures, and surveillance of correctional officers and administrative officials. We might imagine that, because religious programming is largely staffed by volunteers and protected as a freedom from state regulation, religion would be outside the scope of carcerality. In practice, however, state actors vet religious volunteers, scrutinize and limit ritual objects, and may cancel religious programs at any moment, needing only to cite "security risk." Just as carceral control is designed to saturate every aspect of the lives of the incarcerated, from where women live to what they wear, read, and consume, it inflects the programming brought inside by religious staff and volunteers, patterning religious practice through bureaucracy, permissions, and preference.

This is where we see secondhand carcerality in action. Secondhand carcerality warps noncarceral institutions that come into contact with the carceral system in ways that repackage punitive aims. Religion is not immune. Because religious programs must operate in an environment marked by carceral control, they take on a degree of those same principles and ways of doing things. At Mapleside, Protestant teachings putting God in control describe state agents, including judges, parole boards, and even correctional officers, as acting in a manner consistent with God's will. Interpreting incarceration as part of "God's plan" legitimizes carceral control by the highest authority. Religious messages also promulgate secondhand carcerality when it comes to gender-traditionalist messages about femininity, heteronormativity, and paternalism around women's sexual relationships and their motherhood. Finally, in an environment with finite material resources and limited opportunities for status and dignity, access to such resources through religion (and Protestant Christianity in particular) is de facto limited for others. Although religious volunteers and staff may enter Mapleside and other prisons with their own notions regarding reform and redemption, they have no choice but to operate within the bounds laid out by state actors, if they are to enter these facilities at all. The result is a pervasive tension, mediated through religion, offering freedom and imposing constraint.

RELIGION, THE STATE, AND THE COMPETITION FOR INSTITUTIONAL PRIMACY

Sociologist of religion Korie Edwards calls on scholars to stake greater inquiry "in explicating how religion matters for power," on the grounds that "religion is a central institution through which power is produced, deconstructed, and distributed. Power, who gets it and how they can use it when they get it, is the way of the world."[3] Beyond its ability to provide individuals with a set of values and beliefs that guide their behavior, Edwards reminds us that religion is a vehicle of power. We cannot lose sight of religion's "double function" in both challenging and supporting the status quo.[4]

When it comes to incarcerated women, religion's liberating potential involves a certain undermining of state discourses—it asserts the humanity, dignity, and worth of individuals, regardless of the state's willingness to call them irredeemable and lock them away. Within prisons, it also echoes the state's punitive paternalism, naturalizes carceral control as part of God's plan, and imports social inequalities that privilege some people over others, amplifying the cruel contours and competitions of this low-resource environment.

Religious programs focused on personal, bootstraps-type rehabilitation also subtly chip away at the idea that the U.S. needs comprehensive, structural prison reform. The individualism of religion at Mapleside is a meaningful counterpoint to the de-individualizing rhetoric of prison officials. Yet social scientists know as well as anyone that individual-level solutions cannot solve structural-level problems like poverty, addiction, and racism. Researchers have enumerated a set of women's common "pathways" to prison, revealing that many engage in criminal behavior as a response to these structural problems. When jobs are scarce and grossly underpaid, women may turn to the illegal economy to support themselves and their families. So, too, when addiction rears its head, and they take actions to avoid withdrawal. When violent relationships turn life-threatening, women's life-saving measures can also come with life sentences.

When constant police surveillance means being targeted for the sorts of small infractions that are undetected or waived-off when committed by the more privileged, it follows that marginalized and minoritized individuals end up overrepresented in jails and prisons (despite having the same or lower crime rates than white counterparts and wealthier populations).[5] The individual-level interventions and responsibilization discourses most often offered by religious clergy and volunteers reinforce state messages and can dampen urgent calls for structural change. No matter how important they are for incarcerated women, no matter how personally liberating and uplifting, these particular messages do not seek to spur systemic, structural change—nor could any such message be equipped to adequately challenge carceral control from the inside.

At Mapleside, religion is one of the few aspects of prison life that acknowledges the humanity of the women confined inside. It purposely offers dignity and moral worth in an environment designed to strip all of that away. It is a source of light in the darkest of places. At the same time, religion is ill equipped to solve *all* of the problems associated with prisons. Religion cannot undo histories of trauma, abuse, fear, and coercion. Religion cannot erase the past nor restore harms to victims. Religion cannot physically lift women out of prison, but instead must come inside and bow to the rules of the carceral context.

When we consider how the state privileges certain faith traditions over others, both through formal facilitation and everyday interaction, we might consider the case of religious life at Mapleside as a more highly concentrated version of the relationship between religion and the state in today's America. Religious freedom is written into the First Amendment to the Constitution, yet religious pluralism frequently gives way, in practice, to the idea that the U.S. is a fundamentally "Christian nation." Increasingly, religious freedom has been enacted in ways that support freedom for Christians at the expense of other faith traditions. "Christian nationalism," for example, is a belief system among a subset of white Christians whose political participation is guided toward privileging Protestant ideology in public institutions and preserving white supremacy. A full 46 percent of Americans in the 2017 Baylor Religion Survey agreed that "the federal government should advocate Christian values."[6] Politicians court the white evangelical voting bloc and use religious freedom as a rhetorical shield to curtail rights for LGBTQ+ citizens.[7] Reproductive politics have long been embattled with religious advocacy on both sides of racism and women's autonomy.[8] Consistent with the notion of religion as a vehicle for power, the state and Protestant religion continually jockey for institutional primacy, with each seeking to draw on the other's rhetoric and practices toward its own aims.

SECONDHAND CARCERALITY AND ITS APPLICATIONS

I have introduced and defined secondhand carcerality as a reiteration of carceral control by a noncarceral actor that happens by virtue of that actor's contact with the criminal justice system. I argue that it is a process that implicates more than religion alone. Memorably, Foucault writes, "We are in the society of the teacher-judge, the doctor-judge, the educator-judge, the 'social worker'-judge."[9] Punishment is no longer confined to prison walls, but embedded in social systems and across multiple sites of carcerality (what Foucault calls the "carceral archipelago") in an ever-widening net. If carceral control is not the intent of teachers, doctors, and social workers—if, in fact, it is antithetical to their aims—how does it proliferate? I argue that this is the result of secondhand carcerality. Coming into contact with an environment of intractable carceral control, these actors are implicated secondhand, enacting it by proxy.

Take health care, for instance. Drawing on existing research, we can piece together how healthcare professionals like EMTs, nurses, and doctors are affected by secondhand carcerality. This is crystal clear within carceral facilities, where medical anthropologist Carolyn

Sufrin finds "care and discipline not only coexist, but shape each other in unexpected ways." What Sufrin calls "jailcare" is "fundamentally ambivalent ... [it] indexes the mutual coexistence of the violence of punitive discipline with the concern and attention of caregiving."[10] Healthcare providers must be equal parts caregivers and skeptics, discerning medical needs through a lens of ambivalence and mistrust that stems directly from the carceral environment. Thus, as we saw in chapter 4, although Mapleside affords an unusual provision of time and space for mothers to bond with their infants and toddler children, prison officials remain willing to shackle women in labor and remove newborns from their care within hours of their birth. Even beyond jails and prisons, we see secondhand carcerality in emergency rooms, where hospital staff consider patients' justice-involvement when making decisions about care. Nurses triage resources to certain arrestees and incarcerated persons, while policing and delaying resources to others whom they label as "criminal" on axes of race and gender.[11] When ambulances rush to aid those in need, as sociologist Josh Seim specifies, ambulance workers can represent "the state's quick and temporary responses to crises," making EMTs the frontline bureaucrats of top-down decision-making regarding the "governance of urban suffering."[12] As they respond to the symptoms of social problems including violence, addiction, and poverty, EMTs are pressed into police work in instances where officers order them to administer sedatives for the sole purpose of subduing arrestees.[13]

Relatedly, we can consider how secondhand carcerality operates in court-ordered substance abuse treatment programs. One study of a drug treatment program inside a state women's prison found that it mirrored prison officials' views of women as deviant, inherently damaged, and worthy of degradation.[14] Another study comparing a substance abuse rehabilitation program located within the criminal legal system found that justice-involved women were defined as "broken" and undeserving, compared to wealthier, white women treated in a private rehabilitation facility, who left with their dignity intact.[15] Drug treatment program providers often stigmatize and condemn justice-involved individuals in many of the same ways as prison staff do, suggesting elements of secondhand carcerality even in treating the disease of addiction.

Secondhand carcerality is on display in the educational system, too. The "school-to-prison" pipeline has been well established, with the harsh and surveilling aspects of primary and secondary education in criminalized communities leading youth toward future incarceration.[16] Sociologist Jerry Flores further identifies "institutional partnerships" between carceral and educational systems, a "multi-institution, multiagency set of dynamic barriers, through which [young women] can be criminalized and subsequently incarcerated."[17] So, too, in the thick of the "youth control complex," where educational personnel surveil young boys as adults.[18] The convergence of educational and carceral goals are evidenced by the mounting presence of armed "school resource officers" in public school settings,[19] and by mandatory reporting laws requiring educators and school administrators to call in justice-adjacent social service actors should they suspect abuse. Through these state proxies, regardless of their intent, surveillance quickly transforms into poverty governance among marginalized students and their families.[20] Formerly incarcerated fathers and mothers are understandably wary of secondhand carcerality, with scholars documenting fathers' avoidance of and mothers' concerted involvement in school systems as twin responses to the fear of state interference, including CPS intervention and the potential loss of custody.[21]

As a final example, consider the criminal justice system's growing reliance on risk assessment tools. These measurement tools, based in actuarial science, draw on social scientific data to assess and predict the "dangerousness" of a given individual. They are used by carceral actors from prosecutors to parole boards, and noncarceral actors from psychologists to social workers. Here, too, the innovation of risk assessment seemed to be introduced with the best of intentions: discourses of risk grew as reformers sought to garner support for community-based sanctions like probation, parole, and GPS monitoring rather than incarceration.[22] However, while risk assessment technology has aimed to identify nondangerous individuals and funnel them out of the correctional system, it has instead reinforced stereotypes using predictive data to legitimize punishment and extend the power of punitive labeling.[23] Criminologist Kelly Hannah-Moffat notes that risk assessment is yet another "reframing of social problems as individual problems," such that "structural barriers conveniently disappear. Systemic problems become . . . individuals' inadequacies."[24] Risk assessment tools categorize individuals, determining who is "manageable" through noncarceral interventions, and those deemed manageable are asked to transform themselves into so-called responsible, law-abiding citizens through neoliberal accountability rhetoric.[25] Those deemed unmanageable are viewed as too risky for society, sometimes labeled the "worst of the worst" and relegated to carceral control.[26] Meanwhile, the state's offloading of risk management and therapeutic interventions to psychologists, mental health professionals, and social workers presses noncarceral actors to weigh in on an individual's dangerousness and mediate social risk by lending their medical expertise to carceral responses.

Can any nonstate actor interact with the carceral system without being affected by secondhand carcerality? My answer is simple: no. Carceral control is too tenacious, too dominant, too fundamental to U. S. state authority. This is why prison abolitionists demand nothing short of uprooting the entire system.[27] Myriad prison reform efforts cast the offloading punishment onto noncarceral actors as an opportunity: perhaps well-meaning, noncarceral actors will be less punitive. Perhaps the harms will be less severe. Perhaps fewer individuals will get caught in the system. As it turns out, the opposite has occurred. The net is widening—not shrinking—and through secondhand carcerality, we see reiterations of carceral control and punishment, however unintended or indirect, in innumerable institutions that touch our lives.

WHERE DO WE GO FROM HERE?

For a justice system to be unjust, it doesn't need to
convict the wrong individual; it only needs to judge in
the wrong way.
Michel Foucault[28]

The criminal justice system is at a crossroads. Mass incarceration in the United States is beginning to decline for the first time in decades—at least among men. The COVID-19 pandemic alerted the American public to some harrowing truths about imprisonment: most urgently, that crowded correctional facilities are a public health hazard. For those who lived and worked inside, prisons emerged as some of the worst hotbeds for coronavirus outbreaks. The Covid Prison Project reported that well over half a million incarcerated persons tested positive for COVID-19 and, as of this writing, nearly 3,000 incarcerated men and women died of coronavirus, rendering their prison sentences into death sentences.[29] Throughout the pandemic, mediation measures were scarce inside jails and prisons: testing was limited, contract tracing was practically nonexistent, effective cleaning supplies were scant, and social distancing was impossible.[30] Politicians and prison officials bungled their responsibilities to wards of the state, making it abundantly clear that the lives of incarcerated people were less valuable than the goals of retribution and constituents' perceptions of public safety.

These staggering coronavirus numbers broadened preexisting calls for decarceration, already present in a growing push for community sanctions like probation, house arrest, and electronic monitoring. While releasing people from correctional facilities may be priority number one, it is also important to remember that decarceration does not mean the disappearance of carceral control. We must tread cautiously, searching criminal justice reforms for their potential to reproduce many of the same harms as incarceration. As writers Maya Schenwar and Victoria Law put it, we must be on the lookout for creeping iterations of control, or "prison by any other name."[31]

Overall, I took three major lessons from my study at Mapleside that I believe are crucial for policymakers, correctional practitioners, and concerned citizens. First, *words matter*. To be sure, incarceration hurts life chances and damages communities in tangible ways. Yet a groundswell of scholarship also points to the concomitant narrative harms of incarceration. Put simply, both the lived experience and the interpretive experience of incarceration are punitive. Power and control in prison rely on the rhetorical construction of the incarcerated subject. When prison officials describe incarcerated women and men as "flawed," "irresponsible," or "dangerous,"[32] they are seeking control over individuals' self-narratives, encouraging them to adopt responsibilization logics and "perform a flagellant self."[33] Regardless of whether incarcerated individuals unequivocally embrace, categorically reject, or otherwise navigate and negotiate these top-down discourses, the labels and their implications are a force to be reckoned with.

Throughout this book, I have shared stories illuminating how meaningful religious discourses can be against this punitive backdrop. Religious programs offer competing institutional framings. Against the de-individualizing efforts of prison officials, Protestant messages identify the value of each person, with Bible study lessons and prophetic readings that single out individual characteristics as worthy of praise. Incarceration is cast as part of God's greater plan above and beyond a punishment for a wrongdoing. Religious messages uplift incarcerated women's feminine expression and importance as mothers in an environment that seeks to condemn them on both counts. Religious programs are also organized such that those most active are given attendant roles that confer social status, dignity, and a sense of community.

Words matter when prison officials seek to condemn incarcerated women, and words matter when religious volunteers and clergy seek to subvert those dominant narratives. Future studies should take seriously competing institutional logics that can challenge dominant discourses. Individuals seeking to make a difference within the prison system should invest efforts in these competing paradigms. Moreover, concerned citizens must be cautious when it comes to public safety language about what prisons "should" accomplish. The sooner we collectively acknowledge that prisons primarily address the emotional pull of retribution, then the sooner we accept discourses as the core of what prisons actually "do," and the sooner we can address the practical side of making change.

Second, *the best intentions are no match for carceral control.* As they told it, religious clergy and volunteers entered Mapleside hoping to be a force for good. Religious leaders told me of their ardent desires to remind incarcerated women of their dignity and moral worth. They endeavored to share lessons to help women survive prison and improve their lot in life post-release. Volunteers accepted it as their calling to bring religious ritual and practice into an institution where it would otherwise be absent. "You gotta have a special demeanor to be able to handle this line of work," Reverend Mona once lamented. I had spotted her in the parking lot that day on my way inside. Reverend Mona looked anxious as she explained to me that the officers on post denied her entry: "They won't let me in. They don't have my memo from Chaplain Harper." Her unwavering dedication to prison ministry brought her to Mapleside each week and kept her motivated to battle the red tape that made entering the prison as an outsider nothing short of an obstacle course. Although no social scientist can possibly know a person's true intentions, it seems fair to say that, by and large, those who chose to devote their time and energies to religious ministry at Mapleside gave no impression that they were acting with nefarious goals or anything other than theological and social commitments to their faith traditions.

Despite these largely blameless motives, carceral control was too all-encompassing for volunteers to avoid falling into the prison's patterns of surveillance, regulation, and condemnation. Sociologist Megan Comfort points out a similar dynamic in her studies on the wives, girlfriends, and children visiting incarcerated men, terming their subjection to proximate prisoner status "secondary prisonization."[34] In selecting who is allowed to enter, when they are allowed to enter, what they are allowed to do, and even what they can wear, prison officials already play a key role in sorting and surveilling outside visitors, bending them to carceral control.

The same was true for the religious volunteers I met at Mapleside. Once inside, religious staff and volunteers saw that their programs were necessarily shaped by the prison context. Sermons and scripture regularly drew on themes of incarceration as a response to deviant behavior, and liturgy and rituals were subject to standards of security that often distorted the tone of the practice. Anne, a Catholic woman, put this process into words when she complained: "I am just *so sick* of everything being adapted to prison." As I have argued, religious programs shaped by secondhand carcerality ultimately reproduced some of the very forms and narratives of carceral control that they sought to undermine—especially when it came to the meaning of incarceration, normative expectations of femininity, family, and sexuality, and the material experience of resource deprivation behind prison walls.

Larger structural forces are strong enough to override individuals' efforts to blaze their own paths. At Mapleside, as appears to be the case in many U. S. prisons, volunteer efforts are largely conducted at the individual- or congregation-level, without much community-level coordination. A collective strategy that organizes and refocuses faith-based energies on shared aims could potentially effect change. Furthermore, volunteers could strategize on how to partner with nonprofits working toward restorative aims, expand the reach of their donated materials to incarcerated persons unaffiliated with their particular faith tradition, or even lend their time to secular voluntary programs that are understaffed and underresourced. Until the prison system is overhauled top to bottom, religious volunteers hoping to make a difference might redouble and/or reorient their efforts in light of the implications of secondhand carcerality.

Finally, *religion is central—not peripheral—to punishment today.* Religion is, and always has been, integral to the way punishment gets doled out in U. S. jails and prisons. In her role as full-time chaplain, Chaplain Harper once sent an email to her list of volunteers asking them to join her in prayer. She prayed that Mapleside administrators would agree to build "a fully equipped chapel" rather than continuing to hold religious services in the prison gym. Chaplain Harper wrote, "This is in agreement with the [state's] . . . goal to reduce recidivism because we believe a changed heart will cause a changed life." In the chaplain's message, emphasizing the shared goals of the prison church and the state, religion should be more than merely permitted or tolerated—it should be encouraged as a ticket to rehabilitation. Describing her belief that a heart "changed" through religious devotion "will cause a changed life," Chaplain Harper aligned her logic with the state's ideology of individual-level responsibility for transformation. Likewise, remarking on a faith-based event, Ms. West, who works full-time as the prison's volunteer coordinator, said, "Programs such as this one prove rehabilitation *does* occur at Mapleside." Religious programs were viewed favorably by both religious actors and prison administrators as operating in support of Mapleside's neoliberal rehabilitative ideal.

Religion is one of the few protected rights guaranteed in U. S. jails and prisons. This legislative protection grants a unique—in fact, unparalleled—position of religious practice compared to any other activity, save for access to healthcare and legal texts. Historians have convincingly documented how religion played a monumental role in prison reform, from the early days of the American penitentiary throughout the nineteenth and into the early twentieth century.[35] We have seen how the Nation of Islam and evangelical Christian groups were active in securing religious freedom for the incarcerated population in the mid-to-late twentieth century.[36] Finally, as I hope this book has demonstrated, we can acknowledge that religion is alive and well in a twenty-first-century U. S. women's prison. Religion is a vital component of the experience of punishment at Mapleside. Where secular programming has diminished under withering state funding, the prevalence of religious volunteers has allowed the prison to relocate this form of service provision to outsiders.

Although the specific experiences of the women at Mapleside are unique, there are good reasons to believe that religion—Protestant religion in particular—operates similarly and occupies a place of primacy within other correctional facilities elsewhere. A study of men serving life sentences at Graterford Prison in Pennsylvania reveals comparable patterns of how religion structures one's day, offers respite from the "pains of imprisonment," and answers important existential questions.[37] So, too, a study of men's and women's prisons in Texas, Louisiana, and Florida echoes similar themes of religion-based personal transformation.[38] Christian programs like Kairos and the Association for the Protection and Assistance of the Convicted operate in prisons across the world—Canada, Costa Rica, England, Wales, Brazil, and South Africa.[39]

On the subject of prison ministry and outreach with justice-involved populations across the U. S., historian Aaron Griffith states, "Evangelicals . . . are the ones who show up."[40] Indeed, evangelical programming is widespread in U. S. prisons.[41] Ongoing debates about the preferential treatment of Protestants in state and federal prisons suggest further generalizability. Louisiana State Penitentiary in Angola (the nation's largest maximum-security prison) operates its own Christian seminary behind prison walls.[42] An evangelical Christian rehabilitation program in Iowa came under fire for privileging Christian men above those of other faiths,[43] while in Alabama, a Muslim man was denied the right to have an imam present at his execution (a Christian chaplain was made available at the moment of death, instead).[44] Faith-based housing units and Bible colleges function in similar ways across men's and women's prisons, again privileging some over others.[45] Muslims in a Virginia prison filed a lawsuit against a Christian "God Pod" that offered better housing and privileges based on religious affiliation.[46] As some of the best publicized examples, they are indicative of Christianity's standing in the prison system well beyond Mapleside.

Prison policies and religious freedom legislation have brought us here. But how do we move forward? Doing away with religion in prison is hardly the answer. It would not resolve the underlying problems of scarcity and deprivation that lead to the inequalities brought about by differential accommodation of religions and the social hierarchies that stem from religious practice. Nor would it be ethically and morally desirable by any measure. The ability to practice religion is a hard-won right that must be protected insofar as we hope to adhere to the fundamental values of this country or attend to the spiritual needs of the confined population. Furthermore, banishing volunteers and relegating labor back onto the state is impractical. Surely an infusion of state funding and hiring more paid chaplains from a variety of religious backgrounds could help, as would an influx of volunteers and donations from religious organizations beyond Protestant Christian churches, ministries, and parachurch organizations. Yet all these potential, if partial, fixes are destined to repeat some of the same pitfalls brought about by secondhand carcerality. So long as religion and other institutions operate within an environment of carceral control, we will see the harms of carceral control reinscribed. It is instead the prison system itself that requires wholesale change.

.   .   .   .   .

"There are as many prisons as there are prisoners," writes Gresham Sykes, "that each man brings to the custodial institution his own needs and his own background and each man takes away from the prison his own interpretation of life within the walls."[47] Yet this is not what I found in the year I spent getting to know the women confined to Mapleside Prison.

The "interpretation of life within the walls" is not under the sole control of the incarcerated person, despite what individualistic state and religious discourses imply. Institutional forces shape the prison experience, with religion among the most central. Scholars, practitioners, and reformers alike would be remiss to overlook the impact of religion within prison life, let alone the potential of secondhand carcerality to spread American punishment beyond its official purveyors. Without such careful inquiry, deconstructing the problems of incarceration may leave intact untold forms of carceral control.

Epilogue

OUT OF THE HOUSE OF BONDAGE

There is a superstition at Mapleside that a woman who sees a correctional officer drop their keys is going home soon. A keyring clanging on cold, hard tile represents the sound of freedom. In prisons, much of the lore focuses on two things: getting out, and getting out unscathed.[1] That is likely because incarcerated women know that their experiences in prison matter beyond the short term. Their experiences will travel with them when they return home, reverberating in their successes and setbacks, rippling through their families and communities.

A natural question arises about the women's stories chronicled in this book: *What happened next?* As months and years elapsed after the conclusion of my study, I reconnected with some women who returned home, who reported on their own well-being, and shared updates on others they had come to know at Mapleside. Several women saw their sentences reduced thanks to policy reforms to juvenile sentencing and illicit substance possession charges, including Ruby, Deanna, Vanessa, and Ronnie. Each of them came home and never looked back. Reentry programs and personal support systems rallied around them as they worked hard to rebuild their lives. Other women, like Laurelle and Ja, were released but struggled with addiction and financial duress, cycling "in and out of county jail" as one woman reported, experiencing the revolving door of the carceral system for years on end. For these women, incarceration did not come close to treating any underlying needs and, if anything, worsened their personal strains. Tragically, Esther, the ardent evangelist and beloved friend to many, passed away from a terminal illness while at Mapleside. Someone close to her told me that prison staff ignored her pleas for medical treatment until it was too late. "She kept telling them something was wrong, but they didn't believe her. She was begging for treatment. They wouldn't give it to her." Esther was 43. Her vivacious zeal as a true believer touched many lives, including my own. I cherish the wisdom Esther shared one evening during a Baptist Bible study: "I will never understand why He makes you go through some of the things you go through." She chortled softly with a tender smile. Then, paraphrasing a gospel tune, she continued, "But you will still have the joy that the world didn't give you. They can't take that away from you."

.   .   .   .   .

We now know that religion is inextricable from the prison experience. As such, another natural follow-up question is one frequently posed to me, whether I am speaking at an academic conference or talking with acquaintances around the dinner table: *How does religion matter in reentry? Does religion "stick"?*

The study participants I spoke with described a range of relationships with religion post-release. Some immediately joined local churches, providing continuity with the spirituality they felt inside. Carla volunteers with a faith-based ministry to help the homeless. Sabina has secured a full-time job through a Protestant volunteer she met at Mapleside. Adelaide attends weekly ministry classes, and leans on her faith community on a regular basis. Reverend Mona's church has become a major source of support for Rashida, and her career has flourished under their mentorship.

Other women explained that their faith remains central to their lives, but congregational participation is on the back burner. An array of pressing issues demand more immediate attention, like securing housing and employment, and working to regain custody of their children.

One such woman is Lexi, a white woman now in her early 40s, introduced in chapter 1. She was incarcerated for four years, then released to home detention, a strict community-based supervision meant as a transitional environment for people leaving prison. It is not a halfway house, but a rental on the standard market with an ongoing relationship with the DOC, constantly cycling through women reentering from Mapleside. We reconnect a year after I finished my fieldwork.

Before my visit, Lexi cautions me that she is staying in a "dangerous neighborhood" dotted by what her friend Genevieve calls "abandos"—abandoned and foreclosed homes, their windows smashed out or boarded up, roofs caving in. Raised in a middle-class family, Lexi grew up with narratives of violent crime in poor urban neighborhoods. Now, by virtue of her contact with the criminal legal system, she has been funneled into one such neighborhood where she worries over local crime reports, replicating some of the very same class- and race-based discourses that she encountered as a ward of the state herself. When I arrive, I find a cozy, fully furnished home, with three bedrooms, one bathroom, and a kitchen with all of the essentials. All three residents, owing to their time at Mapleside, are impeccably tidy. Lexi rolls her eyes: her housemates scrub the place clean every single day, just like their prison cells, so their tight quarters always smell like cleaning fluid.

Lexi is confined here 24 / 7, except for her once-weekly, mandatory home detention meetings, when she travels to a government office several miles away, carefully staying within the allotted travel time laid out by her supervising officers. As a condition of home con-finement, even though her convictions have nothing to do with drugs or alcohol, she must undergo a biweekly urine test and she can be breathalyzed at random. Failing either test could mean being remanded to prison, as any use of drugs or alcohol is a violation of conditional release. Officers are allowed to show up at any hour, day or night, ensuring that Lexi is detained at home, and that she is absolutely sober. Lexi remembers her terror when she awoke to offic-ers banging on her door to demand a breathalyzer test at 5 am, the morning after St. Patrick's Day.

Cash is tight, and Lexi's to-do list sounds overwhelming. To jump-start her post-prison life will mean paying thousands of dollars in restitution and keeping up with her $450 / month rent. She needs to get a driver's license and open a bank account, find an employer will-ing to hire her despite her criminal record, secure longer-term hous-ing, and, crucially, file the reams of paperwork required to regain custody of her son. Genevieve, who was released a few months before Lexi, advises her, "It'll get easier. It's like a mountain. Chip away at a little bit each day."

Getting a job is incredibly important—not getting one would be a violation, as would losing her housing if she cannot make rent. Lexi has found the employment search grueling so far. She wonders aloud, *Who would hire someone with a record, if there was an equally qualified candidate without a felony record competing for the same job in such a tight economy?* Since she is not permitted out of the house, even to seek employment, she can only submit applications over the phone or online. That means she is compelled to disclose her criminal record without ever having met a prospective employer face-to-face. Lexi believes that an in-person meeting, where she can demonstrate her amiable personality, might give her the leg up she needs to get an interview. Lexi makes an executive decision: en route to her next home detention meeting at the parole office, she will hop off the bus, run into the nearest Starbucks, quickly introduce herself, and ask for an application. If she times it right, she will still get to her home detention meeting in the allotted window. Of course, the coffee shop managers will eventually need to speak to her supervising officer, but at least they will have seen her smiling face. In making this plan, Lexi shows she is willing to do whatever it takes to fulfill one requirement of her release, even if it means risking a different violation.[2] Notably, Lexi has the resources to do whatever it takes. What is more, as a white woman, her advantage in a discriminatory job market means that although the stigma of a criminal record would sting, it would sting less compared to women and men of color with a criminal record.[3]

For the nearly five million adults in the U.S. on probation and parole, the stigma of a criminal record is impossible to avoid. Even in states that "ban the box," where companies cannot ask about prospective employees' criminal history before the interview stage of hiring, their status will eventually be disclosed for those under community supervision. At some point in the hiring process, probation and parole officers will speak with employers to confirm the job offer and approve the work schedule. Ultimately, it is this call that prevents Lexi from getting the Starbucks position. Her in-person application effort worked—she got an interview—then apparently someone in higher management decided against hiring her after learning of her conditional release status. Lexi says with a disheartened smile, "I come with a disclaimer."

Several months later, Lexi tells me she is doing much better. She has secured a job at Panera, where she hopes to rise through the ranks. Home confinement restrictions have been lifted, and she is planning to move in with an old friend from high school who is going through a divorce. This way, they can both save money on rent while Lexi reconnects with people from her past.[4] She is teaching community yoga classes, too, an outgrowth of her introduction to the practice at Mapleside.

In many ways, Lexi's reentry after prison represents a best-case scenario.[5] She is white, a woman, and in her early 40s—she is more likely than others to be able to restart a career without racism and ageism compounding her criminal record on the job market. She is also college-educated, has social support, and is savvy in her job search. Even with these advantages—what social scientists call social and cultural capital—her reentry feels far from easy. She faces a long road ahead, along which she will be surveilled and regulated by the state every step of the way. Miss a parole appointment, sip a beer, or send the rent check late, and she can be reincarcerated. Most painfully, as of this writing, Lexi's husband has still not permitted her any contact with their son.

So what happened next in terms of religion? When we met at Mapleside, Lexi told me that she was raised without religion. "After the Holocaust, I had many family members who died. My grandfather was in a labor camp," she explains. "After that they just turned away from Judaism." Even so, Lexi checked the "Jewish" box on Mapleside's Religious Preference Form during her intake process. "My father was Catholic, but for some reason I wasn't interested in that. This sounds crazy, but when I first got [to the prison], I thought that it might be God punishing me for my grandparents turning away from Judaism." Lexi shakes her head somberly, "I thought that I was being punished and it was time to get back to being Jewish."

As readers may recall, Mapleside's Jewish community was small. When Lexi attended Jewish study forums and worship services, there were rarely more than one or two other attendees. Moreover, Jewish volunteers were few and far between: the prohibition against driving on the Sabbath and holy days meant that observant Jews were unlikely to volunteer at the prison. Lexi, recalling a Passover observance, called it a "Dr. Seuss nightmare": "The rabbi had brought the condensed version [of the *haggadah*] to use, but we were bouncing around. It was such a mess." Lexi laughs at the memory. "Nobody wanted to read [the passages]. God, it was horrible." As Passover neared this year, Lexi submitted a request to the home detention office to attend a *seder* at the local *Chabad*. Her request was denied; her case manager deemed it too distant from home.

Although Lexi had never practiced Judaism prior to her incarceration and did not rush to join a synagogue upon her release, religion remains important to her. Her connection to the Jewish faith was not temporary, nor was it some kind of strategic effort to access kosher meals or doughnuts on Chanukah. Instead, she participated in the Jewish community at Mapleside because it was both available—a byproduct of constitutional religious freedom—and meaningful—a way to cope with the emotional havoc of becoming incarcerated, separated from her child, and otherwise stripped of autonomy. It was not that Lexi turned away from religion on the outside, but no longer were religious activities a way to fill her schedule and occupy her mind, nor were they convenient and abundant, as they had been inside the prison. Lexi needed to attend to more immediately pressing concerns: housing, employment, and family. For the time being, struggling to manage a system that seemed designed to let her fail, Lexi would prioritize getting the essentials together. Her spiritual life would have to wait.

· · · · ·

It has been several years since Estrella came home. Also introduced in chapter 1, Estrella is a Latina woman in her mid-40s. Compared to Lexi, Estrella has had more time to reestablish her life. Estrella resides in a medium-size metropolitan area with vast suburban sprawl, the same community where she grew up. It is a car-dependent town, and Estrella suggests a convenient meeting point at a coffee shop in a strip mall. Big box stores dot the horizon, as far as the eye can see. Everything looks shiny and new. Estrella recommends this location since she is mere days away from selling her home and moving to a new place—all of her possessions are currently stowed away in boxes.

Whereas Lexi tells me she has sworn off khaki owing to its ubiquity at Mapleside, Estrella arrives wearing a tan front-zip hoodie. I admire her sparkly earrings and lustrous wedding band, studded with two rows of emerald-cut diamonds. With a joyful grin, Estrella shares that she has been married for five years, having met her husband after she returned home from prison. Her petite stature, curly hair, and friendly smile are the same as I remembered.

As noted in chapter 3, a judge modified Estrella's sentence, such that she was cleared to leave Mapleside after serving three years of her 10-year term. Estrella tells me what happened after that momentous day in court. Although cleared for release, she had to wait a full year before a bed came available at the court-ordered rehab facility. One full year spent anxiously awaiting her approved release. One full year spent confined and punished even though a judge declared there was no longer a need. As winter, spring, summer, and fall crept slowly by, Estrella never knew which day would finally be her last day at Mapleside.

After her release, the residential, court-ordered substance abuse rehabilitation program was a resounding success for Estrella. For the first time in her life, she recalls, she had access to robust psychological and psychiatric treatment. There, she was diagnosed with depression and anxiety, and that diagnosis really changed things. It put everything into perspective, Estrella explains, and she is finally taking the medication that she needs.

"There was no therapy," Estrella recollects of her time at Mapleside. Short of being confined to the psychiatric ward, "you only saw the therapist on the day you were admitted." Looking back with the wisdom of time, Estrella declares that prison falls short of what it purportedly sets out to accomplish. "They don't do nothing," she asserts, recalling paltry attempts at rehabilitation and her constant fear of the prison staff.

While describing how the court-ordered treatment program yielded major breakthroughs, Estrella signals there is more to the story. Her eyes redden and tears begin to tumble out uncontrollably. I scurry over to the condiment station to procure some napkins. "I haven't talked about this since I got out," she tells me when I return. There is a profound heaviness in Estrella's words.

By all accounts, Estrella is a textbook reentry success story. She has never been rearrested. She got married. She owns a home with her husband. Together, they take care of five enormous, exuberant dogs. She describes "a lot of familial support." She has a steady job and has earned multiple career promotions. She keeps busy but makes sure to connect with her friends. Estrella's son, who is now grown, lives nearby and they spend quality time together. As she enumerates her successes, Estrella casts her gaze downward, watching as her fingers nimbly fold and refold a napkin into an ever-smaller rectangle. Her downtrodden demeanor seems a mismatch for her exemplary accomplishments: she has succeeded by every standard measure.

Estrella explains her melancholy. Her life has been forever changed by her incarceration. Like clockwork, Estrella is jolted awake around 4 in the morning—a holdover from her Mapleside days—and she says she still cannot sleep through the night. Addiction and relapse have reared their unwelcome heads along the road to reintegration. Meanwhile, Estrella has had little time to stop and think. Due to the strict parole stipulation to maintain employment, she began working full-time a mere three days after being released. She started at entry level, but has risen through the ranks to become a general manager of a fast food chain. She has immersed herself in her employment, working exhaustingly long shifts only to get up the next day and do it all over again. Nothing about reentry has come easy.

When it comes to her faith, Estrella is as devout as ever. Chaplain Harper visited her twice in rehab, and that meant a lot. Another minister, one of the religious volunteers, saw that "there really weren't places for us out here" in Estrella's hometown, so she "created a halfway house for me. For a few of us. But at first, I was the only one there." Beaming with gratitude, Estrella reports that she resided in that faith-based halfway house for six months. Then, she completed 18 months of parole supervision without incident. Throughout this time, she reconnected with several Protestant women she met at Mapleside, and there was even a Dance Ministry reunion at a local church.

Estrella had been raised in a Catholic household until her entire family converted to Pentecostal Christianity. An active participant in the Bible Institute, Baptist Bible study, and countless ministry classes, Estrella's faith took shape at Mapleside, developing her scriptural knowledge beyond what she knew before her incarceration. Although a longtime Pentecostal, Estrella says that she no longer agrees with all of the doctrine of her home church. That said, faith has always been more important to Estrella than religious affiliation. "I don't think as much by denomination," she remarks. "It's about your relationship with Jesus." She tells me she will eventually search for a new congregational home. Her faith is "not dependent on the people around me," she explains, so for now, she finds meaning in her spiritual salvation through Christ and continues to talk to God daily through prayer.

Religion remains important to Estrella's everyday routine. She maintains social connections with members of her Christian community from Mapleside, and a religious volunteer even helped her find transitional housing when the time came. Spirituality is a constant in her life. But now that she is home, Estrella's religious beliefs and practices are no longer mediated by secondhand carcerality. They are completely untangled from the freedoms and constraints that tinge religious life within the carceral system. Reflecting on the relationship between prison officials and religious programs, Estrella commented with dismay, "They use religion to promote compliance. It's what is favored." Today, Estrella says with a steadfast resolve, "My relationship with God has grown." She crosses her fingers tightly to demonstrate: "We're still like this."

Acknowledgments

My deepest gratitude is owed to Chaplain Harper and the women at Mapleside for welcoming me with open arms. I am reminded of the ethnographer's imperative described by sociologist Elijah Anderson at the 2019 Annual Meeting of the American Sociological Association: "Our job as ethnographers is to . . . comprehend local knowledge . . . and to represent it accurately." I hope I have done so, knowing that this book was only possible because so many women trusted me to do their stories justice. Additional thanks to Estrella, Lexi, and Adelaide: the three participants who completed member checks, offering invaluable feedback on drafts of this manuscript.

I am also thankful to the trio of mentors who constituted my dissertation committee, supervising the study that would become this book. Melissa Wilde, my dissertation chair, deserves the utmost acknowledgment. From this study's initial conception through drafts too numerous to mention, from talks over lunch to phone calls whenever I needed them, Melissa has been an outstanding mentor for a decade and counting. She has sharpened my writing, encouraged big-picture thinking, and promoted meticulous analysis. Annette Lareau's astute insights profoundly shaped the methods of this study. Her comprehensive guidance shepherded my project, from gaining access to writing field notes to searching for disconfirming evidence. Annette went to great lengths to support my project: she accompanied me to a full board review meeting of the IRB, offered thorough, line-by-line feedback at each and every stage, and chaired an immensely productive book conference. Finally, Randall Collins offered unparalleled wisdom and guidance on the theoretical aspects of this study. He challenged me to be precise and never forget historical context. Randy's lessons on the emotions of writing are ones that I return to, again and again, in trying moments. This book is the result of careful attention from these exceptional advisors.

Research is built through intellectual communities. The following scholars have also served as important mentors: Dave Grazian, Beth Huebner, Dorothy Roberts, and Sandra Susan Smith. Aline Rowens and Audra Rodgers, along with Nancy Bolinski, Sang Chung, Katee Dougherty, Charlene Werner, and Marcus Wright, offered administrative support and the utmost kindness. As I revised this manuscript from a dissertation to a book, I am grateful to my colleagues at the University of Missouri–St. Louis (and my friends from WashU) for their exceptional advice; in particular, Caity Collins, Steph DiPietro, Elaine Doherty, Heidi Grundetjern, Ariela Schachter, and Kyle Thomas. My colleagues at the University of Maryland have offered their steadfast support, with special thanks to my entering cohort: Brooklynn Hitchens and Rob Stewart. The design and framing of this project were enriched by conversations with Orit Avishai, Ram Cnaan, Stefanie DeLuca, Josh Dubler, Kathy Edin, Malitta Engstrom, Shawn Flower, Kathy Hall, John Jackson, Armando Lara-Millán, John MacDonald, Omar McRoberts, and Jason Schnittker. Amada Armenta, Jerry Flores, Andrew Johnson, and Kimberly Welch showed remarkable generosity in providing feedback on chapter drafts. Last but not least, this would have been a completely different book without intensive feedback from the distinguished scholars who commented on the entire manuscript: Waverly Duck, Jamie Fader, Jill McCorkel, and Tia Noelle Pratt—your insights and encouragement have been transformative.

This study was further shaped by a number of brilliant colleagues I am lucky to call friends. Many thanks to my UPenn classmates-in-arms, particularly Sarah Adeyinka-Skold, Valerio Baćak, Yi-Lin Elim Chiang, Sabrina Danielsen, Tuğçe Ellialti-Köse, Lindsay Glassman, Peter Francis Harvey, Liv Hu, Hyejeong Jo, Doga Kerestecioglu, Radha Modi, Bridget Nolan, Frank Prior, Juliana Truesdale, Bethany Weed, and Sarah Zelner. My writing group—Phil Garboden, Anna Rhodes, Eva Rosen, and Emily

Warren—kept me accountable and offered camaraderie along the way. An extra debt of gratitude to my closest academic compatriots, who read untold drafts and workshopped the trickiest sticking points in this manuscript: Betsie Garner, Aliya Rao (who has done all of the above, with bells on), Patricia Tevington, and Junhow Wei.

Several funding organizations supported this project. Data collection and analysis was supported by the Graduate Research Fellowship from the National Science Foundation [DGE-0822], the Constant H. Jacquet Research Award from the Religious Research Association, the Joseph H. Fichter Research Grant from the Association for the Sociology of Religion, and the Gertrude and Otto Pollak Summer Research Fellowship from the University of Pennsylvania. Several completion fellowships enabled the writing and polish of this work: the Mellon Dissertation Completion Fellowship from the American Council of Learned Societies, an Honorary Charlotte W. Newcombe Doctoral Dissertation Fellowship from the Woodrow Wilson National Fellowship Foundation, an Honorary Dissertation Fellowship from the Louisville Institute, and an Honorary Dissertation Fellowship from the University of Pennsylvania.

Naomi Schneider at UC Press has been an indelible editor, along with Paul Tyler's diligent copyediting. I am indebted to the close reading and brilliant wordsmithing of Lisa Crayton (who edited the entire book as a sensitivity reader), Elise Gallagher (proofreader), Tracy C. Gold (chapter 3), and Letta Page (the entire book). Casey Caruso offered skillful design input. Several doctoral research assistants contributed to background work, including Amanda Miller and Tori Inzana at UMSL and Carol Chen, Kristin Reque, and Torri Sperry at UMD. Chapters of this manuscript were workshopped at the CAGSRC at Loyola University Chicago (with special thanks to Courtney Irby, Chez Rumpf, and Rhys Williams), the John C. Danforth Center on Religion and Politics Colloquium at Washington University in St. Louis, the Louisville Institute 2017 Winter Seminar, the Poverty and Inequality Research Lab at Johns Hopkins University, the Social and Moral Cognition Lab at Columbia University, the Sounding Sea Writers' Workshop led by D. Watkins, and a number of workshops at the University of Pennsylvania, including the Gender, Sexuality, and Women's Studies Interdisciplinary Colloquium, the Urban Ethnography Workshop, and the Culture and Interaction Workshop.

Finally, I am grateful beyond compare to my parents, Natalie and Charlie Ellis. To my friends, family, and confidantes along the way, your cheerleading has meant the world: Anna Bank, Rachel Blank, Joey Ellis, Lizzie Ellis, Molly

Franz, Linda and Scott Franz, Jessica Garner, Rachel Hart, Mike Hauss, Shira Hecht, the Aronson / Maher family, Megan McCarthy, Sarah "Penny Intercostals" Murray, Megan Miller, Bryan "Dr. RC" Percivall, Gabby Rathz, Ellen and Mark Romanoff, and Francine Yutsis. To Dave Maher, who has witnessed and workshopped nearly every stage of this study, my heartfelt thanks for being the very best support system and spouse.

Methodological Appendix

"Do you ever feel like you can't ask us the tough questions 'cause you don't want to offend us?" Estrella inquired. We were in the Main Hall's computer lab, and I was already six months into my research year at Mapleside. "Like, if I were in your shoes, I could see you looking at us and saying, '*Really, guys?*'" At this, she eyed me with a look of playful bemusement. I replied that as an ethnographer, my job was to be curious, not skeptical or suspicious. I was there to learn what is normal at Mapleside, to ask about the social world of incarcerated women as they experience it. Estrella nodded, saying, "It really is its own little society. Its own little world."

In this appendix, I detail the nuts and bolts of the methods I used in this study, starting with my process of securing the necessary permissions to gain access, then detailing the steps I took to seek informed consent. I then describe how I coded and analyzed my field notes. Throughout, I consider what social scientists call "positionality," referring to how a researcher's background and position in the social world influence all aspects of a study, from what they observe to how they interpret and report on those observations.[1] In closing this book, I grapple with the complicated role of the never-incarcerated prison ethnographer and take a sober look at the ethics of conducting research inside prisons. As I have argued, even well-meaning outside actors and organizations that come into contact with carceral institutions are influenced by secondhand carcerality. When researchers like me, whose own career interests are at stake, gather data from vulnerable populations whose consent to participate is mediated by this punitive institution, we have a responsibility to continually interrogate whether and how our work may cause harm or reinforce carceral control.

GETTING IN

Between careful regulation by universities' Institutional Review Boards (IRBs) and the strict scrutiny of Departments of Corrections (DOCs), access to prisons for research is highly restricted.[2] I have written elsewhere about the long, bureaucratic process of gaining permission to enter Mapleside Prison.[3] In brief, it involved piles of paperwork and a great deal of interactional labor as prison officials scrutinized my scholarly legitimacy and political orientations. Because research approval hinges on administrative approval, as ethnographers Michael Gibson-Light and Josh Seim write of their work in men's prisons, "the researcher must often—at least partially—articulate the world as seen by penal authority. This usually means promising to keep a relative distance from the dominated and to remain obedient, and somewhat loyal, to the dominant."[4] Seeking access offered my own glimpse into secondhand carcerality: in this case, in the sorting process of prospective researchers, which sought to ensure that any approved study would conform to—or at least not directly contradict—carceral aims.

My project proposal was subjected to a full review by my university IRB's Human Subjects Research committee, which included a prisoner representative. Securing approval from Mapleside took six months from the first phone call with a prison official to the day I entered as a researcher. My study proposal underwent multiple rounds of reviews, revisions, and rejections before ultimately being accepted by Warden Davis and the assistant warden.

Speaking with DOC officials, I got a taste of secondhand carcerality, though I did not yet think of it in those terms. These administrators were centrally concerned with my legitimacy as a researcher, as measured by my study protocol and affirmed by my university affiliation. But the latter also invited scrutiny, with officials seeming to continually gauge my attitude toward prisons. One administrator said she wanted to be sure "you don't come in with a negative outlook, thinking that prison is only a bad thing.

Of course, we want to learn about the good and the bad, but some people come in thinking prison doesn't help anything." Eyeing me, she assessed: "It doesn't seem like you're that way." It was as though, even at this stage, the DOC needed me to understand that I had to play by their rules. Another administrator emphasized the importance of using the language prison officials deemed appropriate—for instance, I was told that those I call "incarcerated women" in this book should be referred to as "female inmates" or "female offenders." Other administrators variously cautioned that, rather than conducting ethnographic observations, I should study "measurable" things, using "evidence-based practices" to examine the "efficacy of different [religious] programming." In my field notes, I wrote: "I need to be ... prepared to speak their language of recovery, behavior, and recidivism." I had to "talk the talk," as I wrote in a reflection memo, to signal the alignment of my proposal with institutional gatekeepers' outcomes of interest and perspectives on incarceration.[5]

This tactic leveraged my positionality and privilege. I am a gender-conforming white woman, 5'2" tall, often assumed to be even younger than my actual age, which was mid-twenties at the time. My shared identities with a number of DOC gatekeepers, including whiteness, educational attainment, and middle-class status, may have facilitated their trust. So, too, my effusive demeanor—quick to smile, with a nervous energy—likely persuaded the gatekeepers that I was eager to please rather than their stereotype of the critical academic.

After processing the paperwork that granted my entrée, the next step was to seek informed consent from prospective participants. The majority of my research participants were incarcerated women—a vulnerable population who, as I have shown throughout this book, are rarely afforded the autonomy of saying "yes" or "no" to institutional requests. In compliance with both IRB requirements and my own research ethics, I handled informed consent as follows: I gave a brief introductory speech to every religious or secular program I observed, then recited a verbal "Informed Consent Form," having determined that keeping a written record of participants posed an undue confidentiality risk. Verbal consent stated the study's purpose (to learn about religion in prison), described the nature of participation (observation and/or interview), and outlined the confidentiality protections (including, for instance, the use of pseudonyms and restricted-access field notes). I also made it clear that participation was voluntary and subjects could withdraw from the study at any time. Furthermore, due to DOC rules, I could not compensate the research participants and noted that participation would not involve any benefits in terms of quality of life or chances at making parole.

Although administrators said they thought about designating an officer to escort me around the facility as a condition of my access, this idea never materialized, to my great relief as an ethnographer. I was allowed to circulate throughout the Main Hall's common areas without institutional surveillance. This independence helped divorce administrators' support for the project from prospective participants' decisions about whether to consent to participate. When I was introduced at my very first Protestant worship service, Rashida, the emcee that morning, said, "Rachel Ellis is a student who is here to observe us, and we welcome you and hope you keep coming back." Handily, she noted my role and purpose, like Asabi, who told her ministry class, "Ms. Rachel . . . is not a spectator. Be yourselves." With introductions like these from incarcerated women in leadership roles, the way was cleared for my speech about informed consent and an opportunity for prospective participants to ask for more information. On our second meeting, Brigit, a young Muslim woman, intoned, "I got some questions for you, little woman." I was heartened by her words, as I was when a few women declined to participate in my study. Both were signs that incarcerated women understood their participation as dynamic, voluntary, and revocable.

Because being a researcher was an anomalous role in the prison and because I frequently discussed my research goals, participants were aware of my unusual purpose. This, too, facilitated ongoing consent, reflected in the women's continual comments and questions about my work. One incarcerated woman asked, "Are you getting everything you need for your project?" and another, having made a bawdy remark, teased with a wagging finger, "I don't know if you want to put that in your paper!" Another woman told me about a prison ministry program that she had discovered, explaining, "It would be good for your project if you went to their planning meetings." The women in my study took an active role in checking in on my study and suggesting further avenues for inquiry—which I took as their clear understanding of my research purposes.

FITTING IN?

All studies have limitations when it comes to the positionality of the researcher vis-à-vis the research participants. There are limitations to being an "outsider" to the group being studied, just as there are limitations to being an "insider." The limitations are especially apparent in studies with greater social distance between the two parties. This study is no exception. When sociologist Forrest Stuart takes up the question of positionality, he argues that there is no readymade solution for this enduring tension. Instead, Stuart recommends that "ethnographers are better served by more fully embracing our unique position and its capacity to generate novel analyses. . . . Reflexivity . . . constitutes a powerful analytical tool."[6] Using reflexivity as an analytical tool calls me to reflect on how my identities shaped what I was privy to, what was beyond my ken, and what new insights I may have gained or overlooked.

Readied with formal approval and verbal consent, my primary agenda was to be an empathetic listener to the women in custody—an agenda I embodied by embracing my positionality. On my first day at Mapleside, someone who greeted me with a hug commented, "Oh, you're so small. You're fragile!" She reminded me of what I already knew: petite can mean unintimidating. This made me work doubly hard to be taken seriously in college classrooms, but here my physicality allowed me to appear young and nonthreatening. Once during her weekly class, Ms. J asked the attendees to raise their hands if they woke up in the morning with chronic pain, announcing, "All of us do, except maybe for Rachel. You need to have fat on your body for that pain!" Wanda, seated beside me, nudged her elbow and teased, "You're gonna let her talk to you like that?" I laughed with Wanda, but of course I would let Ms. J talk to me like that. Being an ethnographer often means stripping away pride and ego, prioritizing rapport over other interactional imperatives.[7] I took the teasing comment as yet another indication of familiarity, a sign I was welcome.

Above all, I strove for consistency: I spent up to four days a week at Mapleside, for up to nine hours a visit. One Friday, for instance, I noticed that Joan was not present for the Muslim worship services and Ronnie explained she was "in property." Brigit and Ronnie laughed when I asked what that meant: "I forget that [Rachel] don't know 'cause she don't live here!" Joan was picking up a package from the mail room.

Over time, participants seemed increasingly comfortable with my presence. I got to know some of the study participants very well, talking with them almost daily. Maria, for one, seemed to relish joking about my "lead leg" after I disclosed that I had gotten a speeding ticket. More sentimentally, she once shared in a quiet moment, "We appreciate you. People like you coming in here, we can talk about what's going on—what it's like in the real world. It makes me feel like I'm not locked up!" She turned her head away with a laugh, dabbed under her eye, and muttered, "Look, I'm gonna cry." Despite a three-decade age gap and different racial backgrounds, religious identities, and sexual orientations, Maria and I built a connection and spoke regularly. So when she said "people like you," I took it to mean not that I was white, Jewish, or straight, but that, to her, I was an "interested outsider."[8]

Importantly, my unusual role meant I was not entangled in the prison's social system in a limiting way. I had the leeway to sit and talk for hours, about everything from the latest episode of *Scandal* to the best food to order at Taco Bell. Despite being outside of Mapleside's social order, however, I was conscious of the power dynamics implicit in my exchanges. When asking questions, I often employed a method called "interviewing by comment," indirectly inviting a response rather than compelling a reply through direct questions.[9] This conversational approach to field interviews evoked a process of interactional consent in which women responded only if they wished to. For example, when I once commented, "That was a nice service this Sunday," Asabi replied with a smirk, "It was *different* . . . . This time the [Holy] Spirit didn't flow." From there, I was able to ask why she found this worship service less meaningful. Other times, and especially as familiarity grew, I asked women to define prison- and faith-specific terms in their own words, and I never shied away from asking clarifying questions or checking in with women for updates on their lives.

During observations, I tried to avoid guiding group conversations, only inserting myself to contribute to conversations already in progress. If there was a lull, I might take the opportunity to run an impromptu "focus group" and invite participants to evaluate ideas from existing scholarship and themes emerging from my observations in the field. Thus, when Maria, Nevaeh, and Estrella's conversation fizzled as they waited around before an afternoon ministry class, I offered, "I've been reading this book about another women's prison where the author talks about 'renting out your head.'[10] Do you know that term?" Nevaeh giggled and clapped a hand over her grin—she said it sounded "dirty." I laughed along and clarified that it was a name for telling officials what they want to hear when they try to control how women in prison see themselves: "fake it until to you make it." Still tickled by her mistake, Nevaeh ended up co-signing the term: "No, we don't say that. But I like that. I do that all the time."

As an ethnographer, I not only wanted to get to know key participants well but also to glean perspectives from as many people as possible. I went out of my way to introduce myself to new faces, and I routinely made sure to talk to women from as many backgrounds and life experiences as possible: I interviewed women who came from deep disadvantage and had lower educational attainment as well as middle-class women who earned professional degrees, women just old enough to buy cigarettes and women in their golden years, women who did not have children to mothers of four. Likewise, I sought the perspectives of prison staff and volunteers. As a nonincarcerated outsider, I was treated to the candor of prison officials, and I engaged in "inconvenience sampling," going out of my way to talk with respondents who had the ability to jeopardize the identity I was cultivating in the field.[11] I solicited officers' opinions on my research topic to understand their perspectives on the role of religion at Mapleside. I sat on post with Officer McLean to observe her surveillance and control strategies, asking plenty of follow-up questions.

Even so, managing competing allegiances—or, at least, trying to maintain the trust and goodwill of several different, even oppositional groups—was a balancing act. I experienced several moments of "identity rupture" that threatened that equilibrium. For instance, I cultivated congenial rapport with Officer Greene, a Black woman in her 30s who was normally on post between the Gatehouse and the Main Hall, as she buzzed me in from one building to another. I got to know her from behind the bulletproof glass of the "bubble," establishing enough rapport that I could ask after her kids each time I saw her. "You're back?" she would smile, and I would reply, "Always!" I was not prepared, however, for the day she was on foot patrol in the Main Hall and spotted me observing a ministry class. Freed from the confines of her desk, Officer Greene burst into the classroom squealing with joy. "Hi!" she said, prancing over to me with outstretched arms. She squeezed me into a hug and declared, "This one's so nice." Before I could gather my thoughts, Estrella, a ministry class attendee, chided with evident dismay, "You know the *officers*, too."

Mindful that being too closely aligned with officers could erode incarcerated women's trust, I began to curb my sociable interactions with staff. Estrella was also present when an officer on post stopped me en route to a religious movie screening in the Main Hall. She wanted me to be an intermediary, asking the attendees to turn down the TV's volume. When I obliged, Asabi retorted, "Rachel, you need to tell the officer to go. She has got to go!" Estrella emphasized, "She's telling you to get rid of that officer!" I felt like the rope in a game of tug-of-war, each group testing my loyalties. I wanted to prove my alliance with the incarcerated women, but I also knew that officers' discretion could endanger my continued access. They could make it a slow and difficult process to enter the prison each day, order me to leave at a moment's notice, or deny my access altogether. Ultimately, I discontinued my observations of officers on post and limited my field interviews with prison staff. To demonstrate my loyalties more overtly, I also made sure to mention to the women all the various times I was reprimanded by officers. There was no shortage, as I was constantly breaking unspoken rules: I was caught with a lunch tray and chastised for eating "state food." I ran afoul of the assistant warden when I used the wrong copy machine at Chaplain Harper's direction. Plenty of times, officers capriciously dictated my movements, ordering me to stop in a hallway until directed to continue or refusing to make eye contact until they were ready to examine my "entrance memo." Although officers had far less control over me, the incarcerated women enjoyed a chuckle at my expense and the stories seemed to help them see me as an ally.

Evangelizing the Observer

Managing my identity in the "little world" of prescribed roles included responding to other people's curiosity about my own religious background and beliefs. It was only natural that they would ask—I attended and participated in religious programs of a variety of faiths almost daily. I shared that I identified as Jewish, but I grew up in an interfaith household: my father was raised Catholic, telling tales of his Catholic school days and the nuns who disciplined him, and my mother was raised Jewish, in a modern orthodox congregation of which my grandparents were founding members. From what I attribute to this interfaith upbringing, I explained that I find all religions interesting. Like a lot of people in their late teens and early 20s, I had shopped around for a spiritual home when I went to college. I explored a number of different faiths. I attended Catholic mass, megachurch worship, and Divine Life meditation services. I went on an interfaith trip to Jerusalem and tried out a *kirtan* chanting service at a yoga retreat. Incidentally, this was the exact same life stage when many marginalized young people have their first formal contact with the adult criminal legal system.[12] Had I been at Mapleside in those years, I would have had no latitude to experiment. New admits may check only one box on the Religious Preference Form.

My interfaith background helped me connect with some women. Hearing the story of my mother's Jewish background and my father's Catholic background, Carla shared that her mother was Muslim and her father,

Christian. Sabina had a Jewish mother, she said, until a recent afternoon when Sabina "saved" her over the phone. Wanda, who grew up near Carla, pointed out that she "used to work for a Jewish [person] for five years," to which Carla added, "Yeah, that's Jew-town." My interfaith upbringing understandably caused a fair amount of confusion as well. Judaism has a number of "strains," like Christianity, and people's assumptions can be powerful. Estrella was excited to learn that I was Jewish, exclaiming, "My chiropractor was a Messianic Jew!" As I readied myself to explain the differences between Messianic Judaism and the kind of Jewish faith I adhered to, she cut me off: "I feel the same way [as you]. To me, it's all about God and that other stuff doesn't matter." That did not quite represent my own beliefs, however: Judaism aligns strongly with history and culture, such that belief in God is not a requirement for affiliating as Jewish, at least in my circles, the way it is in Protestant Christianity.

As helpful as my interfaith background might have been in participating in different groups, it was important to acknowledge the limits of my understanding as a religious outsider, as someone not enmeshed in the practices or theologies of this system. To women who believed that salvation stemmed from accepting Jesus Christ as Lord, their oft-repeated refrain, "It's about relationship [with Christ], not religion," meant that I would be classified squarely in the realm of nonbeliever. In fact, when I asked if anyone could introduce me to atheists or nonbelievers to interview, one woman suggested I speak to Mapleside's Jewish group. In this context, many of the research participants focused not on religious affiliation as much as on salvation through Christ.

One of the early signs that my salvation would be a focal point of my fieldwork was when Pastor O'Neill asked me to read a passage from the book of Esther during a Sunday worship service. I wondered if I was asked to recite this passage because it was from the Old Testament and the pastor knew I was Jewish. At least from prior Purim holiday celebrations, I felt confident about my pronunciation of ancient names like Mordechai and King Ahasuerus. When I finished, a woman in the front row gave me a thumbs-up and whispered, "That's the first step!" Her efforts to "save" me would escalate in the coming weeks—evidently my participation in the reading was "the first step" to my conversion.

Protestant women asked directly, "Are you a Christian?" or "Are you a follower of Christ?" Proselytizing was a core component of their religious practice. Early on, Pastor Thompson introduced me as a student "writing her doctoral dissertation on religious healing." Internally, I questioned whether that was an accurate description, but my thoughts were inter-rupted as the pastor pivoted. He instructed the congregants, "Lift your arms up towards her. Let's pray for Rachel that not only will she success-fully complete her project, but that her spirit will find Christ in the pro-cess." Nearly the entire congregation stood up and raised their hands in witness. Just because my goal was to conduct a research study did not mean the social world of religious life at Mapleside disappeared. My research aims did not exclude me from participating in the religious land-scape at Mapleside as the incarcerated women themselves navigated and negotiated it. Since I did not identify as a "saved" Christian, my Protestant salvation was a frequent topic of conversation, consistent with the preva-lent theological beliefs of the research participants.

During another Protestant worship service, Esther, a church official, asked me pointedly, "Are you saved?" I said no. "Now's the time!" she exclaimed, "Go on up there." Esther was encouraging me to stand at the front of the congregation during the "altar call," a weekly opportunity for churchgoers to "dedicate their life to Christ" (described in chapter 2). I politely declined. "Are you sure?" she asked. I nodded. "Are you one hun-dred percent? I'm gonna ask you again, are you positive?" Esther asked urgently. I insisted, "I'm positive," and she let up. Two weeks later, Esther spotted me entering another service. "I got your seat in the first row, Ms. Rachel!" Throughout the months that followed, her efforts never waned. Whenever I declined an altar call, she would whisper encouragement: "You tell me when you're ready. I'll go up there with you."

In ethnography, there is a continuum between "participant" and "observer."[13] In part, efforts to proselytize me grew out of the ambiguity of my place on that continuum. During worship services, I alternated between sitting with congregants and sitting up front with the volunteers. I partici-pated in worship and rituals when invited and when it did not require affiliation (for instance, I joined in singing hymns but did not take com-munion). The Catholic and Jewish groups' liturgy was somewhat familiar to me, but when I was invited to participate in the Muslim study forum, we read holy texts and the women answered my questions about not only their personal beliefs but the Islamic faith in general. The learning curve was steepest with the Protestant group, the primary focus of my research and the largest religious group in this closed society. I sought participants' advice when it was time for me to procure a Bible (the overwhelming rec-ommendation among Christians at Mapleside was the NIV, or New Inter-national Version).

After months of regular attendance at Bible studies, ministry classes, and worship services, some devout women said they discerned a religious transformation. "You are starting to get more into it, I can tell," Esther ventured. "The way you are at the service, I can just tell the Word [of God] is getting to you." Another night, as I sidled into Baptist Bible study, she joked, "You can't get enough of us, can you? You thought you were coming for your project, but then it *changed* you." Rashida used similar words as she led a group prayer in Discipleship class: "Rachel thought she was coming in for one thing and is getting a whole other thing." One time, Estrella commented, "You should think about becoming a chaplain after this project," and Hanna added, "I've noticed it too, in the questions she's asking." Catholic volunteers prayed in other moments for me to "find Christ and come ever closer to following His path," and Ronnie once teased Brigit for trying to convert me to Islam. To be sure, though I was certainly developing an even deeper appreciation for a variety of faith traditions, my inquiry remained academic. When one woman took to calling me "Chaplain in Training," I doubled down on repeating my research purposes.[14] It was essential to ongoing consent that I continually reminded participants of my role as a researcher, whether or not that aligned with their perceptions of me as a prospective convert.

THE COMPLICATED ROLE OF THE PRISON ETHNOGRAPHER

A long-standing tradition has brought researchers into prisons, hoping to uncover what happens in a punitive place hidden by design, and researchers often use their findings to urge reforms of one kind or another. Yet it has always been necessary that a never-incarcerated ethnographer critically interrogate the very fact of their doing research inside a prison. As sociologist Timothy Black reflects on the inherently problematic nature of scholarship on marginalized communities, "All ethnographies are exploitative in nature, because . . . they advance professional careers and status on the backs of others, often the powerless. Researchers are notorious for going into poor communities and taking but rarely giving back—or, as local activists sometimes say, for 'cutting and running.'"

There are very real potential harms that could arise from research on vulnerable populations and on the subject of prison, specifically. My own argument throughout this book, that secondhand carcerality leads noncarceral actors and institutions to end up replicating carceral aims in their work despite their nonpunitive intentions, raised alarms about my own study, which amplified the longer I grappled with my positionality. Every time I visited Mapleside, every hour I spent analyzing the data, and every word I put on these pages was accompanied by constant caution. As Gibson-Light and Seim note, "Ethnography helps reveal penal domination, but penal domination also shapes ethnography."[15]

Timothy Black sought to chip away at the one-sided nature of human subjects research by mobilizing his social and cultural capital on behalf of his study's participants. He organized a drug intervention, bailed someone out of jail, testified on their behalf, and offered educational tutoring and research assistantships. Even so, he conceded that his own career, like that of other scholars, would benefit from these relationships in the long term, beyond any temporary intervention he might make in his participants' lives. In my study, given the constraints of strict prison rules, direct material and social supports were off the table. I was restricted to bringing in only a notebook, a pen, a Bible, and personal snacks, and could provide nothing tangible to participants. The vast majority of the women I met had already worn out all their chances at appeals, and so offering legal help was out of the question, nor did I harbor any fanciful notion of swooping in and solving anyone's problems. Moreover, both IRB rules and DOC stipulations limited me from compensating participants in any way. In these situations, some ethnographers assuage their guilt by emphasizing that their interviews might be therapeutic, reasoning that it is beneficial simply to be someone who participants can confide in. I could not lessen my guilt that way: although women at Mapleside told me our conversations were enjoyable, that was hardly a sufficient exchange for their incredible candor.

As best I could, I tried to give back through formal institutional mechanisms, reasoning that even the smallest gestures can be meaningful in an environment defined by deprivation. Whenever I received emails from Chaplain Harper requesting financial donations, I donated, making sure to donate the same amounts when secular program coordinators reached out, for instance giving Home Depot gift cards to benefit the beekeeping program and gathering donations for a coat and glove drive to be distributed to women released during the winter months.

Where my liminal status as a researcher could be beneficial to incarcerated women, I was eager to help. For instance, I could assist in getting the ear of Chaplain Harper regarding religious requests. When the Jewish group ran out of grape juice and Shabbat candles, Dorinda asked me to relay a message to the chaplain, figuring it would be quicker and more effective than if she dropped a note in the part-time chaplain's mailbox. At her request, I also brought in (and returned home with) sheet music to sing Shabbat melodies like "Shalom Aleichem" and "Adon Olam." Likewise, the very fact of my observation helped the Muslim group gain access to material resources, as Maya told me. "Probably because they saw there was a visitor today and it's *embarrassing* that we only have VHS tapes," Maya surmised, noting that on this day, her faith group was finally allowed to select some films from a catalog of religious DVDs. Additionally, I was happy to facilitate any benefits or freedoms through women's association with me. Nevaeh once greeted me in the hallway in front of a CO—by my waving back, Nevaeh later explained that it made the officer think she had permission to be in the Main Hall and afforded her the autonomy she craved. Similarly, Hanna deployed me to ask an officer why a volunteer abruptly departed halfway through Bible study. I was able to find out the volunteer had a family emergency—a small fact that put the mystery to bed, whereas Hanna suspected she would be told it was none of her business. "I'm glad we have you for this spy work," she commented.

I found myself seizing on ways to try to repay the generosity of my participants, even in the most minute of ways. After a woman mentioned to me how she enjoyed seeing the volunteers' colorful clothes compared to the sea of drab beige uniforms, I made a special effort to wear bright colors and interesting patterns (while adhering to the visitor regulations stipulating modest, loose-fitting clothing that covered from the neck to the knee). When they faced health scares or an impending parole hearing, many devout women asked me to pray for them. Although I suspected my prayers might sound different from theirs, I prayed for them anyway. I still do.

None of my efforts were anywhere near enough. Ethnographers tend to operate in this gray area, where their careers depend on their research studies, with few avenues to give back to the population in question. In fact, some have rightfully scrutinized whether a privileged researcher, especially a white, middle-class person who has never been incarcerated, *should* write an ethnography about such a deeply marginalized population from the comfort of the academic ivory tower. To be sure, one of the obvious limitations to telling this story as an outsider is an incomplete understanding of carceral control. I do not know what punishment feels like when there is no end in sight, what interactions with prison staff look like when no one is watching, and how authority crosses into coercion. I have not endured family separation, nor a dark cloud of guilt and regret, made even darker by the never-ending imperative to demonstrate remorse and perform rhetorical self-flagellation in the name of accountability. As Reuben Jonathan Miller puts it, "proximity is a gift."[16] There is no way to fully understand the experience of being punished without living it, and I would always be an outsider because I was free to exit at any time.

To believe otherwise would be myopic. That is what a lifetime of socialization into a patriarchal culture of white privilege and class inequality creates: a situation in which one does not know what one does not know. Anne Warfield Rawls and Waverly Duck describe the tacit racism of unobserved privilege: "People who are not aware of the racism embedded in the interactional processes of their own daily lives *cannot change* what they are not aware of . . . the big problem is the deeply embedded tacit racism that we don't see and therefore don't believe we are acting on."[17] To produce knowledge, to truly listen, and to explore how religion becomes enmeshed within carcerality even as it alleviates some of its pains, I had to contend with both my immense, intersectional privilege and its potential effects on the data I gathered. As sociologist Victor Rios states, "A reflexivity of whiteness calls for all researchers to reflect on how their identity and colorblindness might be whitewashing the research process and in turn tainting the knowledge production process—creating one-dimensional caricaturized images of the urban 'other' and limiting our ability to systematically understand the populations we study."[18]

Ultimately, reflexivity calls on me to interrogate my own privileges, working against socialization and stereotypes, while acknowledging that there will always be blind spots that may never come into focus. For this study, I worked to sharpen my vision by devouring the literature on the racialized roots of the U. S. criminal legal system and its interwoven relationship with poverty. Even more importantly, I oriented myself toward learning from the women of Mapleside, granting them my implicit trust and respect as the only true source when it comes to knowing the experience of criminalization and incarceration. To that end, I hired three study participants who had since reentered the community to conduct "member checks" to verify the facts and arguments presented in this book.

Contemplating my positionality and privilege when it comes to the ethics of prison ethnography, more questions than answers emerge. At this point, with the research conducted and the ink dried, these questions guide my thinking as I reflect on the goal of this project. The goal has been to shine a light on how religion helps women cope with one of the most stringent tools of domination—the prison—especially as it relates to a broader system of inequality around race, gender, and social class, while also exploring how this ameliorative effect is dampened by the reproduction of state goals through religious practice. Indeed, as sociologist and activist Beth Richie writes on ethnographies of women in prison, "Nearly all of the manifestations of gender domination . . . exploited labor, inadequate healthcare, dangerous living conditions, physical violence, sexual assault—are revealed at once . . . . The convergence of disadvantage, discrimination, and despair is staggering."[19] Insofar as it reveals new mechanisms of disadvantage and presents openings for meaningful change, we ultimately need more research on prisons, not less, and most pressingly from those who have experienced incarceration themselves. The challenges of positionality, privilege, and potential harms are many—especially when they are not carefully considered, thoughtfully enacted, and reflexively questioned—but the need to examine the lived experience of carceral control remains urgent.

DATA ANALYSIS

The introductory chapter of this book detailed the observations and field interviews I conducted for this study. Here, I explain how these observations and interviews became data. From the first day at my research site, I kept a notebook of handwritten "jottings," short phrases that would jog my memory alongside verbatim quotes scrawled in real time. At the end of each day, I returned home to convert the jottings into typed field notes. It was essential to finish writing field notes before returning to the field to preserve chronologies, avoid any confusion about what happened when and to whom, and to be sure I recorded key phrases, poignant looks, and body language. The process of writing field notes could stretch into the wee hours, after which I would commute back to Mapleside during the morning rush.

Field notes help to capture the qualitative essence of situations—not only what transpires but also the emotional atmosphere and the unspoken social dynamics in a given interaction. They also contain a great deal of quantitative detail, as I recorded things like the time I spent in the field each day (down to the minute), the precise number of participants in each program I observed, and the demographic details shared by staff, officers, volunteers, and incarcerated women. On days when I conducted an in-depth interview, I took my field notes as usual, only putting words in quotations if I had been able to scribble them down, word for word, during the interview. Tape recorders were not allowed, so I took a conservative approach in transcription. I am confident the quotes in this book are verbatim and properly contextualized. In the end, nearly 500 hours spent at Mapleside amounted to some 900 single-spaced, typewritten pages—which became my data for analysis.

Periodically, throughout data collection, I drafted two other kinds of documents: methodological reflection memos and analytical memos. The former, methodological reflection memos, involved freewriting about my own experiences in the field related to my positionality and the choices I was making. From social gaffes and frustrations to moments of clarity and bonding, I used these memos to consider my role, take a broader view, and think creatively about how I could embrace my positionality to work against preconceived notions and potential blind spots.

My analytical memos provided space for sorting through preliminary findings during fieldwork. How did my observations fit with existing social scientific knowledge? More importantly, because I used an abductive approach that focused on surprises and unanticipated outcomes, I attended to the ways my observations *did not* fit with current literature. Unlike grounded theory, which generates hypotheses based on emergent themes in the field, an abductive theoretical approach acknowledges that researchers enter the field with presuppositions and a degree of existing knowledge on their topic of study. Surprising observations are thus used to consider competing hypotheses. In short, the logic of abduction goes: "Unexpected fact C is observed. But if A were true, C would be a matter of course. Hence, there is a reason to suspect that A is true."[20] Before, during, and after my research at Mapleside, I read voraciously: ethnographies of women's and men's prisons alongside studies on religious practice. Examining current scholarly debates lay the foundation to construct what was "surprising" in the field and the conditions under which "C" would or would not follow from "A."[21]

Analytical memoing during data collection allowed me to return to the field to "test" nascent themes. I paid special attention to patterns and searched for disconfirming evidence. I could also run my working theories by the women at Mapleside (the way I sometimes I did with the aforementioned informal "focus groups"). For instance, when I started to really absorb that religion might be a method of survival in an oppressive environment, I asked Hanna what she thought about the survival of women who did not participate in religion. She turned the question over in her mind: "How do people get through it without God? Maybe they get through it, but those who have God . . . they have had a fuller, more transformative experience. Rather than just getting through, they *grow* from it." I ran the survival hypothesis by Estrella, too. She replied, "A lot of it is hope. Or it's a coping mechanism. It's how people cope with being here. Like, during my last bid [at Mapleside], I'm not saying [my religious faith] wasn't real, but it wasn't the same. Finally this time, I was ready." These responses alerted me to a key distinction between narratives of survival versus narratives of transformation, with the latter afforded greater meaning and legitimacy.

Beginning data analysis while still in the field turned out to be consequential for my argument. When I workshopped my emerging ideas at conferences or colloquia, fellow criminologists and sociologists repeatedly questioned the focus on religion, viewing it as a distraction from the "real" problems of incarceration, or a side topic of little importance. To be sure, in this book, I focus on religion's imposition of secondhand carcerality without focusing squarely on the prison system as the *primary* source of carceral control. This is in no way meant to detract from the overt and troubling forms of control perpetuated by state officials, but to underscore secondhand carcerality as one of the more insidious mechanisms of carceral control. It is crucial to identify these subtler manifestations if we are to paint a full picture of state control among justice-involved individuals.[22] When I workshopped the same themes with the incarcerated women I spoke to, few agreed with those academics. By gaining proximity, troubleshooting evolving ideas, and taking seriously women's testimonies, I was gifted the perspective that religion matters because it matters to the women sentenced to months, years, or lifetimes behind bars. "For me, it was front and center," Estrella would tell me later. "That's how I did my time. It governs so much." Whether or not the research participants knew the scholarly literature, they knew their lives. What is important to research participants must be important to the researchers who wish to write about them.

"Flexible coding" was the next step.[23] The process took me an entire summer of full-time work, with careful and meticulous attention. I printed out all 900-odd pages of my field notes and memos and read them through in full. My memory refreshed, I read through my notes and memos again, this time drafting a list of emergent themes. Gradually, and alphabetically, the list expanded: alienation, anger, behavior in church services, cellmates, conversion, deprivations, family, freedom, friendship, guilt, health, innocence, jealousy, money, parole, rules, security, trauma, volunteers, womanhood, and worship styles, to name only a few.

With 187 emergent topic codes for analysis, I performed a first-round of coding using the qualitative software program Nvivo. I reviewed each and every line of my field notes, identifying the broad themes related to each sentence. Due to IRB stipulations regarding the sensitive data gathered from a vulnerable population, only I could access my field notes. It was impossible to hire a second coder to evaluate reliability. In the next round of coding, I was more granular still, breaking broad themes (coded as nouns) into narrower sub-codes (coded as verbs). For instance, I separated "rules of prison" into analytic codes for breaking the rules and following the rules, so that I could locate variation between individuals and across situations. This ensured that my coding scheme did not privilege upholding prison rules over breaking them and vice versa. The sub-codes for womanhood included expressing femininity, rejecting femininity, discussing gender, and surveilling gender, among others. I continually searched for disconfirming evidence to disprove the patterns I observed and strengthen internal validity.

True to the abductive approach described earlier, surprises informed my inquiry, wherein I compared the utility of different theories as a framework for interpreting the data. For instance, I was surprised to find the sexuality code co-occurred with worship services. I used this co-occurrence to examine the tension between religious teachings on sexual orientation with romantic partners' participation in worship services, as discussed in chapter 4. During this stage, I returned to the literature to compare my empirical findings to the predictions laid out by prior scholars.

Despite seeking surprising findings, I did not want the findings to be surprising to the women whose lived experience I documented. My last step was member checks. As mentioned previously, I recruited three women who figure centrally in this manuscript to read drafts—Adelaide, Estrella, and Lexi. Through member checks, I sought to confirm the accuracy of how I depicted Mapleside, from its rules and routines to the interactions with religious volunteers and staff. Crucially, in terms of bigger-picture arguments, although they innovate on existing scholarship, they surprised none of the participant-readers. I viewed this as lending further credence to the theoretical concepts and contributions. "I never thought about it like that," one woman reflected, "but it really is true. . . . Religion governed the hierarchy . . . It's the system. They're using the system of these religions to promote compliance."

In interpreting the findings, it is true that the patterns related to religion and carceral control in one state women's prison cannot represent *all* state women's prisons. Nor can they represent religion at Mapleside in perpetuity. Nevertheless, prisons are highly standardized institutions. Their architectural plans, building materials, paramilitary staffing structure, daily organization, system of rules and regulations, and contracts with private vendors are quite similar across facilities in the United States. I expect, as discussed in this book's conclusion, that certain aspects of my eventual findings could be relevant to other state prisons. Yet I also expect that my decision to conceal the actual identity of Mapleside Prison means losing a certain specificity in my analysis. Place is consequential to understanding social context. I could write that Mapleside was located in a semi-rural area with a lengthy commute from nearby cities. But how rural? Was there a surrounding community that cropped up around the prison's construction, promising employment and economic opportunity?[24] What were the racial demographics and primary economic sectors of the state in which Mapleside operated? Did the majority of this prison's population come from deindustrialized urban centers, struggling agricultural economies, or vibrant but intensely segregated enclaves? All of this information would undoubtedly enrich my account. But it could also lead to potential harms or further vulnerabilities among those who lived and worked at Mapleside, were they to be identified by location or name. I decided at the outset that the price of nonspecificity was a worthwhile cost.

There are no composite characters in this book, though all the people and places are given pseudonyms (some research participants opted to select their own pseudonyms). I removed or disguised details in the rare cases where they risked revealing a participant's identity, but I never changed or swapped out important aspects of their backgrounds (like their race, age, religious affiliation, sexual orientation, or gender identity). Where I had only partial information about a person or a situation, I reported it as such. For clarity, I removed some "ums" and "likes" from direct quotations, but did not edit any substantive terms.

LESSONS LEARNED UPON LEAVING THE FIELD

I entered the field aware of some of my privilege, and left the field all the more aware. By the time I was a graduate student writing my dissertation on the prison system, I was firmly convinced by a swath of books and articles offering systematic evidence about the direct and indirect harms associated with coming into contact with the criminal justice system. I learned that prisons do not keep "us" any safer, nor do they deter crime.[25] It is difficult to know whether they rehabilitate their wards, but it is clear that they wreak havoc by keeping families apart and severely limiting future life chances.

But what I could not understand until I passed through the guarded gates of Mapleside Prison is the degree to which contemporary discourses from politicians, the media, and the cultural zeitgeist misled me about *who prisons are for* and *what they really accomplish*. Importantly, I benefited from the luxury of having my perspective shaped through books and an academic study of a prison rather than through firsthand experience. Many readers may not have shared this luxury.

Physically leaving Mapleside threw my privilege into sharp relief. There were days when the drudgery of spending nine hours inside a prison felt more daunting than scholarly, when the steel doors that shut behind me made me feel trapped.[26] I was exhausted by the constant anticipation of reprimand. The environment was hostile and cold, and the weight of the stories women shared with me felt crushing. At the same time, I felt the nagging pull of a sense of indulgence. What right did *I* have to feel despondent and wallow in someone else's trauma? I got to go *home*. When I caught myself wrapped up in dread about returning to Mapleside, I did my best to glue on a smile and be cheerful for the women who did not share my ability to leave. Now I will do my best to channel my responses, academic and otherwise, into change.

My final day in the field was Ms. Lonnie's final day on earth. Introduced in chapter 2, Ms. Lonnie was 75 and an occasional attendee at Protestant worship services and programs. As my time at Mapleside neared its end, Ms. Lonnie was diagnosed with lung cancer and transferred to the infirmary to reside full-time. It was painful to see Ms. Lonnie languishing in prison, though some outsiders, like those who testified at her parole hearings, expressed that she deserved this sort of pain, since she was able to go on living while her victim died a violent and premature death. Those who knew Ms. Lonnie at Mapleside wholeheartedly disagreed, speaking of how her gentle demeanor and kind eyes softened the energy in any room, shuffling in quietly behind her walker. That very day, her condition worsened and she was rushed to a local hospital. Chaplain Harper went to sit by her side in her last hours. Later in the evening, Chaplain Harper emailed Mapleside's cadre of religious volunteers:

> I am sad to share that one [of] our residents Lonetta Nelson, fondly known as Ms. Lonnie, has transitioned into paradise. She was a woman of great faith

who we believe is now resting with her Lord and Savior Jesus Christ. She had been ill for several years. Please keep her family both inside and out in your prayers. Many of our ladies will be impacted by her passing.

I was a true outsider by the time I read the email. The moment I walked out of Mapleside that final time, I was officially prohibited by the DOC from maintaining personal contact with the women on the inside. I could not send my condolences to Maria or Hanna or any of the others in Ms. Lonnie's fan club. Her death helped me recalibrate my own importance: in the "little world" of this women's prison, in its housing units and multipurpose classrooms, with its lively Baptist choirs and poorly timed *challahs*, its payphone conversions and Bible study debates, its clockwork counts, clandestine romances, and endless expanse of khaki, this project and the researcher were peripheral. As much as I must consider my own role in this project, the utmost importance is honoring the stories of incarcerated women who were generous in sharing their time—in both senses of the term.

Notes

INTRODUCTION

1. All names of people and places are pseudonyms. Descriptive traits are unchanged. Specific details are omitted in the rare cases where they could jeopardize confidentiality.

2. New International Version.

3. Benns 2015; see also Alexander 2012.

4. For example, Lincoln and Mamiya 1990.

5. There were previous iterations of what became the penitentiary model, but many have identified Eastern State as one of the world's first penitentiaries because it made famous a system of imprisonment that was so markedly different from prior houses of correction (McCorkel and Dal-Cortivo 2018).

6. Bentham [1843] 1995; McCorkel and DalCortivo 2018.

7. Beaumont and Tocqueville 1833, 93.

8. The role of Quaker principles in guiding the construction of the separate confinement system of punishment is well documented. Rubin (2021), however, suggests that Quaker influences have been overemphasized, and that some Quaker reformers ultimately eschewed Eastern State's system of

separate confinement. For more on the role of Christianity in penal reform, see Snodgrass 2019; Rothman 2002; Sullivan 2009.

9. For more, see Applegate et al. 2000; Grasmick and McGill 1994; Skotnicki 2000.

10. Davis 2003, 48.

11. Graber 2011.

12. At the time, women convicted of crime were viewed as a "moral menace" who must be reformed through evangelical Christian ideals of domesticity and submissiveness (Hannah-Moffat 2001). For more on the history of women's prisons, see Rafter 1983.

13. Griffith 2020.

14. Irwin 2005; McCorkel 2013.

15. "Nation of Islam" FBI report from October 1960, quoted in Colley 2014.

16. Cooper v. Pate, 378 U.S. 546 (1964). For a detailed history and analysis, see Colley 2014.

17. Congressional Record—S. 14462, 103rd Cong. (1993).

18. Religious Freedom Restoration Act, 42 U.S.C. § 2000bb *et seq.* (2018). For further discussion, see Erzen 2017.

19. Religious Land Use and Institutionalized Persons Act, 42 U.S.C. § 2000cc *et seq.* (2018).

20. Erzen 2017; Sullivan 2009.

21. According to an official White House release, "President Bush created the White House Office of Faith-based and Community Initiatives and Centers for Faith-Based and Community Initiatives in eleven Federal agencies to lead a determined attack on need by strengthening and expanding the role of FBCOs in providing social services. The Federal government has worked to accomplish this mission through an array of regulatory and policy reforms, legislative efforts, and public outreach to FBCOs .... The ultimate beneficiaries are America's poor, who are best served when the Federal government's partners are the providers most capable of meeting their needs" ("White House Faith-Based & Community Initiative" 2002).

22. Becci and Dubler 2017; Beckford and Gilliat 1998.

23. Aday, Krabill, and Deaton-Owens 2014; Clear et al. 2000; Cooney and Phillips 2013; Dubler 2013; Hallett et al. 2017; Johnson 2017; Kerley 2014; Lempert 2016; Maruna, Wilson, and Curran 2006; Thomas and Zaitzow 2006; Walker 2016.

24. Flores 2018; Giordano, Cernkovich, and Rudolph 2002; Giordano et al. 2008; Johnson 2004, 2011; Johnson, Larson, and Pitts 1997; Kerley, Matthews, and Blanchard 2005; Maruna 2001; O'Connor 2004; Sumter 2006; Trusty and Eisenberg 2003; Young et al. 1995.

25. Dye et al. 2014.

26. Beckford and Gilliat 1998; Sullivan 2009.

27. Erzen 2017. As Erzen and others have warned (Davis 2003; Gilmore 2007; Guzman 2020), we must interrogate how a focus on individual-level salvation can obscure the fight against structural inequality in the modern-day criminal legal system.

28. Johnson 2017.

29. Kerley 2014; Owen 1998; Snodgrass 2019.

30. Pew 2020b.

31. In the 2016 *General Social Survey*, 92 percent of women respondents reported believing in God or "some higher power" with or without a degree of doubt (see Smith, Hout, and Marsden 2017). Ninety-seven percent of Black women respondents reported believing in God or "some higher power" with or without a degree of doubt. See also Chatters, Taylor, and Lincoln 1999.

32. Susan Crawford Sullivan (2012) found that socioeconomically disadvantaged mothers lean on faith to make sense of their circumstances, even when busy schedules and costly transportation make worship at formal religious institutions nearly impossible. Even those who feel alienated by formal religious institutions outside prison may welcome its presence inside prison walls.

33. See Erzen (2017) for a background and Sullivan (2009) for a critique.

34. Burnside et al. 2005.

35. Williams and Liebling 2018, 280.

36. Becci and Dubler 2017, 246.

37. Goodman, Page, and Phelps 2017. For more on the four main goals of corrections, see also Tonry 2006.

38. Allen 1981; Garland 2001.

39. Hirschi 1969; Janowitz 1975.

40. Kaufman, Kaiser, and Rumpf 2018.

41. Goffman [1961] 2007.

42. Flores 2016; Miller 2014; Rios 2011.

43. Beckett and Murakawa 2012.

44. Brayne 2014; Haskins and Jacobsen 2017; Shedd 2015.

45. Lara-Millán 2014; Seim 2020.

46. Miller 2014, 327. See also Gustafson 2011; Kaufman, Kaiser, and Rumpf 2018; Schept 2015.

47. Van Cleve and Mayes 2015. The ever-widening net of carceral control should not be interpreted as a coordinated, conspiratorial effort, but instead a fractured, fragmented amalgamation of overlapping institutions (Rubin and Phelps 2017).

48. Flores 2016; McCorkel 2013.

49. Sufrin 2017.

50. Hannah-Moffat 2005; Harcourt 2007; Phelps 2018.

51. Hicks 2012, 639.

52. Secondhand carcerality is distinct from Comfort's (2008) concept of "secondary prisonization," which builds on Clemmer ([1940] 1958) to demonstrate how nonincarcerated individuals are subject to some of the "pains of imprisonment" when coming into contact with the prison system. Secondhand carcerality, by contrast, focuses on the alignment of institutions and institutional actors connected to the carceral system in a subordinate hierarchy. The unit of analysis differs, as do implications for the logics of punishment.

53. Rathbone 2006; Wacquant 2002.

54. Durkheim [1912] 2001, 46.

55. Wilde and Glassman 2016, 408.

56. Reutter and Bigatti 2014, 56.

57. For example, Ammerman 2007; Hall 1997.

58. Africa v. Commonwealth of Pennsylvania, 662 F.2d 1025, 1032 (3d Cir. 1981); Malnak, *supra*, 592 F.2d at 207 (concurring opinion).

59. New York State Department of Corrections and Community Supervision 2015.

60. Virginia Department of Corrections 2018.

61. Montana State Prison Department of Corrections 2016.

62. Virginia Department of Corrections 2018.

63. In Illinois, for example, the statute states, "Committed persons may only attend the religious activities of their designated religion or nondenominational religious activities" (Illinois DOC, 20 Illinois Administrative Code, ch. 1, pt. 425).

64. For example, Montana State Prison Department of Corrections 2016, 3. If denied, incarcerated persons may file a grievance to contest the denial.

65. New York State Department of Corrections and Community Supervision 2015; Virginia Department of Corrections 2018; Montana State Prison Department of Corrections 2016.

1. *THOU SHALT NOT*: A DAY IN PRISON

1. Sykes [1958] 2007.

2. Carson 2020.

3. As of 2019, 107,955 women were incarcerated in state and federal prisons (Carson 2020) while 110,500 women were confined in local jails (Zeng and Minton 2021).

4. Muhitch and Ghandnoosh 2021.

5. See McCorkel 2017. On the prison-industrial complex, see Gilmore 2007; Schlosser 1998.

6. Mai and Subramanian 2017.

7. Disadvantage accumulates throughout the life course as a function of contact with police and the criminal legal system (Kurlychek and Johnson 2019).

8. Bureau of Justice Statistics 2014; Gelman, Fagan, and Kiss 2007.

9. According to the Hamilton Project 2021. See also Beckett, Nyrop, and Pfingst 2006; Tonry 2011.

10. Berdejó 2018.

11. Kutateladze et al. 2014.

12. Demuth and Steffensmeier 2004; Everett and Wojtkiewicz 2002.

13. Carson 2020.

14. Ulmer, Kurlychek, and Kramer 2007.

15. Nellis and King 2009.

16. Per Carson (2020), in 2019, Black women were incarcerated at 1.7 times the rate of white women, and Hispanic women were incarcerated at 1.3 times the rate of white women.

17. Crawford 2000.

18. Boppre and Harmon 2017.

19. Davis 2003, 46. See also Simes 2021.

20. Porter, Voorheis, and Sabol 2017.

21. Couloute 2018.

22. Lageson 2020.

23. Kohler-Hausmann 2018.

24. Clair 2020; Feeley [1979] 1992; Van Cleve 2016.

25. Feigelman, Howard, Li, and Cross 2000.

26. Jennings, Piquero, and Reingle 2012. The victim-offender overlap is especially prevalent in homicides, where victims are 4–10 times more likely to have been previously arrested (Broidy et al. 2006).

27. Those convicted of homicide, for example, have lower rates of recidivism for any offense, including subsequent violent or homicide offenses, after release from prison (Liem 2013; Liem, Zahn, and Tichavsky 2014).

28. Porter and DeMarco 2019; Sugie and Turney 2017.

29. Pager 2003; Smith 2018; Smith and Simon 2020; Western et al. 2015. Educational opportunities and career advancement are limited, too, given evidence of discrimination in college admissions based on criminal record (Stewart and Uggen 2020).

30. Allard 2002; Harding, Morenoff, and Herbert 2013; Mauer and Chesney-Lind 2003; Petersilia 2003; Uggen, Manza, and Thompson 2006.

31. See Harris (2016) for extensive analysis of legal financial obligations. Wages may be garnished to pay fines and fees, exacerbating the economic hardships that stem from the shadow carceral state (Friedman 2021).

32. Rearrest within three years is likely for about half of all those who leave prison, most of whom are rearrested within in the first six months (Petersilia 2003; Western 2018).

33. Miller 2021. On carceral citizenship, see also Miller and Stuart 2017.

34. Enns et al. 2019.

35. Baćak and Kennedy 2015; Comfort 2008; Roberts 2004; Turney and Wildeman 2015.

36. For more on prison labor, see Gibson-Light 2017; Haney 2010b.

37. In Pennsylvania's state prisons, for instance, print books have been replaced by e-books, with incarcerated persons required to purchase tablets should they wish to read—a change made in the name of security (Armstrong 2018).

38. Friedman 2021; Harris 2016.

39. See Haney (2018) on "incarcerated fatherhood" through the entanglement of the correctional and child support systems.

40. The rhetoric of a mandatory "naptime" hearkens back to the infantilizing treatment of adult women in American prisons (Belknap 2010; Bosworth 1999; Carlen 1983; Haney 2010a; Hannah-Moffat 2001).

41. Conover 2001, 18.

42. Sufrin (2017) demonstrates the complexity and contradiction implicit in balancing care, coercion, and condemnation by officers and staff in a carceral environment.

43. As Foucault (1977) argues, the invisibility of what happens inside prison to the wider public makes this sort of treatment possible.

44. Britton 2003, 119.

45. Sykes [1958] 2007, 77.

46. See Collins (2009) on the escalation of violence and Skarbek (2014) on gangs in men's prisons.

47. Goffman [1961] 2007, 56.

48. Sufrin 2017, 209.

49. Sufrin 2017, 209.

2. *LET THERE BE LIGHT*: RELIGIOUS LIFE BEHIND BARS

1. Becci and Dubler (2017) trace the rise of religious programming and examine its tensions with principles of religious freedom.

2. Attributed to Rev. Dr. Martin Luther King Jr. See also Dougherty 2003; Emerson and Smith 2001.

3. Wilde (2018) defines "complex religion" as the ways that race, ethnicity, and social class intersect with religious affiliation. See also Wilde and Glassman 2016; Wilde and Tevington 2017.

4. Pratt 2019; Shelton and Cobb 2017; Steensland et al. 2000.

5. Ewert and Wildhagen 2011; Pettit and Western 2004.

6. Comfort 2008.

7. Goffman [1961] 2007, 42.

8. Elsewhere, I explore the notion of prisons as "porous" rather than "total" institutions: the metaphor of porosity evokes predefined openings in the structure of the prison institution, as we see with the case of religious identity and practice (Ellis 2021a; see also Crewe 2009; Martin and Jefferson 2019).

9. Hinton (2011, 30) characterizes prophecy in the Black Church as "a critical, lamenting voice to cry out against the current status quo . . . an energizing voice to offer hope."

10. See Nelson (2005) on ritual and emotion in AME worship.

11. Although it is prohibited in publicly funded prisons, nearly three-quarters of chaplains in Pew's (2012) national survey reported that proselytizing among incarcerated persons is somewhat or very common.

12. New International Version.

13. Collins 2004.

14. Becci and Dubler (2017, 245–46) explain that prison "chapels refuse and transcend the carceral order," but that more research is needed on the "religious gray zones" beyond formal spaces of worship. The ethnographic data presented in this book illuminates aspects of these "gray zones," where faith and practice are activated outside of formal religious institutions.

3. *THE LORD IS MY SHEPHERD*: PROTESTANT MESSAGES OF GOD'S REDEMPTIVE PLAN

1. Fleetwood 2014; Goodman, Page, and Phelps 2017; Stevens 2012.

2. McCorkel 2013; Schept 2015.

3. Sections of this chapter adapt and extend Ellis (2021b), which interrogates religious discourses in light of responsibilization narratives.

4. Miller, Carbone-Lopez, and Gunderman 2015; Presser and Sandberg 2015; Sandberg and Ugelvik 2016.

5. Valentino 2021, 6.

6. Irwin 2005. On rhetoric of gang violence as a fearmongering policing and prosecutorial tool, see also Duck 2009.

7. Feeley and Simon 1992, 449.

8. Garland 2001; Simon 1993. As Goodman, Page, and Phelps (2017) argue, discourses adapt to the political, economic, and social interests that drive changing correctional practices.

9. Phelps 2017, 2020.

10. Rhodes 2004.

11. On big data in policing, see Brayne 2020.

12. Hannah-Moffat 2005; Lynn 2021; Werth 2017.

13. Butler 1993, 224n6. See also Foucault [1981] 1994.

14. Fleetwood 2014; Warr 2020, 36.

15. Medwed 2008, 493.

16. Ruhland 2020, 651–52.

17. Soyer (2014) analyzes the dissonance between the detrimental effects of incarceration and narratives of incarceration as a positive, "life-changing event." Crewe and Ievins (2020) explore how some incarcerated men and women narrate imprisonment as a productive force in their identity reconstruction. See also Van Ginneken 2016.

18. Presser and Sandberg 2015; Ugelvik 2014.

19. Du Bois [1903a] 2003.

20. Jacobs 1976, 478.

21. Colley 2014.

22. Goffman [1961] 2007, 66.

23. Erzen 2017; Johnson 2011; Johnson 2017.

24. Aday, Krabill, and Deaton-Owens 2014; Bosworth 1999; Dubler 2013; Dye et al. 2014; Kerley 2014; Maruna, Wilson, and Curran 2006.

25. Cunningham Stringer 2009.

26. Frazier [1963] 1974; Schnabel 2021; Whitehead and Perry 2020.

27. On the complementarity of religion and the state, see McRoberts 2002; Sered and Norton-Hawk 2014. For more on correctional perceptions of religious transformation as a legitimate mode of rehabilitation, see Kaufman, Kaiser, and Rumpf 2018; Warr 2020.

28. Becci and Dubler 2017, 244.

29. Sociologist Melissa Guzman (2020) examines how "expanded carceral power masks itself as 'not punishment,' even when it reifies racial, class, and gender hierarchies and legitimizes the construction of stigmatized and criminalized categories of people." Studying a Pentecostal reentry organization in California, Guzman interrogates "spiritual supervision," in which criminalized Latina women were "compelled to perform public degradation ceremonies," sharing religious testimonies highlighting their personal transformation, as part of " 'earning' recovery services" (689–99).

30. See also Sumter 2006.

31. See, for instance, Acoca 1998; James and Glaze 2006.

32. Western 2018, 145.

33. National Center on Addiction and Substance Abuse 2010; Zhang 2003.

34. McClellan, Farabee, and Crouch 1997.

35. Snell and Morton 1994.

36. ACLU of Virginia 2018.

37. Belknap 2010; Carbone-Lopez and Miller 2012; Chesney-Lind and Shelden 2004; Daly 1992; Lopez 2017; Richie 1996; Salisbury and Voorhis 2009.

38. Richie (2000, 7) points to the "unmet social, education, health and economic needs, in addition to a history of victimization."

39. As noted earlier, rhetoric of women's punishment is imbued with pervasive infantilization (Belknap 2010; Bosworth 1999; Carlen 1983; Haney 2010a; Hannah-Moffat 2001).

40. Becci and Dubler 2017, 245.

41. Soyer 2014.

42. Scholarship on gender disparities in sentencing has been mixed. Some studies have found women are likelier to be sentenced to probation or shorter prison terms compared to male counterparts convicted of similar crimes (Griffin and Wooldredge 2006; Lu 2018; Nowacki 2020). Other studies have found gender parity in sentencing for violent crime (Fernando Rodriguez, Curry, and Lee 2006) or harsher sentencing relative to men for women with extensive criminal histories (Tillyer, Hartley, and Ward 2015).

43. Bellah 1970, 12.

44. Durkheim [1912] 2001, 30.

45. Bowler (2013) and Nelson (2005) illustrate Protestant traditions' views on the direct and active role of God and the Devil in daily life.

46. Some branches of Protestant Christianity promote evangelism through social interactions and Christ-like conduct (e.g., Williams 2013).

47. Foucault 1977.

48. Crewe 2009, 10.

49. Incarcerated individuals vary in the extent to which they adopt or subvert dominant carceral narratives (Crewe 2009; Goodman 2012; Rubin 2015; Ugelvik 2014; Werth 2012). While some may narrate personal responsibility to avoid getting caught up in "the mix" (Owen 1998), others cite the inevitability of carceral control, choosing to acquiesce in "surface compliance" (Robinson and McNeill 2008) or "dull compulsion" (Carrabine 2004). Others yet may embrace state responsibilization narratives of their own rehabilitation (Crewe 2009; Goodman 2012; Werth 2012).

50. Foucault 1977.

51. Maruna 2001, 87.

52. For additional examples of religious discourses promoting adherence to state directives, see Armstrong 2016; Fleetwood 2014. Importantly, religious messages are not monolithic. Sociologist Edward Orozco Flores (2018) examines faith-based organizing among formerly incarcerated men, identifying how divergent narratives of "cultural deficits" versus "structural barriers" shaped forms of civic engagement. While I focus primarily on the umbrella Protestant group at Mapleside and the various messages it promoted across situations, future scholarship could tease out denominational differences, with the caveat that the carceral context appears to collapse doctrinal differences, akin to what Dubler (2013) calls the "Protestantization" of the prison chapel.

4. *BLESSED IS THE FRUIT OF THY WOMB*:
GENDER, RELIGION, AND IDEOLOGIES OF
THE FAMILY

1. Haney 2013; Hannah-Moffat 2000, 2001; Lempert 2016; Schur 1984.

2. Britton (2003) reports on officers' attitudes toward women in prison as manipulative and overly emotional. Many officers in Britton's study are so steeped in these patriarchal views that they say they would rather work in men's prisons, where they construe a persistent threat of violence as superior to the emotions and so-called "head games" in women's prisons.

3. McCorkel 2013, 77.

4. When it comes to discourses around what it means to be incarcerated, women are doubly punished: for committing a crime and for violating gender norms by being a woman who committed a crime (Bosworth 1999; Davis 2003; Hannah-Moffat 2000; McCorkel 2003). Paternalistic discourses try to chip away at women's agency (see Belknap 2010; Díaz-Cotto 1996; Haney 2010a; Lempert 2016; McCorkel 2013), reinforcing patriarchal ideas about women's criminality as dependent on men, which myriad research has argued against (e.g., Grundetjern 2015; Kruttschnitt and Carbone-Lopez 2009; Miller 1998, 2001).

5. Crewe, Hulley, and Wright 2017; Daly 1992; Girshick 1999; Lempert 2016.

6. Richie 1996.

7. A substantial share of women serving time for violent crime have been charged as codefendants alongside their boyfriend or husband who engineered the crime (Jones 2008). Becker and McCorkel (2011) found that having a male co-offender increases women's likelihood of participation in a variety of crimes, including burglary, robbery, vehicle theft, and kidnapping.

8. Western 2018, 81; emphasis added. See also Schoenfeld 2016.

9. Annie E. Casey Foundation 2016. Per Glaze and Maruschak (2010), more than 62 percent of women in state prison are mothers to minor children.

10. Glaze and Maruschak 2010, 5. Children with an incarcerated parent face a spate of negative outcomes, including harms to mental health, behavior, and school performance (Haskins 2015; Haskins and Jacobsen 2017; Turney 2014; Turney and Wildeman 2015).

11. Roberts 2012, 1477.

12. Ladd-Taylor and Umansky 1998.

13. For example, Easterling, Feldmeyer, and Presser 2019; Haney 2010a, 2013.

14. Sufrin 2017, 123.

15. McCorkel 2003, 46.

16. Thomas and Lantermann (2019) conducted a comprehensive analysis of current state laws on use of restraints during pregnancy while women are in custody. Based on data from 48 of the 50 U.S. states (data from New Jersey and Michigan were unavailable), 38 states (76 percent) permit handcuffs on pregnant incarcerated women during pregnancy. Up to 29 states (58 percent) permit "shackling," or leg irons and waist chains, during childbirth. Nine states (18 percent) condone restraints during labor and delivery itself, while 28 states (56 percent) condone their use in post-birth recovery. The American College of Obstetricians and Gynecologists (2011) condemned the practice as "demeaning" and warned that it may "compromise health care."

17. See Davis (2003, 62–64) on the practice of the "internal search": "an everyday routine in women's prisons that verges on sexual assault as much as it is taken for granted."

18. Sections of this chapter build on arguments made in Ellis (2020), which examines the interactional dynamics of how religious embodiment can regulate emotions and sexual relationships at Mapleside, and Ellis (2018), which explores how religious volunteers draw on normative constructs of race, class, and gender to craft messages around marriage and the religious self.

19. Sevelius and Jenness 2017; White Hughto et al. 2018.

20. Becker and McCorkel 2011.

21. Maruna 2001; Stone 2016.

22. Bartkowski and Hempel 2009.

23. Pew 2020b; Schulte and Battle 2004.

24. Prison Rape Elimination Act of 2003, 42 U.S.C. § 15601 *et seq.* (2015). See also Gorga and Oehmen 2017.

25. Owen 1998.

26. Freedman 1996; Giallombardo 1966; Ward and Kassebaum 1965.

27. See Bosworth (1999) on sexuality and agency, and Kunzel (2008) for a critique of the academic focus on sexual relationships in women's prisons.

28. Fleisher and Krienert 2009.

29. Moon 2005, 561.

30. For example, Haney 1996, 2013; McCorkel 2003, 2013; Sufrin 2017.

31. Bachman et al. 2016; Liebling 1994; Ward and Kassebaum 1965.

32. Halter 2018; Sufrin, Kolbi-Molinas, and Roth 2015.

33. Glaze and Maruschak 2010, appendix, table 10.

34. Rabuy and Kopf 2015.

35. Aiello and McCorkel (2017) document children's experiences of "secondary prisonization" through visits with incarcerated mothers.

36. Christian, Mellow, and Thomas 2006.

37. King James Version.

38. Not a pseudonym.

39. Other examples in Haney 2013.

40. McCorkel 2003, 56.

5. FOR MANY ARE CALLED, BUT FEW ARE CHOSEN: STATUS AND DIGNITY IN THE PRISON CHURCH

1. Cavendish 2000; Harris 1994.

2. Anderson 1990, 1999.

3. Anderson 2011.

4. From Herberg's (1955) *Protestant—Catholic—Jew* to Wilde and Glassman's (2016) more recent analysis of "complex religion," it is clear that race and ethnicity are fundamentally tied to religious affiliation in the U.S. The racial, ethnic, and class divides of religious groups run deep.

5. Eng, Hatch, and Callan 1985, 85.

6. See Barnes 2014; Brown and Brown 2003; Lincoln and Mamiya 1990.

7. See Du Bois's dynamic, evolving theorizing on the dual functions of religion in Du Bois [1900] 1980, [1903a] 2003, [1903b] 2007; Zuckerman 2000.

8. Walker (2016) demonstrates how jailers use racialization as a form of penal management in the United States. Skarbek (2014) examines how gangs operate as a form of extralegal governance. Johnson (2017) shows how Pentecostal Christianity in Brazilian men's prisons shapes hierarchy in the social order.

9. Conflict polarizes and leads to greater group solidarity (Collins 2004; Durkheim [1912] 2001).

10. Sociologist Erving Goffman ([1961] 2007) might call this a "secondary adjustment" to the deprivations of prison, akin to "knowing the ropes" of the "privilege system" created in the prison (51, 54–55).

11. Clear and Sumter (2002) and Thomas and Zaitzow (2006) write about skepticism concerning the sincerity of religious practice. Access to kosher meals is often cited as a common point of skepticism. As Chaplain Harper commented with a tone of incredulity, "There have been times when there's only one Jewish woman, but once they started with kosher meals a few years ago, all of a sudden there are fifteen Jews." Although many U. S. prisons have decided that they are not in the business of enforcing religious practice, there are regulations in some states to guard against perceived misuse of the kosher meal plan. In Montana, for instance, anyone observed eating nonkosher food is automatically removed from the kosher plan. In Virginia, anyone eating nonkosher food is charged 70 cents per meal (to cover the cost of the religious diet they did not consume; a steep price in light of prison wages). At Mapleside, prior to Ramadan, Muslim women intending to fast are required to submit paperwork for approval to attend early morning *suhoor* and late-night *iftar* meals. During my field work, I was told that one woman's paperwork was denied because she converted to Islam too "recently." If spotted in the cafeteria during daylight hours, Muslim women were immediately removed from this accommodation. There is no room for flexible religious practice.

12. Heffernan 1972; Giordano, Cernkovich, and Rudolph 2002; Johnson 2017; Kerley and Copes 2009; Roberts and Stacer 2016.

13. Anderson 1990, 1999.

14. Blau 1986, 141.

15. Erzen 2017; Griffith 2020; Sullivan 2009.

CONCLUSION

1. Nagin 2013. See also Duck 2015.

2. As of 2020, 203,865 people were serving life sentences in state or federal prisons, including life with parole, life without parole, or virtual life sentences of 50 years or more (Nellis 2021).

3. Edwards 2019, 8.

4. Du Bois [1903a] 2003.

5. Gaston and Doherty 2018.

6. Whitehead and Perry 2020, 6.

7. Kazyak, Burke, and Stange 2018; Whitehead and Perry 2020.

8. For example, Miller 2014; Wilde 2020.

9. Foucault 1977, 304.

10. Sufrin 2017, 233.

11. Lara-Millán 2014.

12. Seim 2020, 27, 172.

13. For example, Mele 2018.

14. McCorkel 2013.

15. McKim 2017.

16. Hirschfield 2008; Sander 2010.

17. Flores 2016, 138.

18. Rios 2011. See also Fader 2013.

19. Shedd 2015.

20. Fong 2020.

21. Brayne 2014; Haskins and Jacobsen 2017.

22. Phelps 2018.

23. Werth 2017. In fact, being defined as a risk can *increase* the likelihood of recidivating in some cases (Werth 2019).

24. Hannah-Moffat 2005, 43.

25. Harcourt 2007; Lynn 2021.

26. Rhodes 2004.

27. Davis 2003; Kaba 2021.

28. Foucault 1994, 429.

29. Covid Prison Project 2022; Equal Justice Initiative 2021.

30. Marshall Project 2021; Novisky, Narvey, and Semenza 2020; Prison Policy Initiative 2021; Schnepel 2020.

31. Schenwar and Law 2020. See also Schoenfeld 2016.

32. Irwin 2005; McCorkel 2013; Phelps 2018.

33. Warr 2020, 36. On the imperative to tell the "right story," see also Stevens 2012; Fleetwood 2014.

34. Comfort 2008.

35. Graber 2011; Rothman 2002.

36. Colley 2014; Sullivan 2009.

37. Dubler 2013.

38. Erzen 2017.

39. Burnside et al. 2005.

40. Griffith 2020, 264.

41. Kerley 2014; Kerley et al. 2010.
42. Hallett et al. 2017.
43. Sullivan 2009.
44. Schwartz 2019.
45. Erzen 2017.
46. Lavoie 2018.
47. Sykes [1958] 2007, 63.

EPILOGUE: *OUT OF THE HOUSE OF BONDAGE*

1. Most incarcerated persons want to "do their time and get out" (Carrabine 2004). On the "afterlife of incarceration" and the hardships faced during reentry, see Miller 2021; Visher and Travis 2003; Western 2018.
2. The young Black men in sociologist Jamie Fader's study (2013) offer a counterexample. Despite their best efforts, their experience was limited due to the unwritten, racialized, and gender-coded rules of the hiring process, and they struggled to find steady employment in the legal economy. See also Smith and Broege 2020.
3. Pager 2003.
4. Western (2018) finds that a social safety net is one of the best predictors of successfully reintegrating and avoiding reincarceration. Yet this process is gendered. Men returning from prison often rely on the women in their lives (wives, girlfriends, mothers, and grandmothers) as a safety net to aid in their reentry, while women returning home from prison have fewer supports in their network. Lexi says she does not have strong familial assistance, but she does have friends who help her.
5. Data from 2010 tell us that 18 percent of all state prisoners were reincarcerated within one year of their release (Durose, Cooper, and Snyder 2014).

METHODOLOGICAL APPENDIX

1. For an analysis of privilege and positionality, see McCorkel and Myers 2003. Stuart (2018) writes about outsider positionality as a "breaching experiment," or an opportunity to generate new insights about a given field. For exemplary discussions of the presentation of self in ethnographic field research, see Duck 2015; Lareau and Rao 2020; Rowe 2014.

2. Rhodes 2001; Wacquant 2002.

3. Ellis 2022.

4. Gibson-Light and Seim 2020, 672.

5. Access and consent can be revoked at any time. For reflections on "broken" access efforts and creative workarounds, see Contreras 2019; Gibson-Light and Seim 2020; Umamaheswar 2014.

6. Stuart 2018, 212–13.

7. Especially among women ethnographers (Hanson and Richards 2019; Hoang 2018). There is an archetype of male ethnographers whose embodiment becomes part of their data, their performance of masculinity calling on them to take up space in their field site. Among female ethnographers, however, embodiment is often erased from their data for fear of sexist interpretations of their actions or from a desire to adhere to a "male neutral" version of normative ethnographic standards.

8. Copes, Hochstetler, and Brown 2013; Liebling 1999; Martin 2013, 2018.

9. Snow, Zurcher, and Sjoberg 1982.

10. McCorkel 2013.

11. Stuart 2016.

12. Bersani and Doherty 2018.

13. On the trade-offs between participant observations versus observant participation, see Seim 2021.

14. This relabeling of the researcher's role does not seem to be an anomaly. In Gibson-Light and Seim (2020), Gibson-Light describes being called an "intern," while both were formally classified as "volunteers" by the prisons they studied even though they made their research intentions clear.

15. Gibson-Light and Seim 2020, 671.

16. Miller 2021, 295–97.

17. Rawls and Duck 2020, 248.

18. Rios 2015, 260.

19. Richie 2004, 438.

20. Peirce 1934, 117.

21. On abductive analysis, see Timmermans and Tavory 2012.

22. Those interested in the profession and practice of correctional control might turn to the many books on prisons and inequality as a primer (e.g., Gilmore 2007; Gottschalk 2015; Rhodes 2004; Schept 2015).

23. Deterding and Waters 2021.

24. Eason (2017) uncovers how state-sponsored narratives of economic opportunity persuade communities to accept the construction of a new prison.

25. Nagin 2013.

26. On the emotions involved in conducting prison research, see Crewe 2009; Gibson-Light and Seim 2020; Liebling 1999; Miller 2021.

References

ACLU of Virginia. 2018. *Women in the Criminal Justice System: Pathways to Incarceration in Virginia*. Richmond: American Civil Liberties Union Foundation of Virginia.

Acoca, Leslie. 1998. "Outside / Inside: The Violation of American Girls at Home, on the Streets, and in the Juvenile Justice System." *Crime & Delinquency* 44(4): 561–89.

Aday, Ronald H., Jennifer J. Krabill, and Dayron Deaton-Owens. 2014. "Religion in the Lives of Older Women Serving Life in Prison." *Journal of Women & Aging* 26(3): 238–56.

Africa v. Commonwealth of Pennsylvania, 662 F.2d 1025, 1032 (3d Cir. 1981); Malnak, supra, 592 F.2d at 207 (concurring opinion).

Aiello, Brittnie L., and Jill A. McCorkel. 2017. "'It Will Crush You Like a Bug': Maternal Incarceration, Secondary Prisonization, and Children's Visitation." *Punishment & Society* 20(3): 351–74.

Alexander, Michelle. 2012. *The New Jim Crow: Mass Incarceration in the Age of Colorblindness*. New York: New Press.

Allard, Patricia. 2002. *Life Sentences: Denying Welfare Benefits to Women Convicted of Drug Offenses*. Washington, DC: Sentencing Project.

Allen, Francis A. 1981. *The Decline of the Rehabilitative Ideal: Penal Policy and Social Purpose*. New Haven, CT: Yale University Press.

American College of Obstetricians and Gynecologists. 2011. "Health Care for Pregnant and Postpartum Women and Adolescent Females." *Obstetrics and Gynecology* 118(5): 1198–202.

Ammerman, Nancy T. 2007. *Everyday Religion: Observing Modern Religious Lives*. New York: Oxford University Press.

Anderson, Elijah. 1990. *Streetwise: Race, Class, and Change in an Urban Community*. Chicago: University of Chicago Press.

———. 1999. *Code of the Street: Decency, Violence, and the Moral Life of the Inner City*. New York: W. W. Norton.

———. 2011. *The Cosmopolitan Canopy: Race and Civility in Everyday Life*. New York: W. W. Norton.

Annie E. Casey Foundation. 2016. *A Shared Sentence: The Devastating Toll of Parental Incarceration on Kids, Families and Communities*. Baltimore: Annie E. Casey Foundation.

Applegate, Brandon K., Francis T. Cullen, Bonnie S. Fisher, and Thomas Vander Ven. 2000. "Forgiveness and Fundamentalism: Reconsidering the Relationship between Correctional Attitudes and Religion." *Criminology* 38(3): 719–54.

Armstrong, Mia. 2018. "Return to Sender: No More Mailing Books to Inmates in Pennsylvania." *Slate*, September 19. https://slate.com/technology/2018/09/pennsylvania-prisons-ban-book-donations-ebooks.html.

Armstrong, Ruth. 2016. "Living in Faith on Parole in Bible Belt USA." In *Parole and Beyond: International Experiences of Life after Prison*, edited by Ruth Armstrong and Ioan Durnescu, 105–39. London: Palgrave Macmillan.

Baćak, Valerio, and Edward H. Kennedy. 2015. "Marginal Structural Models: An Application to Incarceration and Marriage during Young Adulthood." *Journal of Marriage and Family* 77(1): 112–25.

Bachman, Ronet, Erin M. Kerrison, Raymond Paternoster, Lionel Smith, and Daniel O'Connell. 2016. "The Complex Relationship between Motherhood and Desistance." *Women & Criminal Justice* 26(3): 212–31.

Barnes, Sandra L. 2014. "The Black Church Revisited: Toward a New Millennium DuBoisian Mode of Inquiry." *Sociology of Religion* 75(4): 607–21.

Bartkowski, John P., and Lynn M. Hempel. 2009. "Sex and Gender Traditionalism among Conservative Protestants: Does the Difference Make a Difference?" *Journal for the Scientific Study of Religion* 48(4): 805–16.

Beaumont, Gustave de, and Alexis de Tocqueville. 1833. *On the Penitentiary System in the United States and its Application in France*, translated by Francis Lieber. Philadelphia: Carey, Lea & Blanchard.

Becci, Irene, and Joshua Dubler. 2017. "Religion and Religions in Prisons: Observations from the United States and Europe." *Journal for the Scientific Study of Religion* 56(2): 241–47.

Becker, Sarah, and Jill McCorkel. 2011. "The Gender of Criminal Opportunity: The Impact of Male Co-Offenders on Women's Crime." *Feminist Criminology* 6(2): 79–110.

Beckett, Katherine, and Naomi Murakawa. 2012. "Mapping the Shadow Carceral State: Toward an Institutionally Capacious Approach to Punishment." *Theoretical Criminology* 16(2): 221–44.

Beckett, Katherine, Kris Nyrop, and Lori Pfingst. 2006. "Race, Drugs, and Policing: Understanding Disparities in Drug Delivery Arrests." *Criminology* 44(1): 105–37.

Beckford, James A., and Sophie Gilliat. 1998. *Religion in Prison: Equal Rites in a Multi-faith Society*. Cambridge: Cambridge University Press.

Belknap, Joanne. 2010. "Offending Women: A Double Entendre." *Journal of Criminal Law and Criminology* 100(3): 1061–97.

Bellah, Robert N. 1970. *Beyond Belief: Essays on Religion in a Posttraditional World*. New York: Harper & Row.

Benns, Whitney. 2015. "American Slavery, Reinvented." *The Atlantic*, September 21. https://www.theatlantic.com/business/archive/2015/09/prison-labor-in-america/406177/.

Bentham, Jeremy. [1843] 1995. *The Panopticon Writings*, edited by Miran Božovič. London: Verso.

Berdejó, Carlos. 2018. "Criminalizing Race: Racial Disparities in Plea-Bargaining." *Boston College Law Review* 59(4): 1188–249.

Bersani, Bianca E., and Elaine E. Doherty. 2018. "Desistance from Offending in the Twenty-First Century." *Annual Review of Criminology* 1: 311–34.

Blau, Peter M. 1986. *Exchange and Power in Social Life*. New Brunswick, NJ: Transaction Books.

Boppre, Breanna, and Mark G. Harmon. 2017. "The Unintended Consequences of Sentencing Reforms: Using Social Chain Theory to Examine Racial Disparities in Female Imprisonment." *Journal of Ethnicity in Criminal Justice* 15(4): 394–423.

Bosworth, Mary. 1999. *Engendering Resistance: Agency and Power in Women's Prisons*. Brookfield, VT: Ashgate.

Bowler, Kate. 2013. *Blessed: A History of the American Prosperity Gospel.* New York: Oxford University Press.

Brayne, Sarah. 2014. "Surveillance and System Avoidance: Criminal Justice Contact and Institutional Attachment." *American Sociological Review* 79(3): 367–91.

———. 2020. *Predict and Surveil: Data, Discretion, and the Future of Policing.* New York: Oxford University Press.

Britton, Dana M. 2003. *At Work in the Iron Cage: The Prison as Gendered Organization.* New York: NYU Press.

Broidy, Lisa M., Jerry K. Daday, Cameron S. Crandall, David P. Sklar, and Peter F. Jost. 2006. "Exploring Demographic, Structural, and Behavioral Overlap among Homicide Offenders and Victims." *Homicide Studies* 10(3): 155–80.

Brown, R. Khari, and Ronald E. Brown. 2003. "Faith and Works: Church-Based Social Capital Resources and African American Political Activism." *Social Forces* 82(2): 617–41.

Bureau of Justice Statistics. 2014. *Police-Public Contact Survey, 2011.* Ann Arbor, MI: International Consortium for Political and Social Research.

Burnside, Jonathan P., Joanna R. Adler, Nancy Loucks, and Gerry Rose. 2005. *My Brother's Keeper: Faith-Based Units in Prisons.* Cullompton, UK: Willan.

Butler, Judith. 1993. *Bodies That Matter: On the Discursive Limits of "Sex."* New York: Routledge.

Carbone-Lopez, Kristin, and Jody Miller. 2012. "Precocious Role Entry as a Mediating Factor in Women's Methamphetamine Use: Implications for Life-Course and Pathways Research." *Criminology* 50(1): 187–220.

Carlen, Pat. 1983. *Women's Imprisonment: A Study in Social Control.* Boston: Routledge.

Carrabine, Eamonn. 2004. *Power, Discourse, and Resistance: A Genealogy of the Strangeways Prison Riot.* Burlington, VT: Ashgate.

Carson, Elizabeth A. 2020. *Prisoners in 2019.* Washington, DC: Bureau of Justice Statistics.

Cavendish, James C. 2000. "Church-Based Community Activism: A Comparison of Black and White Catholic Congregations." *Journal for the Scientific Study of Religion* 39(3): 371–84.

Chatters, Linda, Robert J. Taylor, and Karen Lincoln. 1999. "African American Religious Participation." *Journal for the Scientific Study of Religion* 38(1): 132–45.

Chesney-Lind, Meda, and Randall G. Shelden. 2004. *Girls, Delinquency, and Juvenile Justice.* Belmont, CA: Wadsworth.

Christian, Johnna, Jeff Mellow, and Shenique Thomas. 2006. "Social and Economic Implications of Family Connections to Prisoners." *Journal of Criminal Justice* 34(4): 443–52.

Clair, Matthew. 2020. *Privilege and Punishment: How Race and Class Matter in Criminal Court.* Princeton, NJ: Princeton University Press.

Clear, Todd R., Patricia L. Hardyman, Bruce Stout, Karol Lucken, and Harry R. Dammer. 2000. "The Value of Religion in Prison: An Inmate Perspective." *Journal of Contemporary Criminal Justice* 16(1): 53–74.

Clear, Todd R., and Melvina Sumter. 2002. "Prisoners, Prison, and Religion: Religion and Adjustment to Prison." *Journal of Offender Rehabilitation* 35(3–4): 125–56.

Clemmer, Donald. [1940] 1958. *The Prison Community.* New York: Rinehart.

Colley, Zoe. 2014. "'All America Is a Prison': The Nation of Islam and the Politicization of African American Prisoners, 1955–1965." *Journal of American Studies* 48(2): 393–415.

Collins, Randall. 2004. *Interaction Ritual Chains.* Princeton, NJ: Princeton University Press.

———. 2009. *Violence: A Micro-sociological Theory.* Princeton, NJ: Princeton University Press.

Comfort, Megan. 2008. *Doing Time Together: Love and Family in the Shadow of Prison.* Chicago: University of Chicago Press.

Congressional Record—Senate S14462; *Religious Freedom Restoration Act,* HR 1308, 103rd Cong., (passed Senate amended October 27, 1993), Public Law No. 103-141 (November 16, 1993).

Conover, Ted. 2001. *Newjack: Guarding Sing Sing.* New York: First Vintage Books.

Contreras, Randol. 2019. "The Broken Ethnography: Lessons from an Almost Hero." *Qualitative Sociology* 42(2): 161–79.

Cooney, Mark, and Scott Phillips. 2013. "With God on One's Side: The Social Geometry of Death Row Apologies." *Sociological Forum* 28(1): 159–78.

Copes, Heith, Andy Hochstetler, and Anastasia Brown. 2013. "Inmates' Perceptions of the Benefits and Harms of Prison Interviews." *Field Methods* 25(2): 182–96.

Couloute, Lucius. 2018. "Nowhere to Go: Homelessness among Formerly Incarcerated People." *Prison Policy Initiative,* August. prisonpolicy .org/reports/housing.html.

Covid Prison Project. 2022. "National Covid Statistics." September 12. https://covidprisonproject.com/data/national-overview/.

Crawford, Charles. 2000. "Gender, Race, and Habitual Offender Sentencing in Florida." *Criminology* 38(1): 263–80.

Crewe, Ben. 2009. *The Prisoner Society: Power, Adaptation, and Social Life in an English Prison.* New York: Oxford University Press.

Crewe, Ben, Susie Hulley, and Serena Wright. 2017. "The Gendered Pains of Life Imprisonment." *British Journal of Criminology* 57(6): 1359–78.

Crewe, Ben, and Alice Ievins. 2020. "The Prison as a Reinventive Institution." *Theoretical Criminology* 24(4): 568–89.

Cunningham Stringer, Ebonie. 2009. "'Keeping the Faith': How Incarcerated African American Mothers Use Religion and Spirituality to Cope with Imprisonment." *Journal of African American Studies* 13(3): 325–47.

Daly, Kathleen. 1992. "Women's Pathways to Felony Court: Feminist Theories of Lawbreaking and Problems of Representation." *Southern California Review of Law and Women's Studies* 2(1): 11–52.

Davis, Angela Y. 2003. *Are Prisons Obsolete?* New York: Seven Stories Press.

Demuth, Stephen, and Darrell Steffensmeier. 2004. "Ethnicity Effects on Sentence Outcomes in Large Urban Courts: Comparisons among White, Black, and Hispanic Defendants." *Social Science Quarterly* 85(4): 994–1011.

Deterding, Nicole M., and Mary C. Waters. 2021. "Flexible Coding of In-Depth Interviews: A Twenty-First-Century Approach." *Sociological Methods & Research* 50(2): 708–39.

Díaz-Cotto, Juanita. 1996. *Gender, Ethnicity, and the State: Latina and Latino Prison Politics.* Albany: SUNY Press.

Dougherty, Kevin D. 2003. "How Monochromatic Is Church Membership? Racial-Ethnic Diversity in Religious Community." *Sociology of Religion* 64(1): 65–85.

Dubler, Joshua. 2013. *Down in the Chapel: Religious Life in an American Prison.* New York: Farrar, Straus, and Giroux.

Du Bois, W. E. B. [1900] 1980. "The Religion of the American Negro." In *On Sociology and the Black Community,* edited by Dan Green and Edwin Driver, 214–25. Chicago: University of Chicago Press.

———. [1903a] 2003. *The Negro Church.* Walnut Creek, CA: AltaMira Press.

———. [1903b] 2007. *The Souls of Black Folk,* edited by Henry Louis Gates, Jr. New York: Oxford University Press.

Duck, Waverly. 2009. "'Senseless' Violence: Making Sense of Murder."
     Ethnography 10(4): 417–34.
———. 2015. *No Way Out: Precarious Living in the Shadow of Poverty
     and Drug Dealing.* Chicago: University of Chicago Press.
Durkheim, Émile. [1912] 2001. *The Elementary Forms of Religious Life,*
     translated by Carol Cosman. New York: Oxford University Press.
Durose, Matthew R., Alexia D. Cooper, and Howard N. Snyder. 2014.
     *Recidivism of Prisoners Released in 30 States in 2005: Patterns from
     2005–2010.* Washington, DC: Bureau of Justice Statistics.
Dye, Meredith, Ronald H. Aday, Lori Farney, and Jordan Raley. 2014.
     "'The Rock I Cling To': Religious Engagement in the Lives of Life-
     Sentenced Women." *Prison Journal* 94(3): 388–408.
Eason, John. 2017. *Big House on the Prairie: Rise of the Rural Ghetto and
     Prison Proliferation.* Chicago: University of Chicago Press.
Easterling, Beth A., Ben Feldmeyer, and Lois Presser. 2019. "Narrating
     Mother Identities from Prison." *Feminist Criminology* 14(5): 519–39.
Edwards, Korie L. 2019. "Presidential Address: Religion and Power—A
     Return to the Roots of Social Scientific Scholarship." *Journal for the
     Scientific Study of Religion* 58(1): 5–19.
Ellis, Rachel. 2018. "'It's Not Equality': How Race, Class, and Gender
     Construct the Normative Religious Self among Female Prisoners."
     Social Inclusion 6(2): 181–91.
———. 2020. "Redemption and Reproach: Religion and Carceral
     Control in Action among Women in Prison." *Criminology* 58(4):
     747–72.
———. 2021a. "Prisons as Porous Institutions." *Theory and Society* 50(2):
     175–99.
———. 2021b. "'You're Not Serving Time, You're Serving Christ': Prot-
     estant Religion and Discourses of Responsibilization in a Women's
     Prison." *British Journal of Criminology* 61(6): 1647–64.
———. 2022. "What Do We Mean by a 'Hard-to-Reach' Population? Legit-
     imacy Versus Precarity as Barriers to Access." *Sociological Methods &
     Research,* Online First. https://doi.org/10.1177/0049124121995536.
Emerson, Michael O., and Christian Smith. 2001. *Divided by Faith:
     Evangelical Religion and the Problem of Race in America.* New York:
     Oxford University Press.
Eng, Eugenia, John Hatch, and Anne Callan. 1985. "Institutionalizing
     Support through the Church and into the Community." *Health Educa-
     tion Quarterly* 12(1): 81–92.

Enns, Peter K., Youngmin Yi, Megan Comfort, Alyssa W. Goldman, Hedwig Lee, Christopher Muller, Sara Wakefield, Emily A. Wang, and Christopher Wildeman. 2019. "What Percentage of Americans Have Ever Had a Family Member Incarcerated?: Evidence from the Family History of Incarceration Survey (FamHIS)." *Socius: Sociological Research for a Dynamic World* 5: 1–45.

Equal Justice Initiative. 2021. "Covid-19's Impact on People in Prison." *Equal Justice Initiative,* April 16. https://eji.org/news/covid-19s-impact-on-people-in-prison/.

Erzen, Tanya. 2017. *God in Captivity: The Rise of Faith-Based Prison Ministries in the Age of Mass Incarceration.* Boston: Beacon Press.

Everett, Ronald S., and Roger A. Wojtkiewicz. 2002. "Difference, Disparity, and Race / Ethnic Bias in Federal Sentencing." *Journal of Quantitative Criminology* 18(2): 189–211.

Ewert, Stephanie, and Tara Wildhagen. 2011. "Educational Characteristics of Prisoners: Data from the ACS." Working paper presented at the Annual Meeting of the Population Association of America, Washington, DC. https://www.census.gov/library/working-papers/2011/demo/SEHSD-WP2011-08.html.

Fader, Jamie. 2013. *Falling Back: Incarceration and Transitions to Adulthood among Urban Youth.* New Brunswick, NJ: Rutgers University Press.

Feeley, Malcolm M. [1979] 1992. *The Process Is the Punishment: Handling Cases in a Lower Criminal Court.* New York: Russell Sage Foundation.

Feeley, Malcolm M., and Jonathan Simon. 1992. "The New Penology: Notes on the Emerging Strategy of Corrections and Its Implications." *Criminology* 30(4): 449–74.

Feigelman, Susan, Donna E. Howard, Xiaoming Li, and Sheila I. Cross. 2000. "Psychosocial and Environmental Correlates of Violence Perpetration among African-American Urban Youth." *Journal of Adolescent Health* 27(3): 202–9.

Fernando Rodriguez, S., Theodore R. Curry, and Gang Lee. 2006. "Gender Differences in Criminal Sentencing: Do Effects Vary across Violent, Property, and Drug Offenses?" *Social Science Quarterly* 87(2): 318–39.

Fleetwood, Jennifer. 2014. "In Search of Respectability: Narrative Practice in a Women's Prison in Quito, Ecuador." In *Narrative Criminology: Understanding Stories of Crime,* edited by Lois Presser and Sveinung Sandberg, 42–68. New York: NYU Press.

Fleisher, Mark S., and Jessie L. Krienert. 2009. *The Myth of Prison Rape: Sexual Culture in American Prisons.* Lanham, MD: Rowman & Littlefield.

Flores, Edward Orozco. 2018. *"Jesus Saved an Ex-Con": Political Activism and Redemption after Incarceration.* New York: NYU Press.

Flores, Jerry. 2016. *Caught Up: Girls, Surveillance, and Wraparound Incarceration.* Berkeley: University of California Press.

Fong, Kelley. 2020. "Getting Eyes in the Home: Child Protective Services Investigations and State Surveillance of Family Life." *American Sociological Review* 85(4): 610–38.

Foucault, Michel. 1977. *Discipline and Punish: The Birth of the Prison,* translated by Alan Sheridan. New York: Vintage Books.

———. [1981] 1994. "To Punish Is the Most Difficult Thing There Is." In *The Essential Works of Foucault, 1954–1984,* vol. 3, *Power,* edited by James D. Faubion, 462–64. New York: New Press.

———. 1994. "The Proper Use of Criminals." In *The Essential Works of Foucault, 1954–1984,* vol. 3, *Power,* edited by James D. Faubion, 429–34. New York: New Press.

Frazier, Edward F. [1963] 1974. *The Negro Church in America.* New York: Knopf.

Freedman, Estelle B. 1996. "The Prison Lesbian: Race, Class, and the Construction of the Aggressive Female Homosexual." *Feminist Studies* 22(2): 397–423.

Friedman, Brittany. 2021. "Unveiling the Necrocapitalist Dimensions of the Shadow Carceral State: On Pay-to-Stay to Recoup the Cost of Incarceration." *Journal of Contemporary Criminal Justice* 37(1): 66–87.

Garland, David. 2001. *The Culture of Control: Crime and Social Order in Contemporary Society.* Chicago: University of Chicago Press.

Gaston, Shytierra, and Elaine E. Doherty. 2018. "Why Don't More Black Americans Offend? Testing a Theory of African American Offending's Ethnic-Racial Socialization Hypothesis." *Race and Justice* 8(4): 366–85.

Gelman, Andrew, Jeffrey Fagan, and Alex Kiss. 2007. "An Analysis of the New York City Police Department's 'Stop-and-Frisk' Policy in the Context of Claims of Racial Bias." *Journal of the American Statistical Association* 102(479): 813–23.

Giallombardo, Rose. 1966. *Society of Women: A Study of a Women's Prison.* New York: John Wiley & Sons.

Gibson-Light, Michael. 2017. "Classification Struggles in Semi-formal and Precarious Work: Lessons from Inmate Labor and Cultural

Production." In *Precarious Work in Research in the Sociology of Work*, vol. 31, edited by Arne L. Kalleberg and Steven P. Vallas, 61–89. Bingley, UK: Emerald.

Gibson-Light, Michael, and Josh Seim. 2020. "Punishing Fieldwork: Penal Domination and Prison Ethnography." *Journal of Contemporary Ethnography* 49(5): 666–90.

Gilmore, Ruth W. 2007. *Golden Gulag: Prisons, Surplus, Crisis, and Opposition in Globalizing California*. Berkeley: University of California Press.

Giordano, Peggy C., Stephen A. Cernkovich, and Jennifer L. Rudolph. 2002. "Gender, Crime, and Desistance: Toward a Theory of Cognitive Transformation." *American Journal of Sociology* 107(4): 990–1064.

Giordano, Peggy C., Monica A. Longmore, Ryan D. Schroeder, and Patrick M. Seffrin. 2008. "A Life-Course Perspective on Spirituality and Desistance from Crime." *Criminology* 46(1): 99–132.

Girshick, Lori B. 1999. *No Safe Haven: Stories of Women in Prison*. Boston: Northeastern University Press.

Glaze, Lauren E., and Laura M. Maruschak. 2010. *Parents in Prison and Their Minor Children*. Washington, DC: Bureau of Justice Statistics.

Goffman, Erving. [1961] 2007. *Asylums: Essays on the Social Situation of Mental Patients and Other Inmates*. Piscataway, NJ: Transaction Books.

Goodman, Philip. 2012. "'Another Second Chance': Rethinking Rehabilitation through the Lens of California's Prison Fire Camps." *Social Problems* 59(4): 437–58.

Goodman, Philip, Joshua Page, and Michelle Phelps. 2017. *Breaking the Pendulum: The Long Struggle over Criminal Justice*. New York: Oxford University Press.

Gorga, Allison N., and Nicole Bouxsein Oehmen. 2017. "Gendered Prisons, Gendered Policy: Gender Subtext and the Prison Rape Elimination Act." In *Gender Panic, Gender Policy (Advances in Gender Research)*, vol. 24, edited by Vasilikie Demos and Marcia T. Segal, 251–71. Bingley, UK: Emerald.

Gottschalk, Marie. 2015. *Caught: The Prison State and the Lockdown of American Politics*. Princeton, NJ: Princeton University Press.

Graber, Jennifer. 2011. *The Furnace of Affliction: Prisons and Religion in Antebellum America*. Chapel Hill: University of North Carolina Press.

Grasmick, Harold G., and Anne L. McGill. 1994. "Religion, Attribution Style, and Punitiveness toward Juvenile Offenders." *Criminology* 32(1): 23–46.

Griffin, Timothy, and John Wooldredge. 2006. "Sex-Based Disparities in Felony Dispositions before Versus after Sentencing Reform in Ohio." *Criminology* 44(4): 893–93.

Griffith, Aaron. 2020. *God's Law and Order: The Politics of Punishment in Evangelical America*. Cambridge, MA: Harvard University Press.

Grundetjern, Heidi. 2015. "Women's Gender Performances and Cultural Heterogeneity in the Illegal Drug Economy." *Criminology* 53(2): 253–79.

Gustafson, Kaaryn S. 2011. *Cheating Welfare: Public Assistance and the Criminalization of Poverty*. New York: NYU Press.

Guzman, Melissa. 2020. "Sanctifying the Expansion of Carceral Control: Spiritual Supervision in the Religious Lives of Criminalized Latinas." *Punishment & Society* 22(5): 681–702.

Hall, David D. 1997. *Lived Religion in America: Toward a History of Practice*. Princeton, NJ: Princeton University Press.

Hallett, Michael, Joshua Hays, Byron R. Johnson, Sung Joon Jang, and Grant Duwe. 2017. *The Angola Prison Seminary: Effects of Faith-Based Ministry on Identity Transformation, Desistance, and Rehabilitation*. New York: Routledge.

Halter, Emily. 2018. "Parental Prisoners: The Incarcerated Mother's Constitutional Right to Parent." *Journal of Criminal Law and Criminology* 108(3): 539–67.

Hamilton Project. 2016. "Rates of Drug Use and Sales, by Race; Rates of Drug Related Criminal Justice Measures, by Race." *Brookings Institution*, October 12. https://www.hamiltonproject.org/charts /rates_of_drug_use_and_sales_by_race_rates_of_drug_related _criminal_justice.

Haney, Lynne A. 1996. "Homeboys, Babies, Men in Suits: The State and the Reproduction of Male Dominance." *American Sociological Review* 61(5): 759–78.

———. 2010a. *Offending Women: Power, Punishment, and the Regulation of Desire*. Berkeley: University of California Press.

———. 2010b. "Working through Mass Incarceration: Gender and the Politics of Prison Labor from East to West." *Signs* 36(1): 73–97.

———. 2013. "Motherhood as Punishment: The Case of Parenting in Prison." *Signs* 39(1): 105–30.

———. 2018. "Incarcerated Fatherhood: The Entanglements of Child Support Debt and Mass Imprisonment." *American Journal of Sociology* 124(1): 1–48.

Hannah-Moffat, Kelly. 2000. "Prisons That Empower: Neo-liberal Governance in Canadian Women's Prisons." *British Journal of Criminology* 40(3): 510–31.

———. 2001. *Punishment in Disguise: Penal Governance and Canadian Women's Imprisonment.* Toronto: University of Toronto Press.

———. 2005. "Criminogenic Needs and the Transformative Risk Subject: Hybridizations of Risk / Need in Penality." *Punishment & Society* 7(1): 29–51.

Hanson, Rebecca, and Patricia Richards. 2019. *Harassed: Gender, Bodies, and Ethnographic Research.* Berkeley: University of California Press.

Harcourt, Bernard E. 2007. *Against Prediction: Profiling, Policing, and Punishing in an Actuarial Age.* Chicago: University of Chicago Press.

Harding, David J., Jeffrey D. Morenoff, and Claire Herbert. 2013. "Home Is Hard to Find: Neighborhoods, Institutions, and the Residential Trajectories of Returning Prisoners." *Annals of the American Academy of Political Science* 647(1): 214–36.

Harris, Alexes. 2016. *A Pound of Flesh: Monetary Sanctions as Punishment for the Poor.* New York: Russell Sage Foundation.

Harris, Frederick. 1994. "Something Within: Religion as a Mobilizer of African-American Political Activism." *Journal of Politics* 56(1): 42–68.

Haskins, Anna R. 2015. "Paternal Incarceration and Child-Reported Behavioral Function at Age 9." *Social Science Research* 52: 18–33.

Haskins, Anna R., and Wade C. Jacobsen. 2017. "Schools as Surveilling Institutions? Paternal Incarceration, System Avoidance, and Parental Involvement in Schooling." *American Sociological Review* 82(4): 657–84.

Havens, R. N. 1846. "Report of the Committee on Detentions." In *Third Report of the Prison Association of New York*, 76–88. New York: Burns & Baner.

Heffernan, Esther. 1972. *Making It in Prison: The Square, the Cool and the Life.* New York: John Wiley & Sons.

Herberg, Will. 1955. *Protestant—Catholic—Jew: An Essay in American Religious Sociology.* Garden City, NY: Doubleday.

Hicks, Allison M. 2012. "Learning to Watch Out: Prison Chaplains as Risk Managers." *Journal of Contemporary Ethnography* 41(6): 636–67.

Hinton, Mary. 2011. *The Commercial Church: Black Churches and the New Religious Marketplace in America.* Lanham, MD: Lexington Books.

Hirschfield, Paul J. 2008. "Preparing for Prison? The Criminalization of School Discipline in the USA." *Theoretical Criminology* 12(1): 79–101.

Hirschi, Travis. 1969. *Causes of Delinquency*. Berkeley: University of California Press.

Hoang, Kimberly Kay. 2018. "Gendering Carnal Ethnography: A Queer Reception." In *Other, Please Specify: Queer Methods in Sociology*, edited by D'Lane R. Compton, Tey Meadow, and Kristen Schilt, 230–46. Oakland: University of California Press.

Illinois Department of Corrections, 20 Illinois Administrative Code, ch. 1, pt. 425.

Irwin, John. [1985] 2013. *The Jail: Managing the Underclass in American Society*. Berkeley: University of California Press.

———. 2005. *The Warehouse Prison: Disposal of the New Dangerous Class*. Los Angeles: Roxbury.

Jacobs, James B. 1976. "Stratification and Conflict among Prison Inmates." *Journal of Criminal Law and Criminology* 66(4): 476–82.

James, Doris J., and Lauren E. Glaze. 2006. *Mental Health Problems of Prison and Jail Inmates*. Washington, DC: Bureau of Justice Statistics.

Janowitz, Morris. 1975. "Sociological Theory and Social Control." *American Journal of Sociology* 81(1): 82–108.

Jennings, Wesley G., Alex R. Piquero, and Jennifer M. Reingle. 2012. "On the Overlap between Victimization and Offending: A Review of the Literature." *Aggression and Violent Behavior* 17(1): 16–26.

Johnson, Andrew R. 2017. *If I Give My Soul: Faith Behind Bars in Rio de Janeiro*. New York: Oxford University Press.

Johnson, Byron R. 2004. "Religious Programs and Recidivism among Former Inmates in Prison Fellowship Programs: A Long Term Follow-Up Study." *Justice Quarterly* 21(2): 329–54.

———. 2011. *More God, Less Crime: Why Faith Matters and How It Could Matter More*. West Conshohocken, PA: Templeton Press.

Johnson, Byron R., David B. Larson, and Timothy C. Pitts. 1997. "Religious Programming, Institutional Adjustment and Recidivism among Former Inmates in Prison Fellowship Programs." *Justice Quarterly* 14(1): 145–66.

Jones, Stephen. 2008. "Partners in Crime: A Study of the Relationship between Female Offenders and Their Co-defendants." *Criminology & Criminal Justice* 8(2): 147–64.

Kaba, Mariame. 2021. *We Do This 'Til We Free Us: Abolitionist Organizing and Transforming Justice*. Chicago: Haymarket Books.

Kaufman, Nicole, Joshua Kaiser, and Cesraéa Rumpf. 2018. "Beyond Punishment: The Penal State's Interventionist, Covert, and Negligent Modalities of Control." *Law & Social Inquiry* 43(2): 468–95.

Kazyak, Emily, Kelsy Burke, and Mathew Stange. 2018. "Logics of Freedom: Debating Religious Freedom Laws and Gay and Lesbian Rights." *Socius* 4: 1–18.

Kerley, Kent R. 2014. *Religious Faith in Correctional Contexts.* Boulder, CO: First Forum Press.

Kerley, Kent R., John P. Bartkowski, Todd L. Matthews, and Tracy L. Emond. 2010. "From the Sanctuary to the Slammer: Exploring the Narratives of Evangelical Prison Ministry Workers." *Sociological Spectrum* 30(5): 504–25.

Kerley, Kent R., and Heith Copes. 2009. "'Keepin' My Mind Right': Identity Maintenance and Religious Social Support in the Prison Context." *International Journal of Offender Therapy and Comparative Criminology* 53(2): 228–44.

Kerley, Kent R., Todd L. Matthews, and Troy C. Blanchard. 2005. "Religiosity, Religious Participation and Negative Prison Behaviors." *Journal for the Scientific Study of Religion* 44(4): 443–57.

Kohler-Haussman, Issa. 2018. *Misdemeanorland: Criminal Courts and Social Control in an Age of Broken Windows Policing.* Princeton, NJ: Princeton University Press.

Kruttschnitt, Candace, and Kristin Carbone-Lopez. 2009. "Customer Satisfaction: Crime Victims' Willingness to Call the Police." *Ideas in American Policing* 12(December): 1–15.

Kunzel, Regina. 2008. *Criminal Intimacy: Prison and the Uneven History of Modern American Sexuality.* Chicago: University of Chicago Press.

Kurlychek, Megan C., and Brian D. Johnson. 2019. "Cumulative Disadvantage in the American Criminal Justice System." *Annual Review of Criminology* 2: 291–319.

Kutateladze, Besiki L., Nancy R. Andiloro, Brian D. Johnson, and Cassia C. Spohn. 2014. "Cumulative Disadvantage: Examining Racial and Ethnic Disparity in Prosecution and Sentencing." *Criminology* 52(3): 514–51.

Ladd-Taylor, Molly, and Lauri Umansky, eds. 1998. *"Bad" Mothers: The Politics of Blame in Twentieth-Century America.* New York: NYU Press.

Lageson, Sarah Esther. 2020. *Digital Punishment: Privacy, Stigma, and the Harms of Data-Driven Criminal Justice.* New York: Oxford University Press.

Lara-Millán, Armando. 2014. "Public Emergency Room Overcrowding in the Era of Mass Imprisonment." *American Sociological Review* 79(5): 866–87.

Lareau, Annette, and Aliya Rao. 2020. "Intensive Family Observations: A Methodological Guide." *Sociological Methods & Research*, Online First. https://doi.org/10.1177%2F0049124120914949.

Lavoie, Denise. 2018. "Lawsuit Says Virginia Jail's 'God Pod' Violates Constitution." *AP News*, November 21. https://www.apnews.com/99516 798d32e49168707e2cebc3c9000.

Lempert, Lora B. 2016. *Women Doing Life: Gender, Punishment, and the Struggle for Identity.* New York: NYU Press.

Liebling, Alison. 1994. "Suicide amongst Women Prisoners." *Howard Journal of Criminal Justice* 33(1): 1–9.

———. 1999. "Doing Research in Prison: Breaking the Silence?" *Theoretical Criminology* 3(2): 147–73.

Liem, Marieke. 2013. "Homicide Offender Recidivism: A Review of the Literature." *Aggression and Violent Behavior* 18(1): 19–25.

Liem, Marieke, Margaret A. Zahn, and Lisa Tichavsky. 2014. "Criminal Recidivism among Homicide Offenders." *Journal of Interpersonal Violence* 29(14): 2630–51.

Lincoln, Charles E., and Lawrence H. Mamiya. 1990. *The Black Church in the African American Experience.* Durham, NC: Duke University Press.

Lopez, Vera. 2017. *Complicated Lives: Girls, Parents, Drugs, and Juvenile Justice.* New Brunswick: NJ: Rutgers University Press.

Lu, Yunmei. 2018. "Rural and Urban Differences in Gender-Sentencing Patterns in Pennsylvania." *Rural Sociology* 82(3): 402–30.

Lynn, Vanessa. 2021. "Prison Autobiographical Narratives: Making Sense of Personal and Social (Racial) Transformation." *Crime, Media, Culture* 17(1): 65–84.

Mai, Chris, and Ram Subramanian. 2017. "The Price of Prisons: Examining State Spending Trends, 2010–2015." Vera Institute, May. https://www .vera.org/publications/price-of-prisons-2015-state-spending-trends/price -of-prisons-2015-state-spending-trends.

Marshall Project. 2021. "A State-by-State Look at Coronavirus in Prisons." June 17. https://www.themarshallproject.org/2020/05/01/a-state-by-state-look-at-coronavirus-in-prisons.

Martin, Liam. 2013. "Reentry within the Carceral: Foucault, Race and Prisoner Reentry." *Critical Criminology* 21(4): 493–508.

———. 2018. "'Free but Still Working in the Yard': Prisonization and the Problems of Reentry." *Journal of Contemporary Ethnography* 47(5): 671–94.

Martin, Tomas M., and Andrew M. Jefferson. 2019. "Prison Ethnography in Africa: Reflections on a Maturing Field." *Politique Africaine* 155(3): 131–52.

Maruna, Shadd. 2001. *Making Good: How Ex-Convicts Reform and Rebuild Their Lives*. Washington, DC: American Psychological Association.

Maruna, Shadd, Louise Wilson, and Kathryn Curran. 2006. "Why God Is Often Found Behind Bars: Prison Conversions and the Crisis of Self-Narrative." *Research in Human Development* 3(2): 161–84.

Mauer, Marc, and Meda Chesney-Lind, eds. 2003. *Invisible Punishment: The Collateral Consequences of Mass Imprisonment*. New York: New Press.

McClellan, Dorothy S., David Farabee, and Ben M. Crouch. 1997. "Early Victimization, Drug Use, and Criminality: A Comparison of Male and Female Prisoners." *Criminal Justice and Behavior* 24(4): 455–76.

McCorkel, Jill A. 2003. "Embodied Surveillance and the Gendering of Punishment." *Journal of Contemporary Ethnography* 32(1): 41–76.

———. 2013. *Breaking Women: Gender, Race, and the New Politics of Imprisonment*. New York: NYU Press.

———. 2017. "The Second Coming: Gender, Race, and the Privatization of Carceral Drug Treatment." *Contemporary Drug Problems* 44(4): 286–300.

McCorkel, Jill A., and Anna DalCortivo. 2018. "Prison Tourism in the Age of Mass Incarceration." *Contexts* 17(3): 63–65.

McCorkel, Jill A., and Kristen Myers. 2003. "What Difference Does Difference Make? Position and Privilege in the Field." *Qualitative Sociology* 26(2): 199–231.

McKim, Allison. 2017. *Addicted to Rehab: Race, Gender, and Drugs in the Era of Mass Incarceration*. New Brunswick, NJ: Rutgers University Press.

McRoberts, Omar M. 2002. *Religion, Reform, Community: Examining the Idea of Church-Based Prisoner Reentry*. Washington, DC: Urban Institute.

Medwed, Daniel S. 2008. "The Innocent Prisoner's Dilemma: Consequences of Failing to Admit Guilt at Parole Hearings." *Iowa Law Review* 93: 491–557.

Mele, Christopher. 2018. "Ketamine Used to Subdue Dozens at Request of Minneapolis Police, Report Says." *New York Times*, June 16. https://www.nytimes.com/2018/06/16/us/ketamine-minneapolis-police.html.

Miller, Jody. 1998. "Up It Up: Gender and the Accomplishment of Street Robbery." *Criminology* 36(1): 37–66.

———. 2001. *One of the Guys: Girls, Gangs, and Gender.* New York: Oxford University Press.

Miller, Jody, Kristin Carbone-Lopez, and Mikh V. Gunderman. 2015. "Gendered Narratives of Self, Addiction, and Recovery among Women Methamphetamine Users." In *Narrative Criminology: Understanding Stories of Crime,* edited by Lois Presser and Sveinung Sandberg, 69–95. New York: NYU Press.

Miller, Patricia. 2014. *Good Catholics: The Battle over Abortion in the Catholic Church.* Berkeley: University of California Press.

Miller, Reuben Jonathan. 2014. "Devolving the Carceral State: Race, Prisoner Reentry, and the Micro-politics of Urban Poverty Management." *Punishment & Society* 16(3): 305–35.

———. 2021. *Halfway Home: Race, Punishment, and the Afterlife of Mass Incarceration.* New York: Little, Brown.

Miller, Reuben Jonathan, and Forrest Stuart. 2017. "Carceral Citizenship: Race, Rights and Responsibility in the Age of Mass Supervision." *Theoretical Criminology* 21(4): 532–48.

Montana State Prison Department of Corrections. 2016. "Operational Procedure: Religious Programming." Effective December 8, 1999. Revised December 5, 2016.

Moon, Dawne. 2005. "Discourse, Interaction, and Testimony: The Making of Selves in the U. S. Protestant Dispute over Homosexuality." *Theory and Society* 34(5–6): 551–77.

Muhitch, Kevin, and Nazgol Ghandnoosh. 2021. *Private Prisons in the United States.* Washington, DC: Sentencing Project.

Nagin, Daniel S. 2013. "Deterrence in the Twenty-First Century." *Crime and Justice* 42(1): 199–263.

National Center on Addiction and Substance Abuse. 2010. *Behind Bars II: Substance Abuse and America's Prison Population.* New York: National Center on Addiction and Substance Abuse at Columbia University.

Nellis, Ashley. 2021. *No End in Sight: America's Enduring Reliance on Life Imprisonment.* Washington, DC: Sentencing Project.

Nellis, Ashley, and Ryan S. King. 2009. *No Exit: The Expanding Use of Life Sentences in America.* Washington, DC: Sentencing Project.

Nelson, Timothy. 2005. *Every Time I Feel the Spirit: Religious Experience and Ritual in an African American Church*. New York: NYU Press.

New York State Department of Corrections and Community Supervision. 2015. "Directive: Religious Programs and Practices." October 19.

Novisky, Meghan A., Chelsey S. Narvey, and Daniel C. Semenza. 2020. "Institutional Responses to the Covid-19 Pandemic in American Prisons." *Victims & Offenders* 15(7–8): 1244–61.

Nowacki, Jeffrey S. 2020. "Gender Equality and Sentencing Outcomes: An Examination of State Courts." *Criminal Justice Policy Review* 31(5): 673–95.

O'Connor, Thomas P. 2004. "What Works: Religion as a Correctional Intervention, Part I." *Journal of Community Corrections* 14(1): 11–27.

Owen, Barbara. 1998. *"In the Mix": Struggle and Survival in a Women's Prison*. Albany: SUNY Press.

Pager, Devah. 2003. "The Mark of a Criminal Record." *American Journal of Sociology* 108(5): 937–75.

Peirce, Charles. 1934. *Collected Papers of Charles Sanders Peirce*, vol. 5., edited by Charles Hartshorne and Paul Weiss. Cambridge, MA: Harvard University Press.

Petersilia, Joan. 2003. *When Prisoners Come Home: Parole and Prisoner Reentry*. New York: Oxford University Press.

Pettit, Becky, and Bruce Western. 2004. "Mass Imprisonment and the Life Course: Race and Class Inequality in U. S. Incarceration." *American Sociological Review* 69(2): 151–69.

Pew Research Center. 2012. *Religion in Prisons—A 50-State Survey of Prison Chaplains*. Washington, DC: Pew Forum on Religion and Public Life. http://www.pewforum.org/files/2012/03/Religion-in-Prisons.pdf.

———. 2020a. *Religion in America: U. S. Religious Data, Demographics and Statistics*. Washington, DC: Pew Forum on Religion and Public Life. https://www.pewforum.org/religious-landscape-study/.

———. 2020b. *Religious Landscape Study: Views about Homosexuality*. Washington, DC: Pew Forum on Religion and Public Life. https://www.pewforum.org/religious-landscape-study/views-about-homosexuality/.

Phelps, Michelle S. 2017. "Mass Probation: Toward a More Robust Theory of State Variation in Punishment." *Punishment & Society* 19(1): 53–73.

———. 2018. "Discourses of Mass Probation: From Managing Risk to Ending Human Warehousing in Michigan." *British Journal of Criminology* 58(5): 1107–26.

———. 2020. "Mass Probation from Micro to Macro: Tracing the Expansion and Consequences of Community Supervision." *Annual Review of Criminology* 3(1): 261–79.

Porter, Lauren, and Laura M. DeMarco. 2019. "Beyond the Dichotomy: Incarceration Dosage and Mental Health." *Criminology* 57(1): 136–56.

Porter, Sonya R., John L. Voorheis, and William Sabol. 2017. *Correctional Facility and Inmate Locations: Urban and Rural Status Patterns.* Washington, DC: US Census Bureau.

Pratt, Tia Noelle. 2019. "Liturgy as Identity Work in Predominately African American Parishes." In *American Parishes: Remaking Local Catholicism,* edited by Gary Adler, Tricia C. Bruce, and Brian Starks, 132–52. New York: Fordham University Press.

Presser, Lois, and Sveinung Sandberg. 2015. "What Is the Story?" In *Narrative Criminology: Understanding Stories of Crime,* edited by Lois Presser and Sveinung Sandberg, 1–20. New York: NYU Press.

Prison Policy Initiative. 2021. "The Most Significant Criminal Justice Policy Changes from the Covid-19 Pandemic." *Prison Policy Initiative,* May 18. https://www.prisonpolicy.org/virus/virusresponse.html.

Prison Rape Elimination Act of 2003, 42 U.S.C. § 15601 *et seq.* (2015).

Rabuy, Bernadette, and Daniel Kopf. 2015. "Separation by Bars and Miles: Visitation in State Prisons." *Prison Policy Initiative,* October 20. https://www.prisonpolicy.org/reports/prisonvisits.html.

Rafter, Nicole H. 1983. "Prisons for Women, 1790–1980." *Crime and Justice* 5: 129–81.

Rathbone, Cristina. 2006. *A World Apart: Women, Prison, and Life Behind Bars.* New York: Random House.

Rawls, Anne W., and Waverly Duck. 2020. *Tacit Racism.* Chicago: University of Chicago Press.

Reiter, Keramet. 2016. *23/7: Pelican Bay Prison and the Rise of Long-Term Solitary Confinement.* New Haven, CT: Yale University Press.

Religious Freedom Restoration Act, 42 U.S.C. § 2000bb *et seq.* (2018).

Religious Land Use and Institutionalized Persons Act, 42 U.S.C. § 2000cc *et seq.* (2018).

Reutter, Kirby K., and Silvia M. Bigatti. 2014. "Religiosity and Spirituality as Resiliency Resources: Moderation, Mediation, or Moderated Mediation?" *Journal for the Scientific Study of Religion* 53(1): 56–72.

Rhodes, Lorna A. 2001. "Toward an Anthropology of Prisons." *Annual Review of Anthropology* 30(1): 65–83.

———. 2004. *Total Confinement: Madness and Reason in the Maximum Security Prison*. Berkeley: University of California Press.

Richie, Beth. 1996. *Compelled to Crime: The Gender Entrapment of Battered Black Women*. New York: Routledge.

———. 2000. "Exploring the Link Between Violence against Women and Women's Involvement in Illegal Activity." In *Research on Women and Girls in the Criminal Justice System*, edited by Beth Richie, Kay Tsenin, and Cathy Spatz Widom, 1–13. Washington, DC: National Institute of Justice.

———. 2004. "Feminist Ethnographies of Women in Prison." *Feminist Studies* 30(2): 438–50.

Rios, Victor. 2011. *Punished: Policing the Lives of Black and Latino Boys*. New York: NYU Press.

———. 2015. "Decolonizing the White Space in Urban Ethnography." *City & Community* 14(3): 258–61.

Roberts, Dorothy E. 2004. "The Social and Moral Cost of Mass Incarceration in African American Communities." *Stanford Law Review* 56(5): 1271–305.

———. 2012. "Prison, Foster Care, and the Systemic Punishment of Black Mothers." *UCLA Law Review* 59(6): 1474–500.

Roberts, Melinda R., and Melissa J. Stacer. 2016. "In Their Own Words: Offenders' Perspectives on Their Participation in a Faith-Based Diversion and Reentry Program." *Journal of Offender Rehabilitation* 55(7): 466–83.

Robinson, Gwen, and Fergus McNeill. 2008. "Exploring the Dynamics of Compliance with Community Penalties." *Theoretical Criminology* 12(4): 431–49.

Rothman, David J. 2002. *Conscience and Convenience: The Asylum and Its Alternatives in Progressive America*. New York: Routledge.

Rowe, Abigail. 2014. "Situating the Self in Prison Research: Power, Identity, and Epistemology." *Qualitative Inquiry* 20(4): 404–16.

Rubin, Ashley T. 2015. "Resistance or Friction: Understanding the Significance of Prisoners' Secondary Adjustments." *Theoretical Criminology* 19(1): 23–42.

———. 2021. *The Deviant Prison: Philadelphia's Eastern State Penitentiary and the Origins of America's Modern Penal System, 1829–1913*. Cambridge: Cambridge University Press.

Rubin, Ashley T., and Michelle S. Phelps. 2017. "Fracturing the Penal State: State Actors and the Role of Conflict in Penal Change." *Theoretical Criminology* 21(4): 422–40.

Ruhland, Ebony L. 2020. "Philosophies and Decision Making in Parole Board Members." *Prison Journal* 100(5): 640–51.

Salisbury, Emily J., and Patricia Van Voorhis. 2009. "Gendered Pathways: A Quantitative Investigation of Women Probationers' Paths to Incarceration." *Criminal Justice and Behavior* 36(6): 541–66.

Sandberg, Sveinung, and Thomas Ugelvik. 2016. "The Past, Present, and Future of Narrative Criminology: A Review and an Invitation." *Crime, Media, and Culture: An International Journal* 12(2): 129–36.

Sander, Janay B. 2010. "School Psychology, Juvenile Justice, and the School to Prison Pipeline." *Communique* 39(4): 4–6.

Schenwar, Maya, and Victoria Law. 2020. *Prison by Any Other Name: The Harmful Consequences of Popular Reforms.* New York: New Press.

Schept, Judah. 2015. *Progressive Punishment: Job Loss, Jail Growth, and the Neoliberal Logic of Carceral Expansion.* New York: NYU Press.

Schlosser, Eric. 1998. "The Prison-Industrial Complex." *Atlantic Monthly,* December. https://www.theatlantic.com/magazine/archive/1998/12/the-prison-industrial-complex/304669/.

Schnabel, Landon. 2021. "Opiate of the Masses? Inequality, Religion, and Political Ideology in the United States." *Social Forces* 99(3): 979–1012.

Schnepel, Kevin T. 2020. *Covid-19 in U.S. State and Federal Prisons: December 2020 Update.* Washington, DC: National Commission on COVID-19 and Criminal Justice.

Schoenfeld, Heather. 2016. "A Research Agenda on Reform: Penal Policy and Politics Across the States." *Annals of the American Academy of Political and Social Science* 664(1): 155–74.

Schulte, Lisa J., and Juan Battle. 2004. "The Relative Importance of Ethnicity and Religion in Predicting Attitudes towards Gays and Lesbians." *Journal of Homosexuality* 47(2): 127–42.

Schur, Edwin M. 1984. *Labeling Women Deviant: Gender, Stigma, and Social Control.* New York: Random House.

Schwartz, Matthew S. 2019. "Justices Let Alabama Execute Death Row Inmate Who Wanted Imam by His Side." *National Public Radio,* February 8. https://www.npr.org/2019/02/08/692605056/supreme-court-lets-alabama-execute-muslim-murderer-without-imam-by-his-side.

Seim, Josh. 2020. *Bandage, Sort, and Hustle: Ambulance Crews on the Front Lines of Urban Suffering.* Oakland: University of California Press.

———. 2021. "Participant Observation, Observant Participation, and Hybrid Ethnography." *Sociological Methods & Research,* Online First. https://doi.org/10.1177/0049124120986209.

Sered, Susan S., and Maureen Norton-Hawk. 2014. *Can't Catch a Break: Gender, Jail, Drugs, and the Limits of Personal Responsibility.* Oakland: University of California Press.

Sevelius, Jae, and Valerie Jenness. 2017. "Challenges and Opportunities for Gender-Affirming Healthcare for Transgender Women in Prison." *International Journal of Prisoner Health* 13(1): 32–40.

Shedd, Carla. 2015. *Unequal City: Race, Schools, and Perceptions of Injustice.* New York, NY: Russell Sage Foundation.

Shelton, Jason E., and Ryon Cobb. 2017. "Black Reltrad: Measuring Religious Diversity and Commonality among African Americans." *Journal for the Scientific Study of Religion* 56(4): 737–64.

Simes, Jessica. 2021. *Punishing Places: The Geography of Mass Imprisonment.* Oakland: University of California Press.

Simon, Jonathan. 1993. *Poor Discipline: Parole and the Social Control of the Underclass, 1890–1900.* Chicago: University of Chicago Press.

———. 2000. "The 'Society of Captives' in the Era of Hyper-Incarceration." *Theoretical Criminology* 4(3): 285–308.

Skarbek, David. 2014. *The Social Order of the Underworld: How Prison Gangs Govern the American Penal System.* New York: Oxford University Press.

Skotnicki, Andrew. 2000. *Religion and the Development of the American Penal System.* Lanham, MD: University Press of America.

Smith, Sandra S. 2018. "'Change' Frames and the Mobilization of Social Capital for Formerly Incarcerated Job Seekers." *Du Bois Review: Social Science Research on Race* 15(2): 387–416.

Smith, Sandra S., and Nora C. R. Broege. 2020. "Searching For Work With a Criminal Record." *Social Problems* 67(2): 208–32.

Smith, Sandra S., and Jonathan Simon. 2020. "Exclusion and Extraction: Criminal Justice Contact and the Reallocation of Labor." *Russell Sage Foundation Journal of the Social Sciences* 6(1): 1–27.

Smith, Tom W., Michael Hout, and Peter V. Marsden 2017. *General Social Survey, 1972–2016* [Cumulative File]. Ann Arbor, MI: ICPSR, NORC. https://doi.org/10.3886/ICPSR36797.v1.

Snell, Tracy L., and Danielle C. Morton. 1994. *Women in Prison: Survey of State Prison Inmates, 1991.* Washington, DC: Bureau of Justice Statistics.

Snodgrass, Jill L. 2019. *Women Leaving Prison: Justice-Seeking Spiritual Support for Female Returning Citizens.* Lanham, MD: Lexington Books.

Snow, David A., Louis A. Zurcher, and Gideon Sjoberg. 1982. "Interviewing by Comment: An Adjunct to the Direct Question." *Qualitative Sociology* 5(4): 285–311.

Soyer, Michaela. 2014. "The Imagination of Desistance: A Juxtaposition of the Construction of Incarceration as a Turning Point and the Reality of Recidivism." *British Journal of Criminology* 54(1): 91–108.

Steensland, Brian, Jerry Z. Park, Mark D. Regnerus, Lynn D. Robinson, Bradford W. Wilcox, and Robert D. Woodberry. 2000. "The Measure of American Religion: Toward Improving the State of the Art." *Social Forces* 79(1): 291–318.

Stevens, Alisa. 2012. "'I am the Person Now I Was Always Meant to Be': Identity Reconstruction and Narrative Reframing in Therapeutic Community Prisons." *Criminology & Criminal Justice* 12(5): 527–47.

Stewart, Robert, and Christopher Uggen. 2020. "Criminal Records and College Admissions: A Modified Experimental Audit Study." *Criminology* 58(1): 156–88.

Stone, Rebecca. 2016. "Desistance and Identity Repair: Redemption Narratives as Resistance to Stigma." *British Journal of Criminology* 56(5): 956–75.

Stuart, Forrest. 2016. *Down, Out, and Under Arrest: Policing and Everyday Life in Skid Row.* Chicago: University of Chicago Press.

———. 2018. "Reflexivity: Introspection, Positionality, and the Self as Research Instrument—Toward a Model of Abductive Reflexivity." In *Approaches to Ethnography: Analysis and Representation in Participant Observation,* edited by Colin Jerolmack and Shamus Khan, 211–38. New York: Oxford University Press.

Sufrin, Carolyn. 2017. *Jailcare: Finding the Safety Net for Women Behind Bars.* Berkeley: University of California Press.

Sufrin, Carolyn, Alexa Kolbi-Molinas, and Rachel Roth. 2015. "Reproductive Justice, Health Disparities and Incarcerated Women in the United States." *Perspectives on Sexual and Reproductive Health* 47(4): 213–19.

Sugie, Naomi F., and Kristin Turney. 2017. "Beyond Incarceration: Criminal Justice Contact and Mental Health." *American Sociological Review* 82(4): 719–43.

Sullivan, Susan C. 2012. *Living Faith: Everyday Religion and Mothers in Poverty.* Chicago: University of Chicago Press.

Sullivan, Winnifred F. 2009. *Prison Religion: Faith-Based Reform and the Constitution.* Princeton, NJ: Princeton University Press.

Sumter, Melvina. 2006. "Faith-Based Prison Programs." *Criminology & Public Policy* 5(3): 523–28.

Sykes, Gresham. [1958] 2007. *Society of Captives: A Study of a Maximum Security Prison.* Princeton, NJ: Princeton University Press.

Thomas, Jim, and Barbara H. Zaitzow. 2006. "Conning or Conversion? The Role of Religion in Prison Coping." *Prison Journal* 86(2): 242–59.

Thomas, Sarah Y., and Jennifer L. Lanterman. 2019. "A National Analysis of Shackling Laws and Policies as They Relate to Pregnant Incarcerated Women." *Feminist Criminology* 14(2): 263–84.

Tillyer, Rob, Richard D. Hartley, and Jeffrey T. Ward. 2015. "Differential Treatment of Female Defendants: Does Criminal History Moderate the Effect of Gender on Sentence Length in Federal Narcotics Cases?" *Criminal Justice and Behavior* 42(7): 703–21.

Timmermans, Stefan, and Iddo Tavory. 2012. "Theory Construction in Qualitative Research: From Grounded Theory to Abductive Analysis." *Sociological Theory* 30(3): 167–86.

Tonry, Michael. 2006. "Purposes and Functions of Sentencing." *Crime and Justice* 34(1): 1–52.

———. 2011. *Punishing Race: A Continuing American Dilemma.* New York: Oxford University Press.

Trusty, Brittani, and Michael Eisenberg. 2003. *Initial Process and Outcome Evaluation of the InnerChange Freedom Initiative: The Faith-Based Prison Program in TDCJ.* Austin: Texas Criminal Justice Policy Council.

Turney, Kristin. 2014. "Stress Proliferation across Generations? Examining the Relationship between Parental Incarceration and Childhood Health." *Journal of Health and Social Behavior* 55(3): 302–19.

Turney, Kristin, and Christopher Wildeman. 2015. "Detrimental for Some? Heterogeneous Effects of Maternal Incarceration on Child Well-Being." *Criminology & Public Policy* 14(1): 125–56.

Ugelvik, Thomas. 2014. "Paternal Pains of Imprisonment: Incarcerated Fathers, Ethnic Minority Masculinity and Resistance Narratives." *Punishment & Society* 16(2): 152–68.

Uggen, Christopher, Jeff Manza, and Melissa Thompson. 2006. "Citizenship, Democracy, and the Civic Reintegration of Criminal Offenders." *Annals of the American Academy of Political and Social Science* 605(1): 281–310.

Ulmer, Jeffery, Megan Kurlychek, and John Kramer. 2007. "Prosecutorial Discretion and the Imposition of Mandatory Minimum Sentences." *Journal of Research in Crime and Delinquency* 44(4): 427–58.

Umamaheswar, Janani. 2014. "Gate Keeping and the Politics of Access to Prisons: Implications for Qualitative Prison Research." *Journal of Qualitative Criminal Justice and Criminology* 2(2): 238–67.

Valentino, Lauren. 2021. "Cultural Logics: Toward Theory and Measurement." *Poetics* 88: 101574.

Van Cleve, Nicole Gonzalez. 2016. *Crook County: Racism and Injustice in America's Largest Criminal Court.* Stanford, CA: Stanford University Press.

Van Cleve, Nicole Gonzalez, and Lauren Mayes. 2015. "Criminal Justice through 'Colorblind' Lenses: A Call to Examine the Mutual Constitution of Race and Criminal Justice." *Law & Social Inquiry* 40(2): 406–32.

Van Ginneken, Esther. 2016. "Making Sense of Imprisonment: Narratives of Posttraumatic Growth among Female Prisoners." *International Journal of Offender Therapy and Comparative Criminology* 60(2): 208–27.

Virginia Department of Corrections. 2018. "Operating Procedure: Offender Religious Programs." Effective March 1, 2018, amended August 1, 2018.

Visher, Christy A., and Jeremy Travis. 2003. "Transitions from Prison to Community: Understanding Individual Pathways." *Annual Review of Sociology* 29: 89–113.

Wacquant, Loïc. 2002. "The Curious Eclipse of Prison Ethnography in the Age of Mass Incarceration." *Ethnography* 3(4): 371–91.

Walker, Michael L. 2016. "Race Making in a Penal Institution." *American Journal of Sociology* 121(4): 1051–78.

Ward, David A., and Gene G. Kassebaum. 1965. *Women's Prison: Sex and Social Structure.* Chicago: Aldine.

Warr, Jason. 2020. "'Always Gotta Be Two Mans': Lifers, Risk, Rehabilitation, and Narrative Labour." *Punishment & Society* 22(1): 28–47.

Werth, Robert. 2012. "I Do What I'm Told, Sort of: Reformed Subjects, Unruly Citizens, and Parole." *Theoretical Criminology* 16(3): 329–46.

———. 2017. "Individualizing Risk: Moral Judgment, Professional Knowledge, and Affect in Parole Evaluations." *British Journal of Criminology* 57(4): 808–27.

———. 2019. "Theorizing the Performative Effects of Penal Risk Technologies: (Re)producing the Subject Who Must Be Dangerous." *Social & Legal Studies* 28(3): 327–48.

Western, Bruce. 2018. *Homeward: Life in the Year after Prison.* New York: Russell Sage Foundation.

Western, Bruce, Anthony A. Braga, Jaclyn Davis, and Catherine Sirois. 2015. "Stress and Hardship after Prison." *American Journal of Sociology* 120(5): 1512–47.

Whitehead, Andrew L., and Samuel L. Perry. 2020. *Taking America Back for God: Christian Nationalism in the United States.* New York: Oxford University Press.

"White House Faith-Based & Community Initiative." 2002. *WhiteHouse. gov.* https://georgewbush-whitehouse.archives.gov/government/fbci /president-initiative.html.

White Hughto, Jaclyn M., Kirsty A. Clark, Frederick L. Altice, Sari L. Reisner, Trace S. Kershaw, and John E. Pachankis. 2018. "Creating, Reinforcing, and Resisting the Gender Binary: A Qualitative Study of Transgender Women's Healthcare Experiences in Sex-Segregated Jails and Prisons." *International Journal of Prisoner Health* 14(2): 69–88.

Wilde, Melissa J. 2018. "Complex Religion: Interrogating Assumptions of Independence in the Study of Religion." *Sociology of Religion* 79(3): 287–98.

———. 2020. *Birth Control Battles: How Race and Class Divided American Religion.* Oakland: University of California Press.

Wilde, Melissa J., and Lindsey Glassman. 2016. "How 'Complex Religion' Can Improve Our Understanding of American Politics." *Annual Review of Sociology* 42: 407–25.

Wilde, Melissa J., and Patricia Tevington. 2017. "Complex Religion: Toward a Better Understanding of the Ways in Which Religion Intersects with Inequality." *Emerging Trends in the Social and Behavioral Sciences* 1–14. https://doi.org/10.1002/9781118900772 .etrds0440.

Williams, Roman R. 2013. "Constructing a Calling: The Case of Evangelical Christian International Students in the United States." *Sociology of Religion* 74(2): 254–80.

Williams, Ryan J., and Alison Liebling. 2018. "Faith Provision, Institutional Power, and Meaning among Muslim Prisoners in Two English High-Security Prisons." In *Finding Freedom in Confinement,* edited by Kent Kerley, 269–91. Santa Barbara, CA: Praeger.

Young, Mark C., John Gartner, Thomas O'Connor, David Larson, and Kevin N. Wright. 1995. "Long-Term Recidivism among Federal Inmates Trained as Volunteer Prison Ministers." *Journal of Offender Rehabilitation* 22(1–2): 97–118.

Zeng, Zhen, and Todd D. Minton. 2021. *Jail Inmates in 2019.* Washington, DC: Bureau of Justice Statistics.

Zhang, Zhiwei. 2003. *Drug and Alcohol Use and Related Matters among Arrestees.* Chicago: National Opinion Research Center at the University of Chicago.

Zuckerman, Phil. 2000. *DuBois on Religion.* Walnut Creek, CA: AltaMira Press.

Index

Founded in 1893,
UNIVERSITY OF CALIFORNIA PRESS
publishes bold, progressive books and journals
on topics in the arts, humanities, social sciences,
and natural sciences—with a focus on social
justice issues—that inspire thought and action
among readers worldwide.

The UC PRESS FOUNDATION
raises funds to uphold the press's vital role
as an independent, nonprofit publisher, and
receives philanthropic support from a wide
range of individuals and institutions—and from
committed readers like you. To learn more, visit
ucpress.edu/supportus.